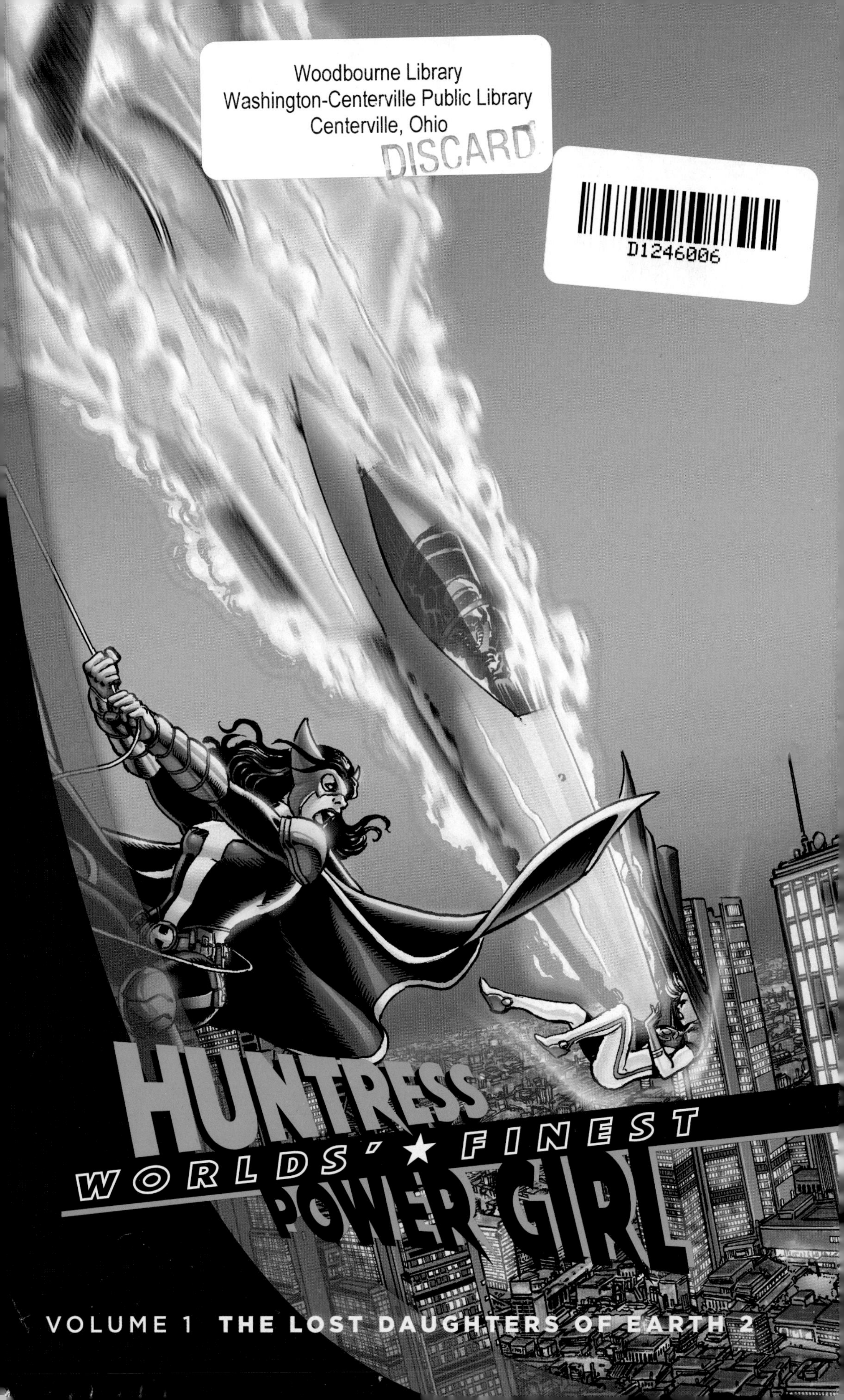
HUNTRESS
WORLDS' FINEST
POWER GIRL
VOLUME 1 THE LOST DAUGHTERS OF EARTH 2

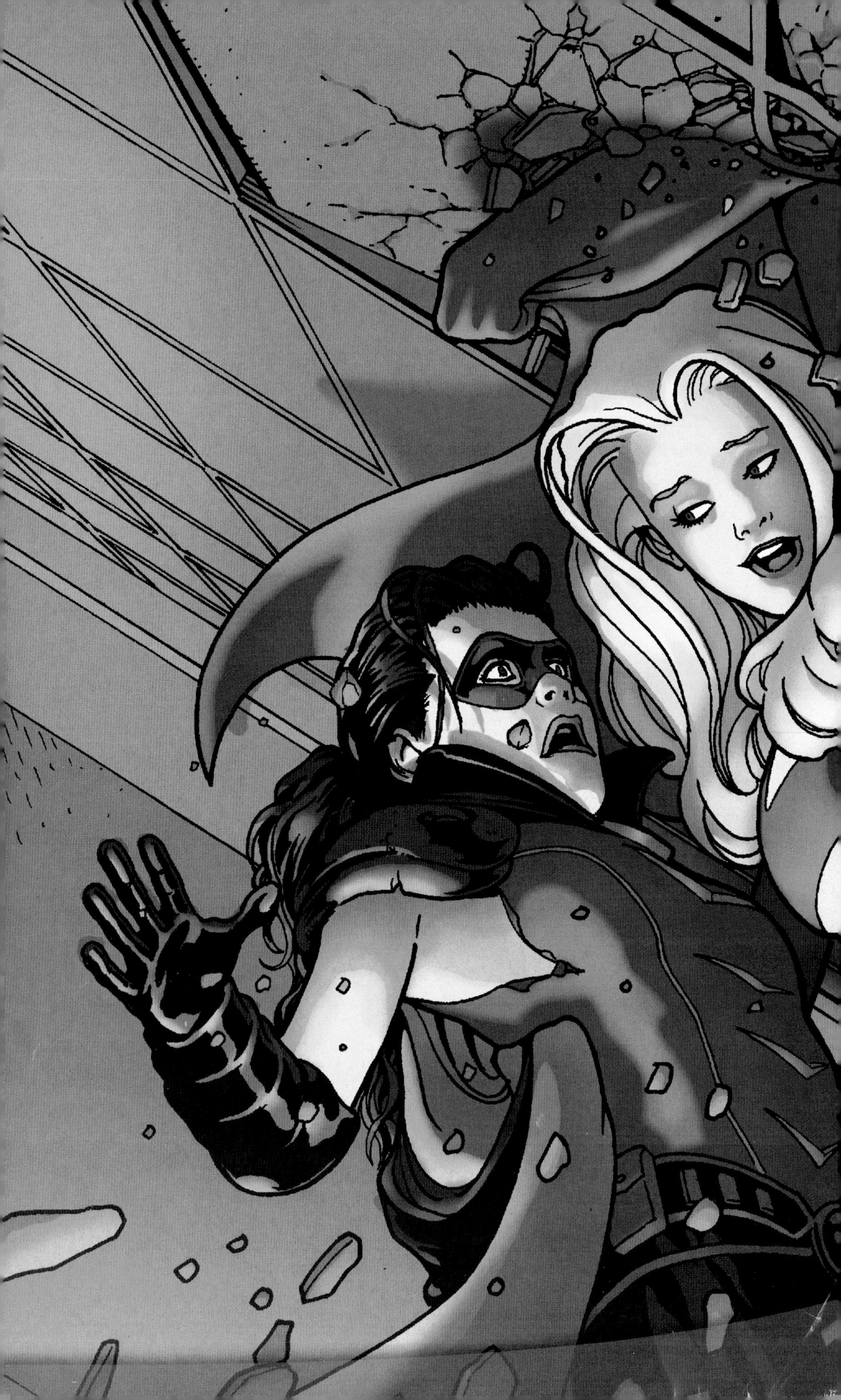

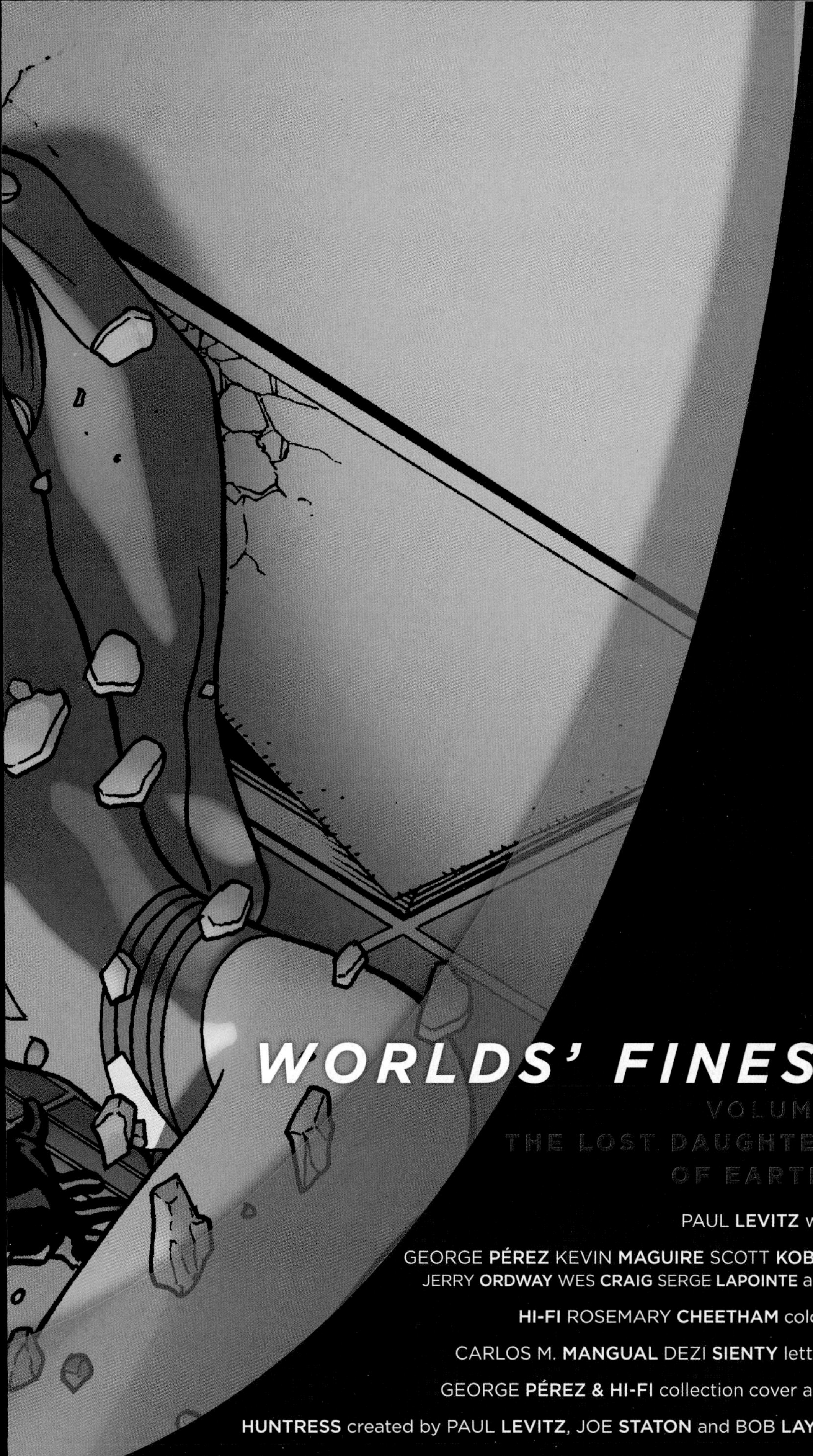

# WORLDS' FINEST

## VOLUME 1
## THE LOST DAUGHTERS OF EARTH 2


PAUL **LEVITZ** writer

GEORGE **PÉREZ** KEVIN **MAGUIRE** SCOTT **KOBLISH**
JERRY **ORDWAY** WES **CRAIG** SERGE **LAPOINTE** artists

**HI-FI** ROSEMARY **CHEETHAM** colorists

CARLOS M. **MANGUAL** DEZI **SIENTY** letterers

GEORGE **PÉREZ & HI-FI** collection cover artists

**HUNTRESS** created by PAUL **LEVITZ**, JOE **STATON** and BOB **LAYTON**

WIL MOSS Editor – Original Series
ROBIN WILDMAN Editor  ROBBIN BROSTERMAN Design Director – Books
ROBBIE BIEDERMAN Publication Design

BOB HARRAS VP – Editor-in-Chief

DIANE NELSON President  DAN DIDIO and JIM LEE Co-Publishers
GEOFF JOHNS Chief Creative Officer  JOHN ROOD Executive VP – Sales, Marketing and Business Development
AMY GENKINS Senior VP – Business and Legal Affairs  NAIRI GARDINER Senior VP – Finance
JEFF BOISON VP – Publishing Operations  MARK CHIARELLO VP – Art Direction and Design
JOHN CUNNINGHAM VP – Marketing  TERRI CUNNINGHAM VP – Talent Relations and Services
ALISON GILL Senior VP – Manufacturing and Operations  HANK KANALZ Senior VP – Digital
JAY KOGAN VP – Business and Legal Affairs, Publishing  JACK MAHAN VP – Business Affairs, Talent
NICK NAPOLITANO VP – Manufacturing Administration  SUE POHJA VP – Book Sales
COURTNEY SIMMONS Senior VP – Publicity  BOB WAYNE Senior VP – Sales

WORLDS' FINEST VOLUME 1: THE LOST DAUGHTERS OF EARTH 2
Published by DC Comics. Compilation Copyright © 2013 DC Comics. All Rights Reserved.

DC Comics, 1700 Broadway, New York, NY 10019
A Warner Bros. Entertainment Company.
Printed by RR Donnelley, Salem, VA, USA. 3/1/13. First Printing.
ISBN: 978-1-4012-3834-6

Library of Congress Cataloging-in-Publication Data

Levitz, Paul.
Worlds' Finest. Volume 1, The Lost Daughters of Earth 2 / Paul Levitz, George Pérez.
pages cm
"Originally published in single magazine form in Worlds' Finest 0-5."
ISBN 978-1-4012-3834-6
1.  Graphic novels.  I. Pérez, George, 1954- II. Title. III. Title: Lost Daughters of Earth 2.
PN6728.W7L48 2013
741.5'973—dc23
                    2012048549

SUSTAINABLE
FORESTRY
INITIATIVE
Certified Chain of Custody
At Least 20% Certified Forest Content
www.sfiprogram.org
SFI-01042
APPLIES TO TEXT STOCK ONLY

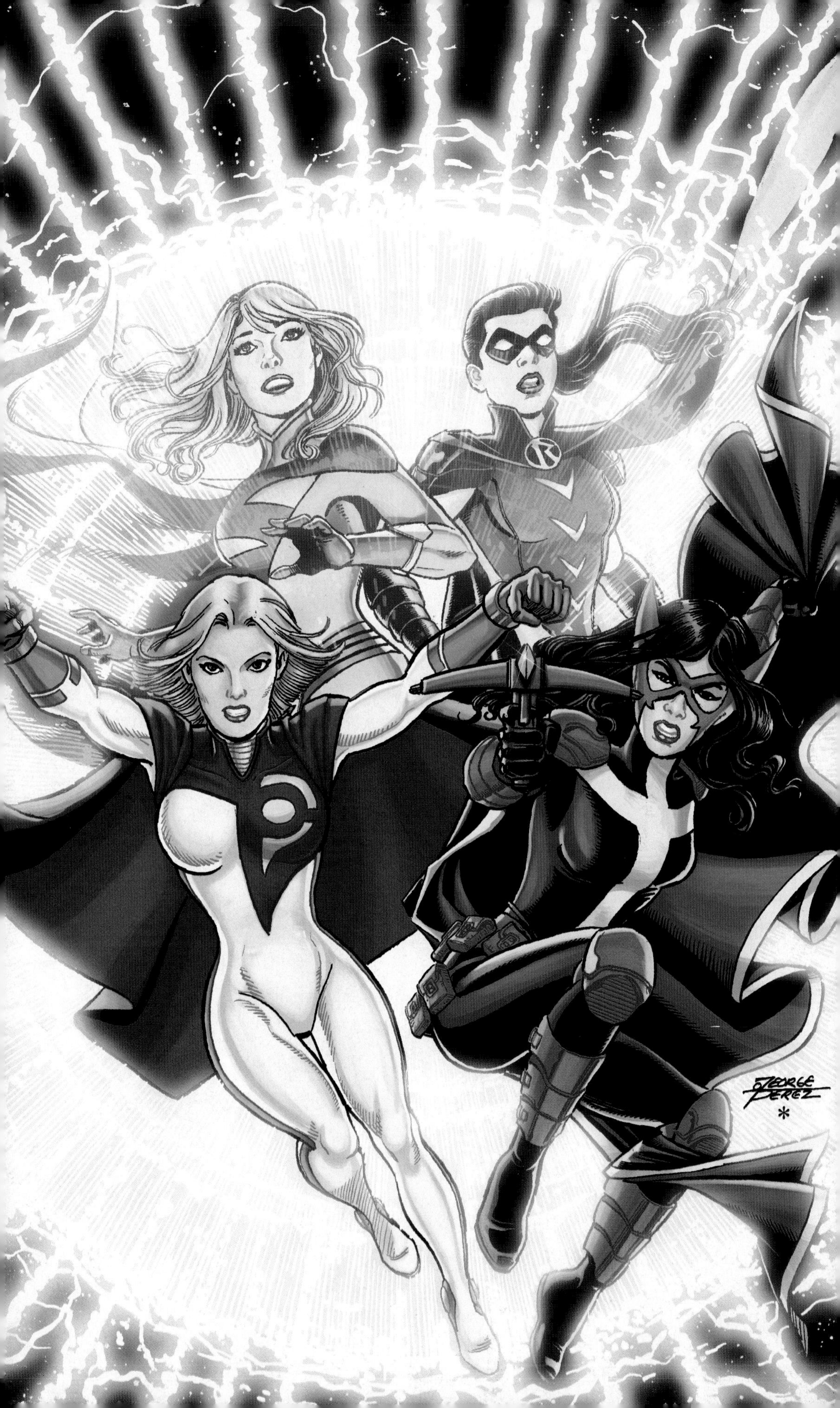

GEORGE PEREZ

**PAUL LEVITZ** writer **GEORGE PEREZ** penciller (present-day sequence)
**SCOTT KOBLISH** inker (present-day sequence) **KEVIN MAGUIRE** artist (flashback sequence)

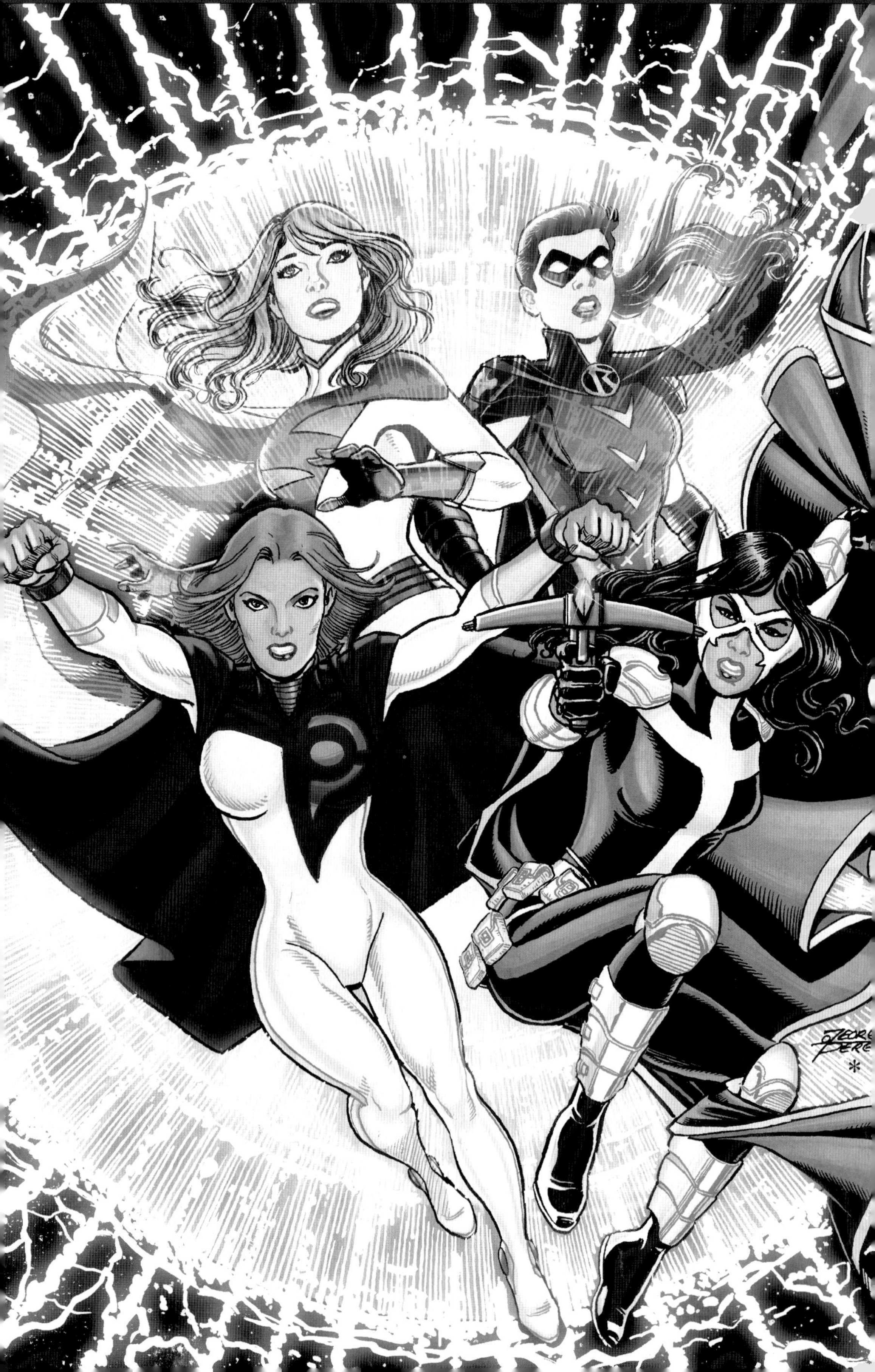

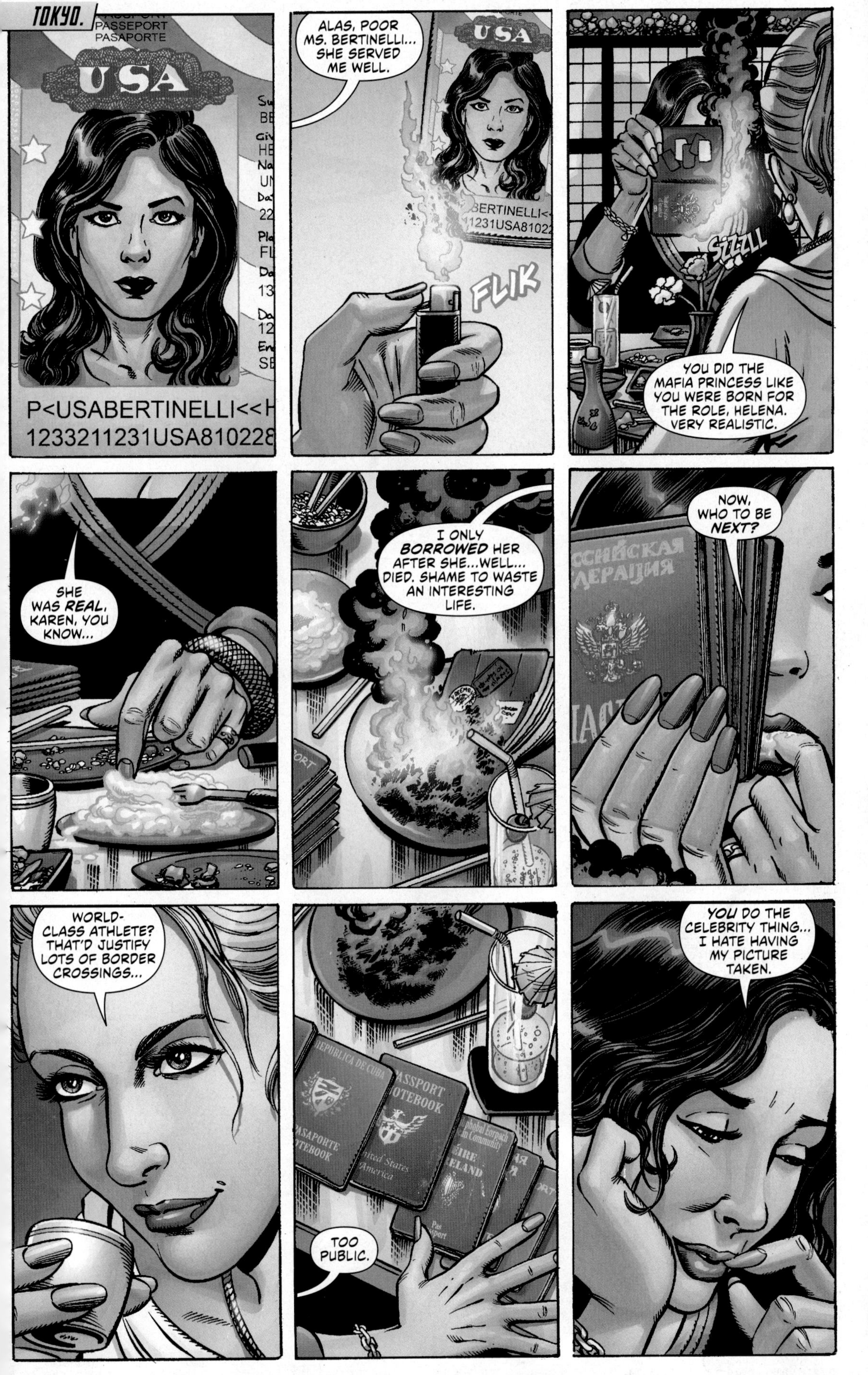
TOKYO.
PASSEPORT
PASAPORTE
USA
P<USABERTINELLI<<H
1233211231USA810228
ALAS, POOR MS. BERTINELLI... SHE SERVED ME WELL.
FLIK
SZZZLL
YOU DID THE MAFIA PRINCESS LIKE YOU WERE BORN FOR THE ROLE, HELENA. VERY REALISTIC.
SHE WAS *REAL*, KAREN, YOU KNOW...
I ONLY *BORROWED* HER AFTER SHE...WELL... DIED. SHAME TO WASTE AN INTERESTING LIFE.
NOW, WHO TO BE *NEXT?*
WORLD-CLASS ATHLETE? THAT'D JUSTIFY LOTS OF BORDER CROSSINGS...
TOO PUBLIC.
*YOU* DO THE CELEBRITY THING... I HATE HAVING MY PICTURE TAKEN.

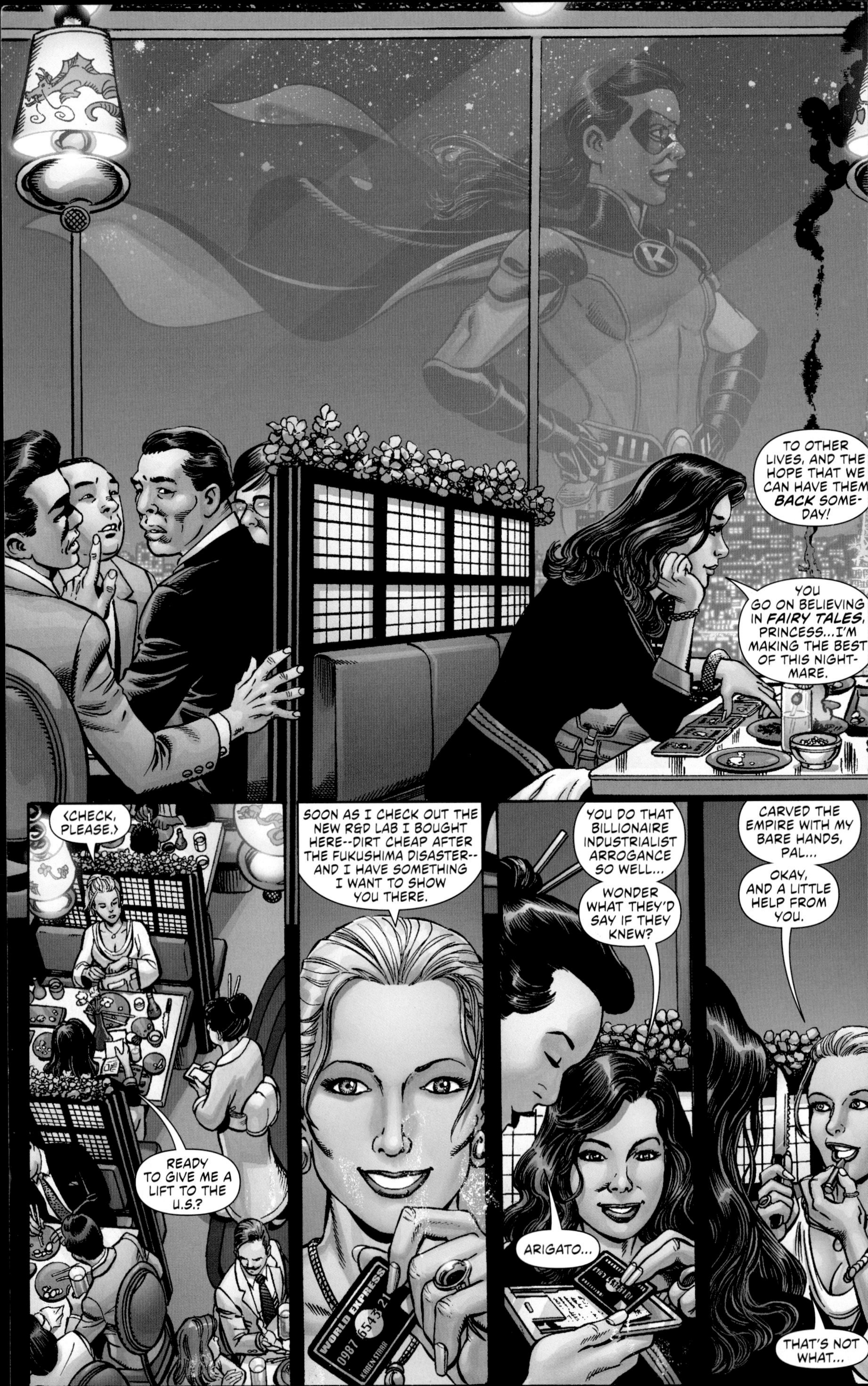
TO OTHER LIVES, AND THE HOPE THAT WE CAN HAVE THEM BACK SOMEDAY!
YOU GO ON BELIEVING IN FAIRY TALES, PRINCESS...I'M MAKING THE BEST OF THIS NIGHTMARE.
<CHECK, PLEASE.>
READY TO GIVE ME A LIFT TO THE U.S.?
SOON AS I CHECK OUT THE NEW R&D LAB I BOUGHT HERE--DIRT CHEAP AFTER THE FUKUSHIMA DISASTER--AND I HAVE SOMETHING I WANT TO SHOW YOU THERE.
WORLD EXPRESS
0987 6543 21
KAREN STARR
YOU DO THAT BILLIONAIRE INDUSTRIALIST ARROGANCE SO WELL...
WONDER WHAT THEY'D SAY IF THEY KNEW?
ARIGATO...
CARVED THE EMPIRE WITH MY BARE HANDS, PAL...
OKAY, AND A LITTLE HELP FROM YOU.
THAT'S NOT WHAT...

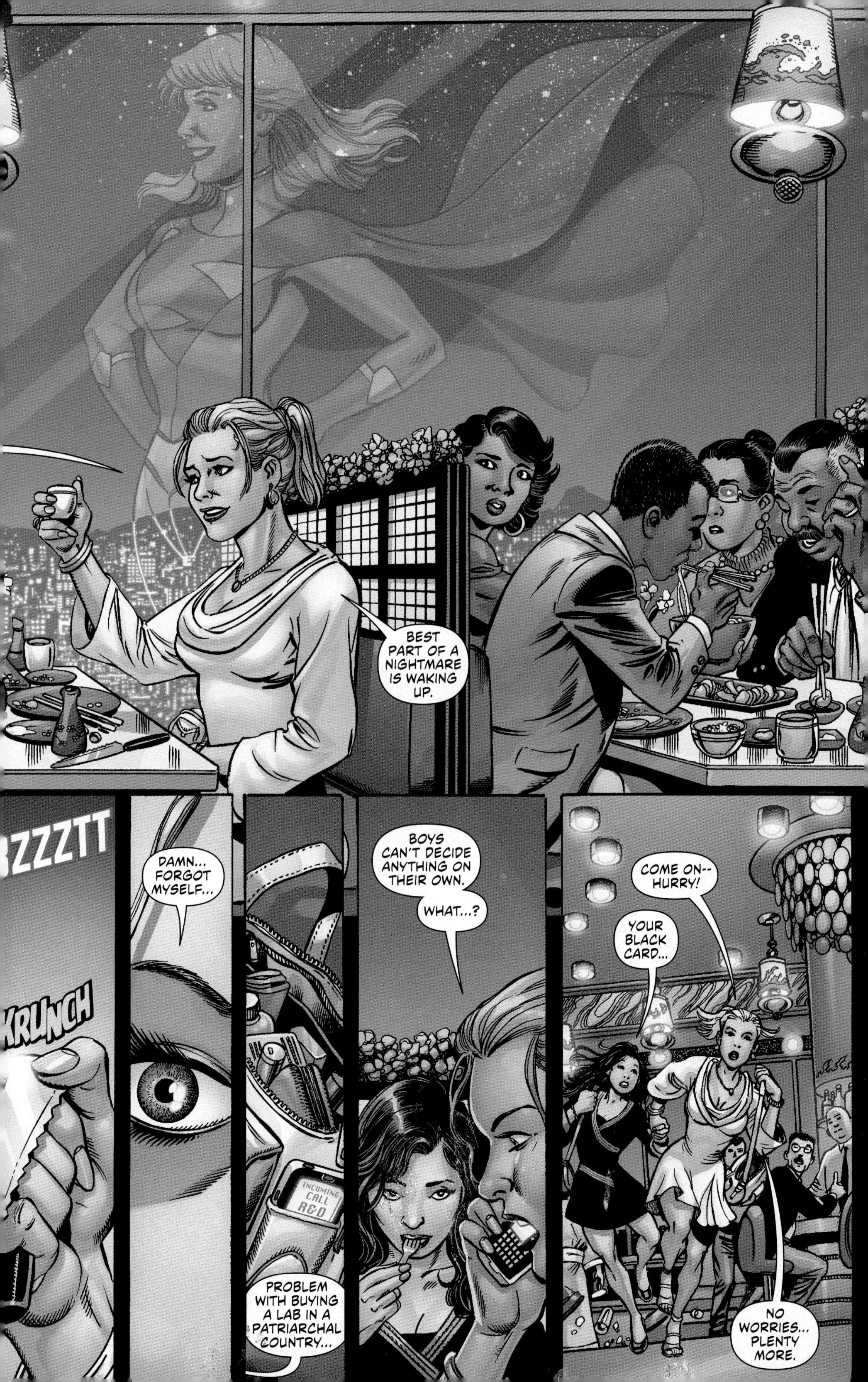
BEST PART OF A NIGHTMARE IS WAKING UP.
BZZZTT
KRUNCH
DAMN... FORGOT MYSELF...
PROBLEM WITH BUYING A LAB IN A PATRIARCHAL COUNTRY...
INCOMING CALL R&D
BOYS CAN'T DECIDE ANYTHING ON THEIR OWN.
WHAT...?
COME ON-- HURRY!
YOUR BLACK CARD...
NO WORRIES... PLENTY MORE.

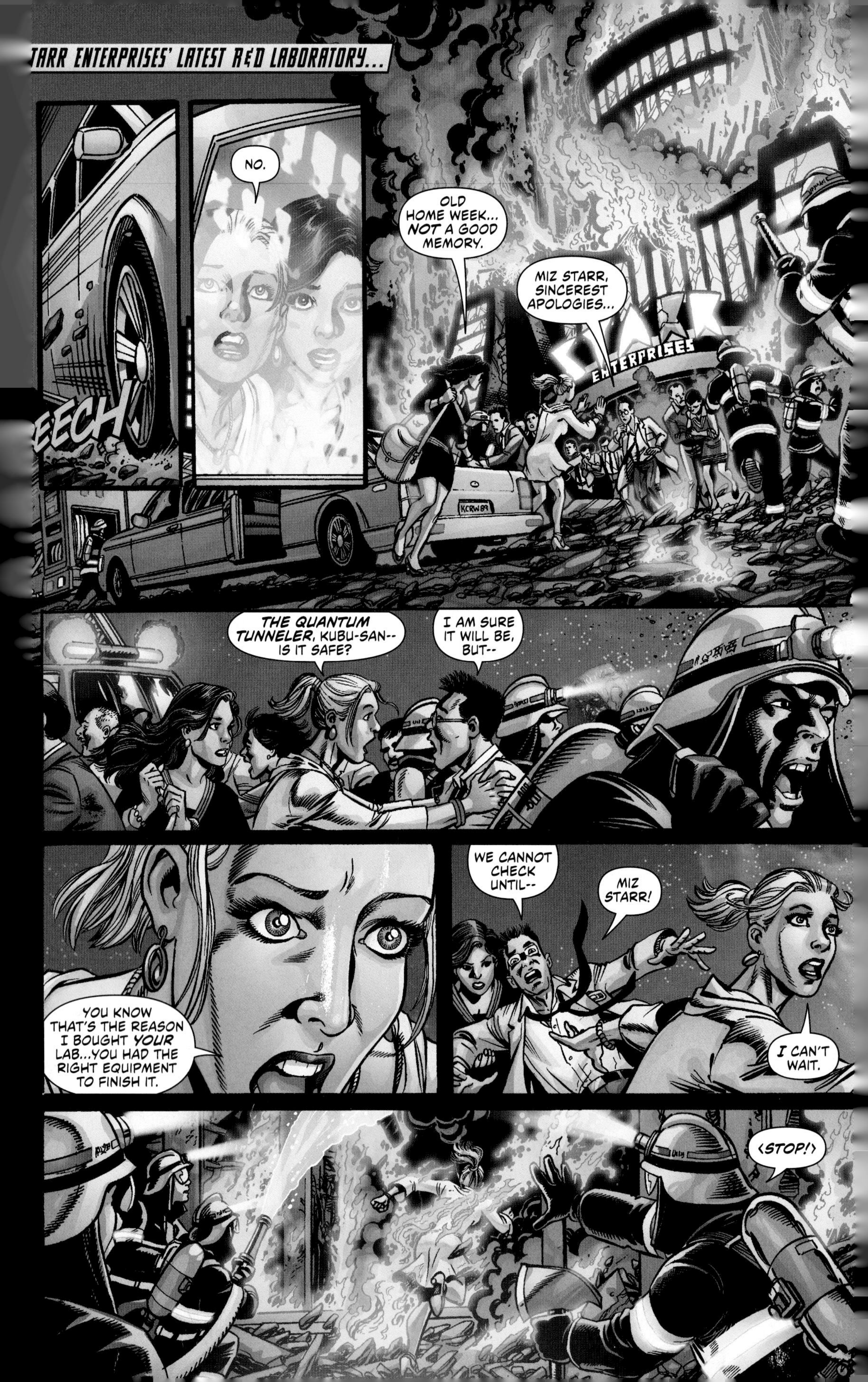

...STARR ENTERPRISES' LATEST R&D LABORATORY...
EECH
NO.
OLD HOME WEEK... NOT A GOOD MEMORY.
MIZ STARR, SINCEREST APOLOGIES...
STARR ENTERPRISES
THE QUANTUM TUNNELER, KUBU-SAN-- IS IT SAFE?
I AM SURE IT WILL BE, BUT--
YOU KNOW THAT'S THE REASON I BOUGHT YOUR LAB...YOU HAD THE RIGHT EQUIPMENT TO FINISH IT.
WE CANNOT CHECK UNTIL--
MIZ STARR!
I CAN'T WAIT.
<STOP!>

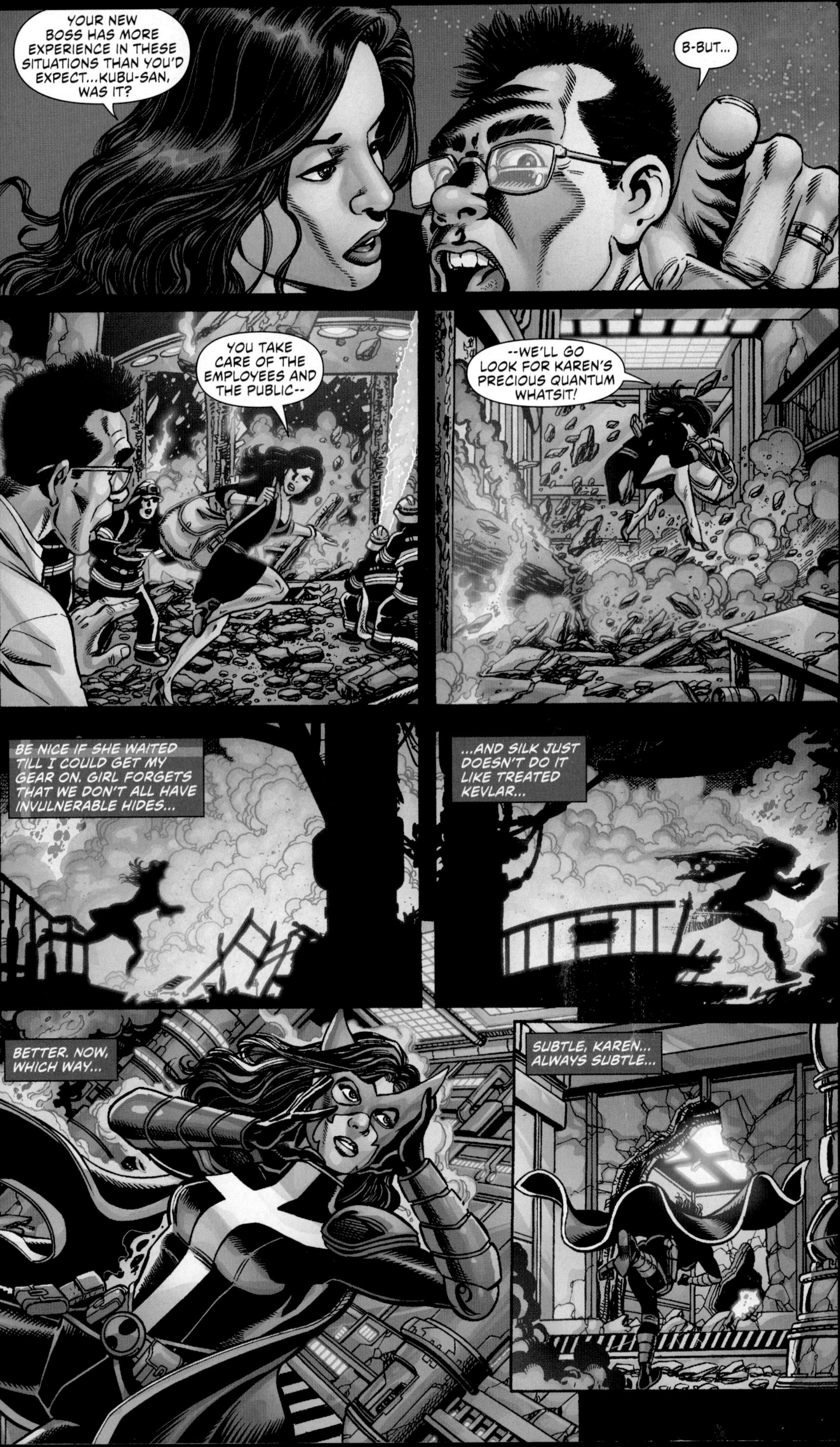
YOUR NEW BOSS HAS MORE EXPERIENCE IN THESE SITUATIONS THAN YOU'D EXPECT...KUBU-SAN, WAS IT?
B-BUT...
YOU TAKE CARE OF THE EMPLOYEES AND THE PUBLIC--
--WE'LL GO LOOK FOR KAREN'S PRECIOUS QUANTUM WHATSIT!
BE NICE IF SHE WAITED TILL I COULD GET MY GEAR ON. GIRL FORGETS THAT WE DON'T ALL HAVE INVULNERABLE HIDES...
...AND SILK JUST DOESN'T DO IT LIKE TREATED KEVLAR...
BETTER. NOW, WHICH WAY...
SUBTLE, KAREN... ALWAYS SUBTLE...

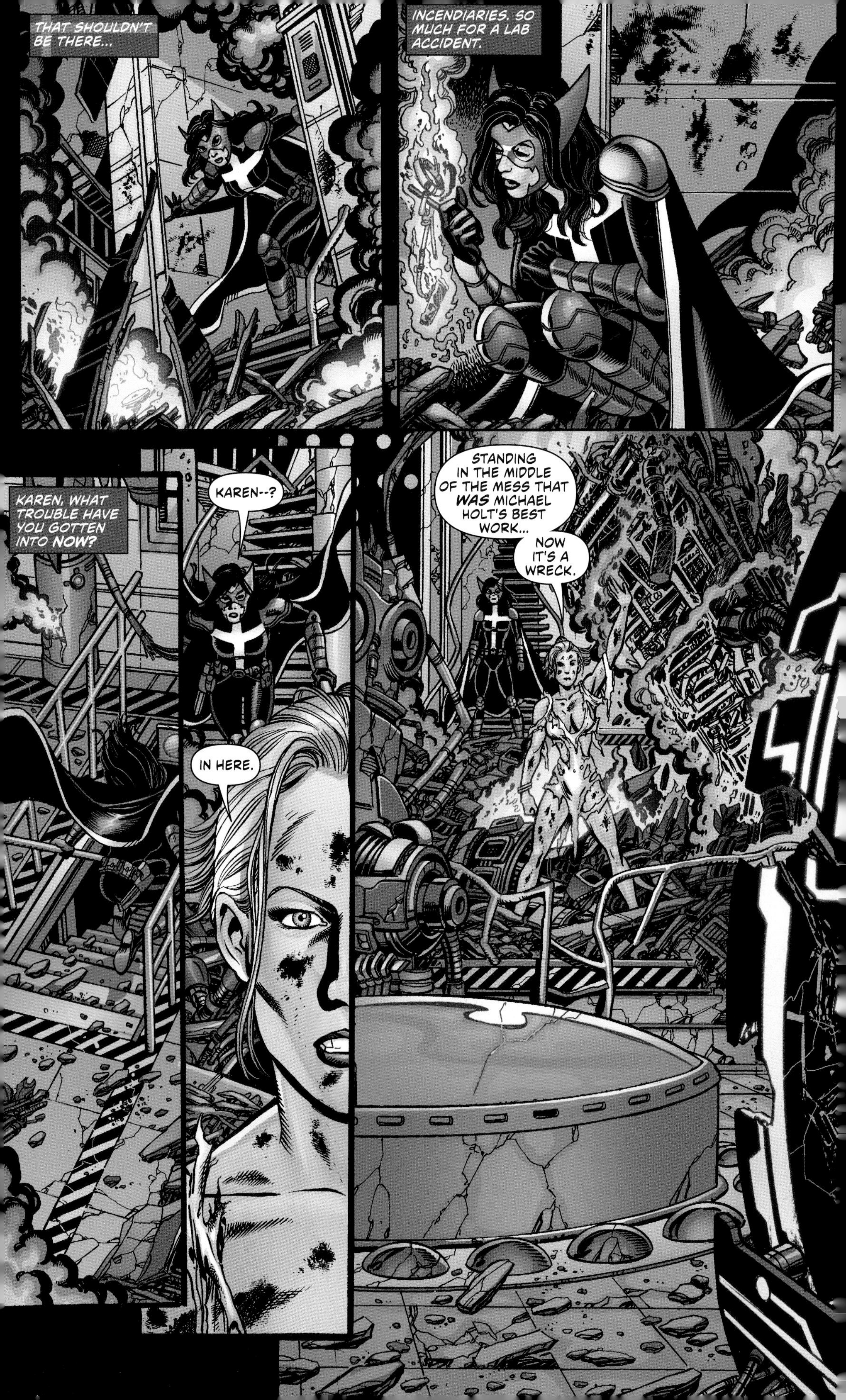
THAT SHOULDN'T BE THERE...
INCENDIARIES. SO MUCH FOR A LAB ACCIDENT.
KAREN, WHAT TROUBLE HAVE YOU GOTTEN INTO NOW?
KAREN--?
IN HERE.
STANDING IN THE MIDDLE OF THE MESS THAT WAS MICHAEL HOLT'S BEST WORK...
NOW IT'S A WRECK.

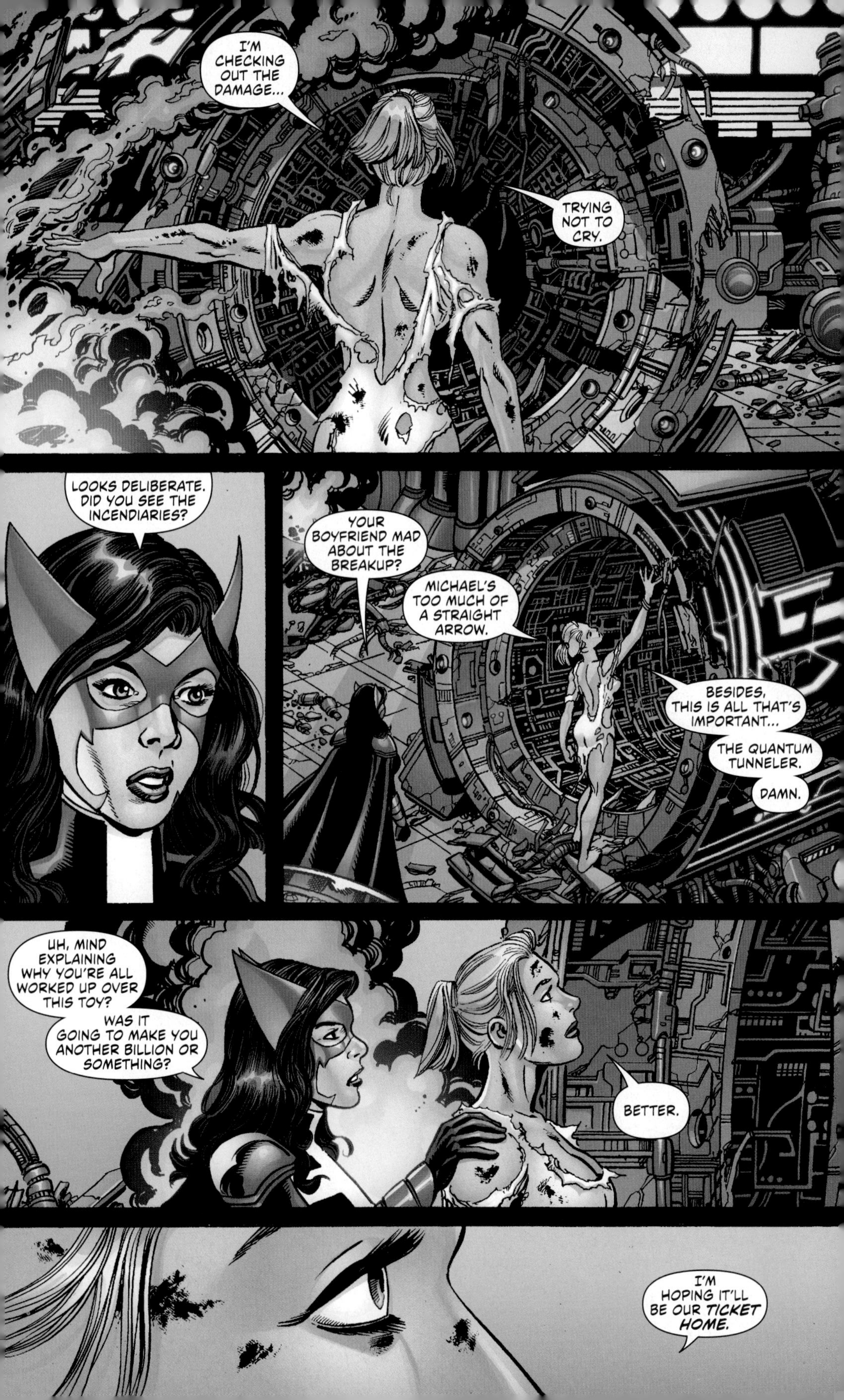
I'M CHECKING OUT THE DAMAGE...
TRYING NOT TO CRY.
LOOKS DELIBERATE. DID YOU SEE THE INCENDIARIES?
YOUR BOYFRIEND MAD ABOUT THE BREAKUP?
MICHAEL'S TOO MUCH OF A STRAIGHT ARROW.
BESIDES, THIS IS ALL THAT'S IMPORTANT...
THE QUANTUM TUNNELER.
DAMN.
UH, MIND EXPLAINING WHY YOU'RE ALL WORKED UP OVER THIS TOY?
WAS IT GOING TO MAKE YOU ANOTHER BILLION OR SOMETHING?
BETTER.
I'M HOPING IT'LL BE OUR *TICKET HOME.*

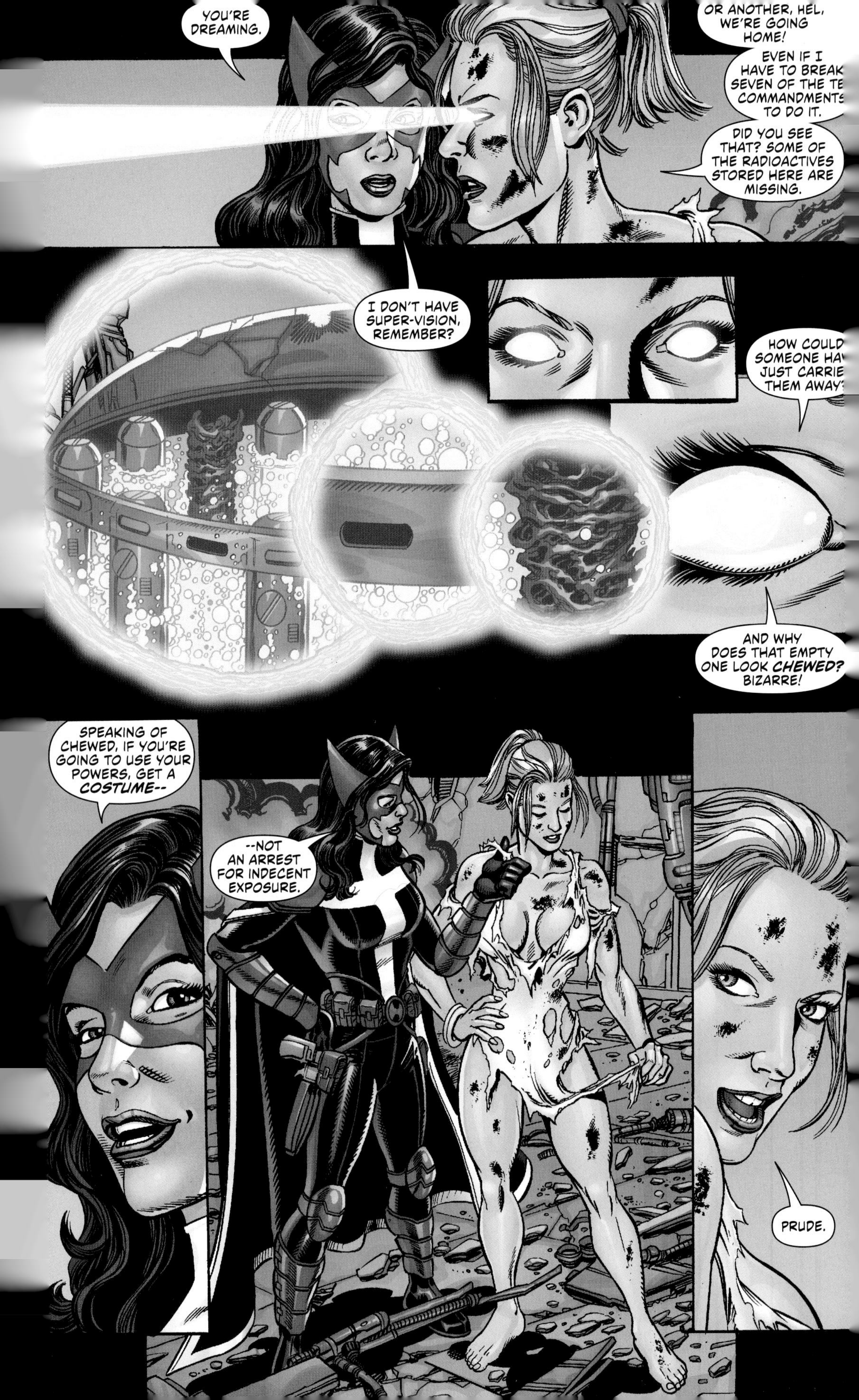
YOU'RE DREAMING.
OR ANOTHER, HEL, WE'RE GOING HOME!
EVEN IF I HAVE TO BREAK SEVEN OF THE TE COMMANDMENTS TO DO IT.
DID YOU SEE THAT? SOME OF THE RADIOACTIVES STORED HERE ARE MISSING.
I DON'T HAVE SUPER-VISION, REMEMBER?
HOW COULD SOMEONE HAV JUST CARRIE THEM AWAY?
AND WHY DOES THAT EMPTY ONE LOOK CHEWED? BIZARRE!
SPEAKING OF CHEWED, IF YOU'RE GOING TO USE YOUR POWERS, GET A COSTUME--
--NOT AN ARREST FOR INDECENT EXPOSURE.
PRUDE.

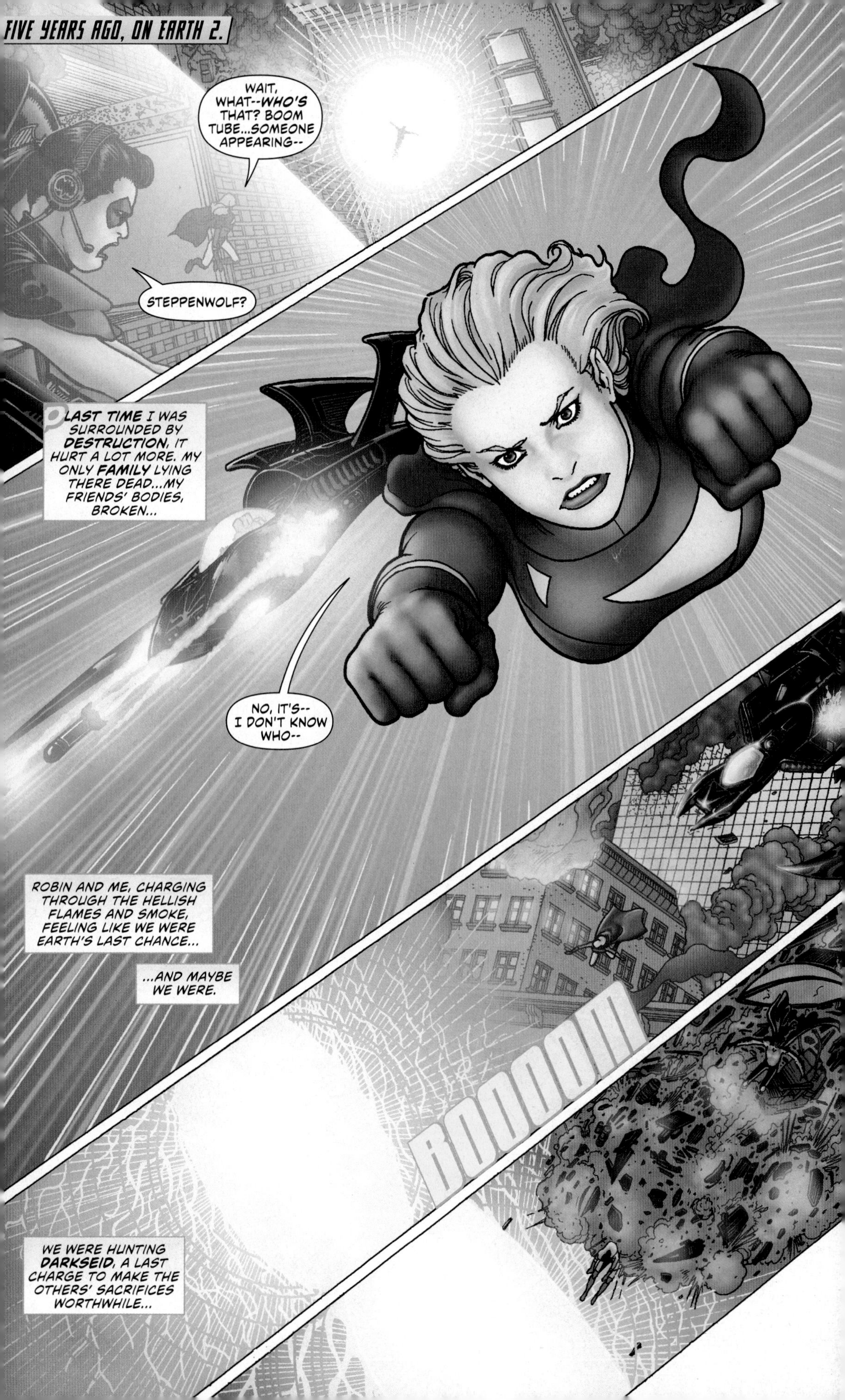
FIVE YEARS AGO, ON EARTH 2.
WAIT, WHAT--WHO'S THAT? BOOM TUBE...SOMEONE APPEARING--
STEPPENWOLF?
LAST TIME I WAS SURROUNDED BY DESTRUCTION, IT HURT A LOT MORE. MY ONLY FAMILY LYING THERE DEAD...MY FRIENDS' BODIES, BROKEN...
NO, IT'S-- I DON'T KNOW WHO--
ROBIN AND ME, CHARGING THROUGH THE HELLISH FLAMES AND SMOKE, FEELING LIKE WE WERE EARTH'S LAST CHANCE...
...AND MAYBE WE WERE.
BOOOOM
WE WERE HUNTING DARKSEID, A LAST CHARGE TO MAKE THE OTHERS' SACRIFICES WORTHWHILE...

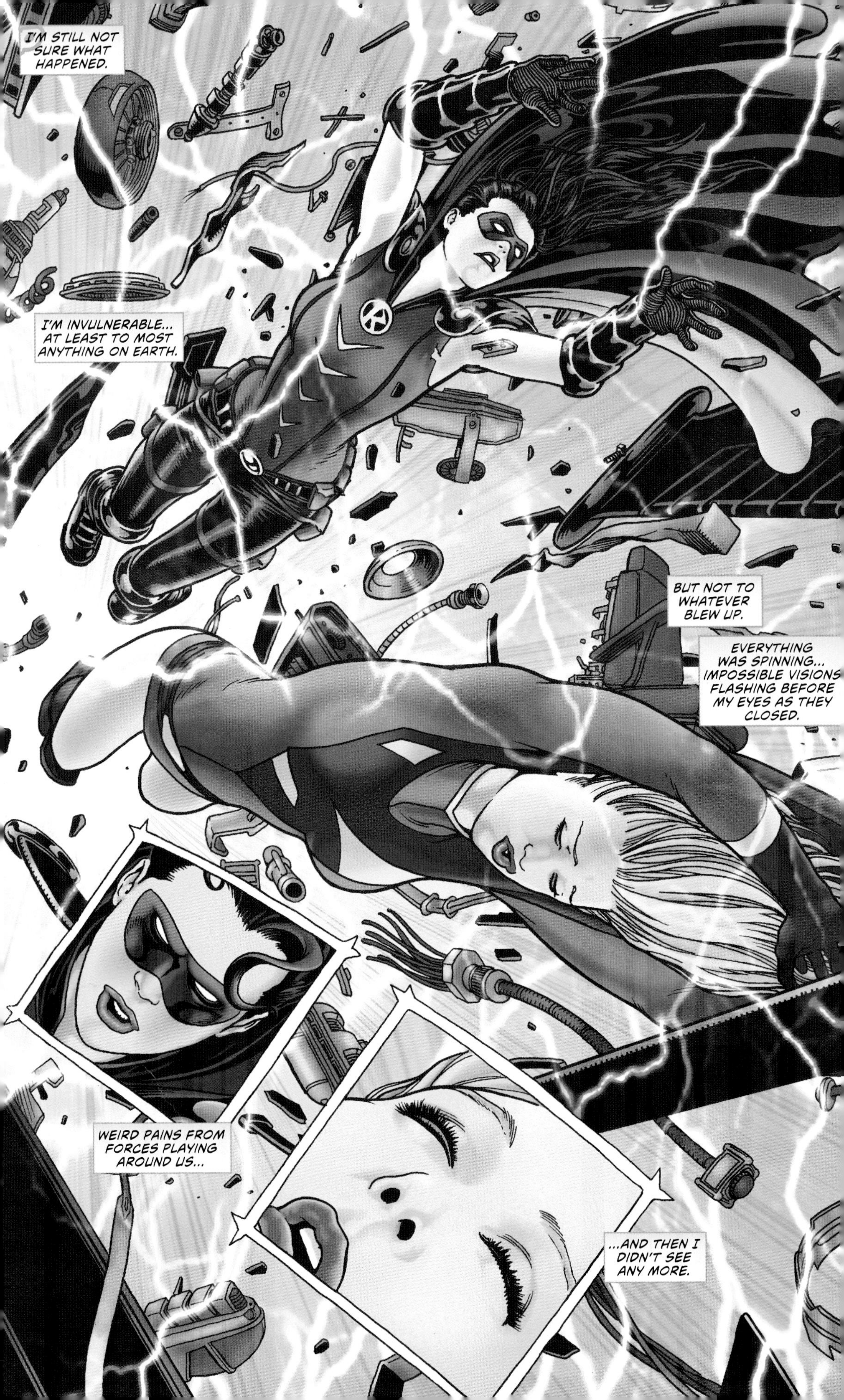
I'M STILL NOT SURE WHAT HAPPENED.
I'M INVULNERABLE... AT LEAST TO MOST ANYTHING ON EARTH.
BUT NOT TO WHATEVER BLEW UP.
EVERYTHING WAS SPINNING... IMPOSSIBLE VISIONS FLASHING BEFORE MY EYES AS THEY CLOSED.
WEIRD PAINS FROM FORCES PLAYING AROUND US...
...AND THEN I DIDN'T SEE ANY MORE.

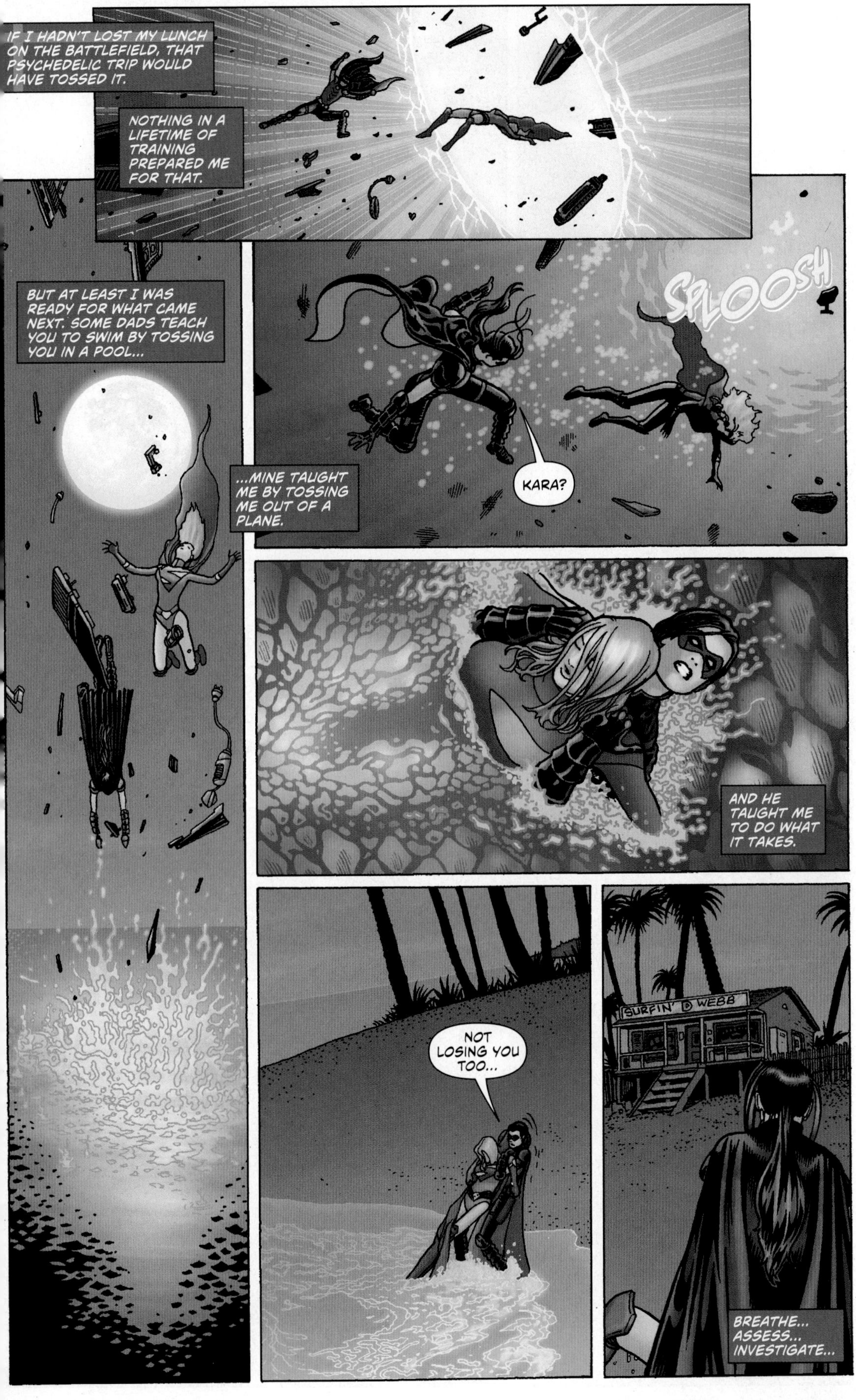
IF I HADN'T LOST MY LUNCH ON THE BATTLEFIELD, THAT PSYCHEDELIC TRIP WOULD HAVE TOSSED IT.
NOTHING IN A LIFETIME OF TRAINING PREPARED ME FOR THAT.
BUT AT LEAST I WAS READY FOR WHAT CAME NEXT. SOME DADS TEACH YOU TO SWIM BY TOSSING YOU IN A POOL...
...MINE TAUGHT ME BY TOSSING ME OUT OF A PLANE.
SPLOOSH
KARA?
AND HE TAUGHT ME TO DO WHAT IT TAKES.
NOT LOSING YOU TOO...
SURFIN' D WEBB
BREATHE... ASSESS... INVESTIGATE...

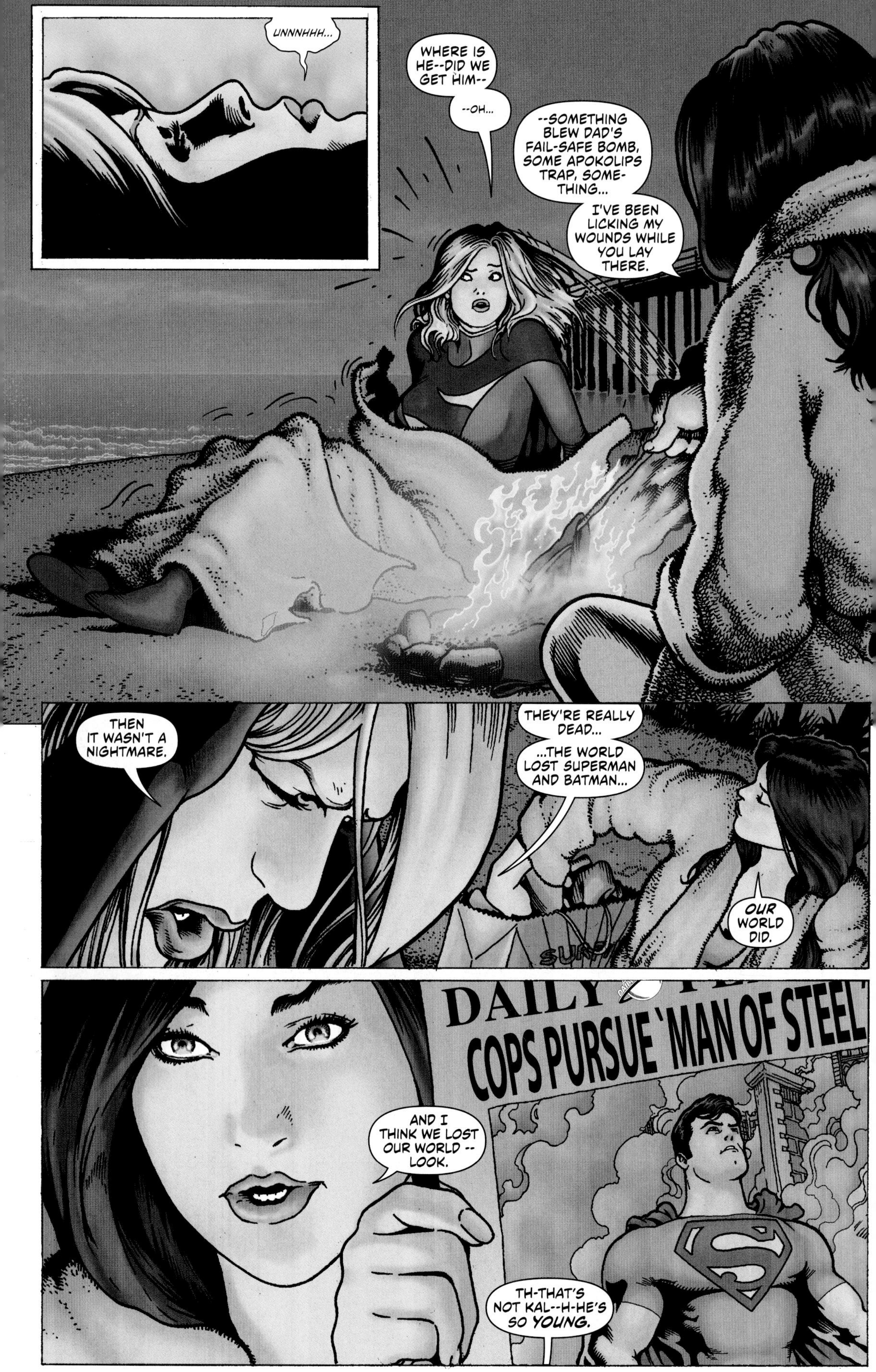
UNNNHHH...
WHERE IS HE--DID WE GET HIM--
--OH...
--SOMETHING BLEW DAD'S FAIL-SAFE BOMB, SOME APOKOLIPS TRAP, SOME-THING...
I'VE BEEN LICKING MY WOUNDS WHILE YOU LAY THERE.
THEN IT WASN'T A NIGHTMARE.
THEY'RE REALLY DEAD...
...THE WORLD LOST SUPERMAN AND BATMAN...
OUR WORLD DID.
DAILY
COPS PURSUE `MAN OF STEEL'
AND I THINK WE LOST OUR WORLD -- LOOK.
TH-THAT'S NOT KAL--H-HE'S SO YOUNG.

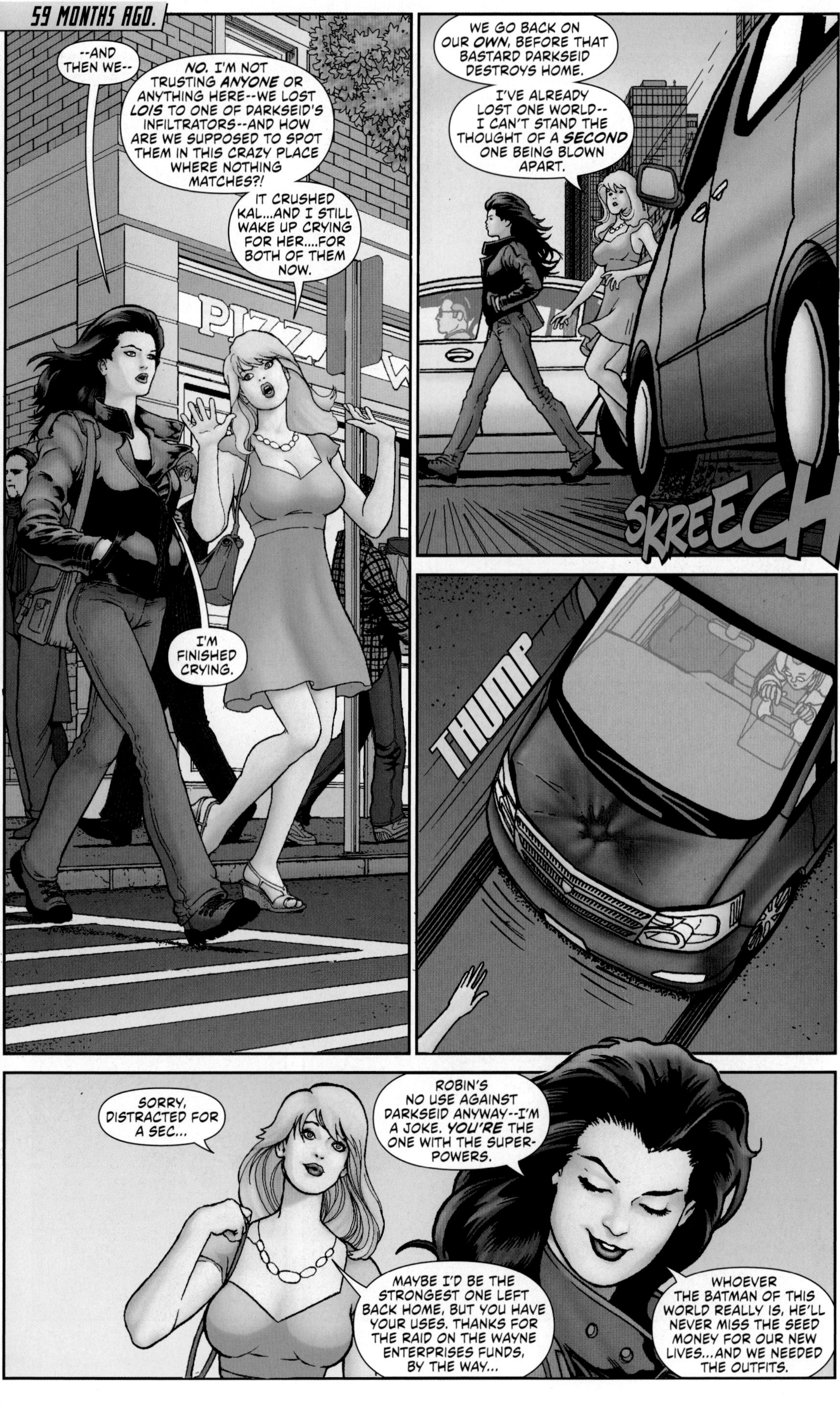
59 MONTHS AGO.
--AND THEN WE--
NO. I'M NOT TRUSTING ANYONE OR ANYTHING HERE--WE LOST LOIS TO ONE OF DARKSEID'S INFILTRATORS--AND HOW ARE WE SUPPOSED TO SPOT THEM IN THIS CRAZY PLACE WHERE NOTHING MATCHES?!
IT CRUSHED KAL...AND I STILL WAKE UP CRYING FOR HER....FOR BOTH OF THEM NOW.
I'M FINISHED CRYING.
WE GO BACK ON OUR OWN, BEFORE THAT BASTARD DARKSEID DESTROYS HOME.
I'VE ALREADY LOST ONE WORLD--I CAN'T STAND THE THOUGHT OF A SECOND ONE BEING BLOWN APART.
SKREECH
THUMP
SORRY, DISTRACTED FOR A SEC...
ROBIN'S NO USE AGAINST DARKSEID ANYWAY--I'M A JOKE. YOU'RE THE ONE WITH THE SUPER-POWERS.
MAYBE I'D BE THE STRONGEST ONE LEFT BACK HOME, BUT YOU HAVE YOUR USES. THANKS FOR THE RAID ON THE WAYNE ENTERPRISES FUNDS, BY THE WAY...
WHOEVER THE BATMAN OF THIS WORLD REALLY IS, HE'LL NEVER MISS THE SEED MONEY FOR OUR NEW LIVES...AND WE NEEDED THE OUTFITS.

# TIME

WHO IS SHE? YOUNG MYSTERY MOGUL

IF SHE WASN'T SO SHY AND RETIRING, THAT GIRL COULD GO PLACES.

GIVE HER WHAT'S DUE...SHE TOOK HER STAKE, USED HER POWERS QUIETLY, AND SHE'S BEEN BUYING UP HALF THE ADVANCED TECHNOLOGY ON THIS PLANET.

AND WHAT SHE COULDN'T BUY...WELL, I GUESS "KAREN" WOULD SAY SHE BORROWED...

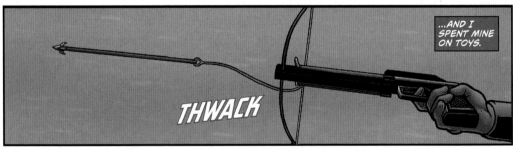

...AND I SPENT MINE ON TOYS.

THWACK

TO EACH.

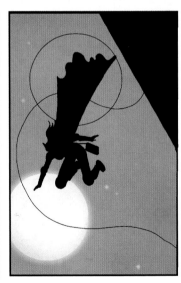

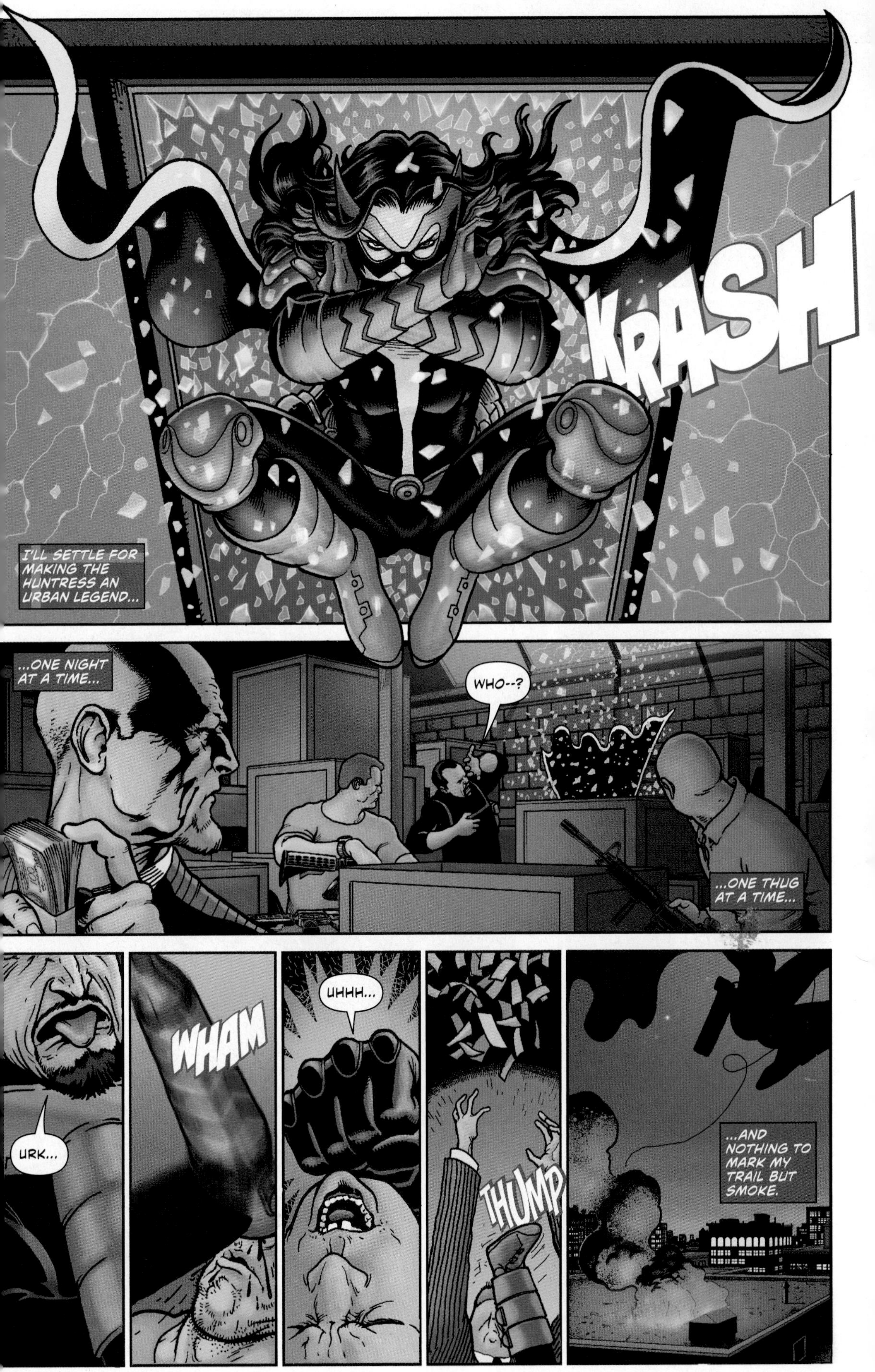
KRASH
I'LL SETTLE FOR MAKING THE HUNTRESS AN URBAN LEGEND...
...ONE NIGHT AT A TIME...
WHO--?
...ONE THUG AT A TIME...
URK...
WHAM
UHHH...
THUMP
...AND NOTHING TO MARK MY TRAIL BUT SMOKE.

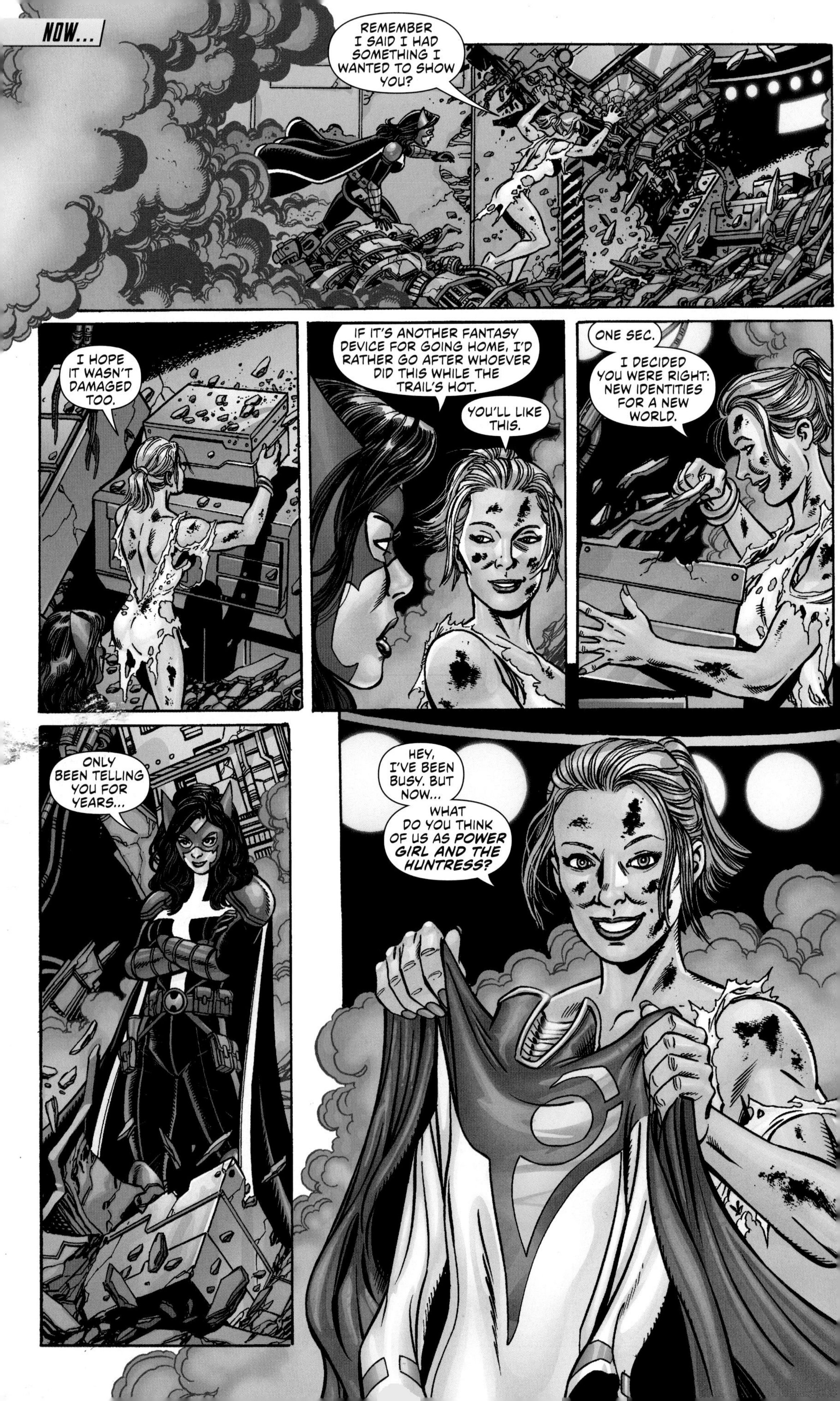
NOW...
REMEMBER I SAID I HAD SOMETHING I WANTED TO SHOW YOU?
I HOPE IT WASN'T DAMAGED TOO.
IF IT'S ANOTHER FANTASY DEVICE FOR GOING HOME, I'D RATHER GO AFTER WHOEVER DID THIS WHILE THE TRAIL'S HOT.
YOU'LL LIKE THIS.
ONE SEC.
I DECIDED YOU WERE RIGHT: NEW IDENTITIES FOR A NEW WORLD.
ONLY BEEN TELLING YOU FOR YEARS...
HEY, I'VE BEEN BUSY. BUT NOW...
WHAT DO YOU THINK OF US AS POWER GIRL AND THE HUNTRESS?

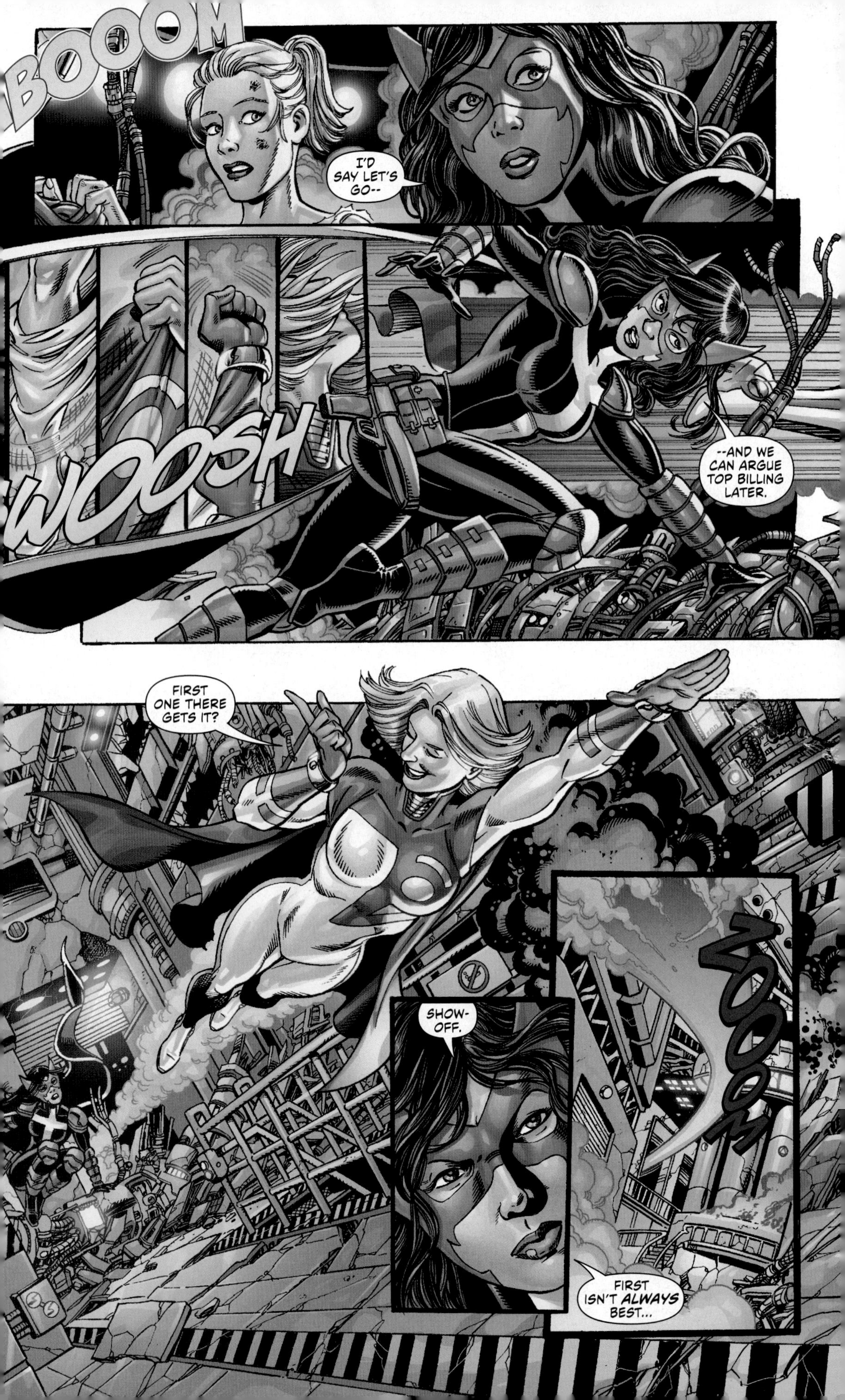
BOOOM
I'D SAY LET'S GO--
WOOSH
--AND WE CAN ARGUE TOP BILLING LATER.
FIRST ONE THERE GETS IT?
ZOOOOM
SHOW-OFF.
FIRST ISN'T *ALWAYS* BEST...

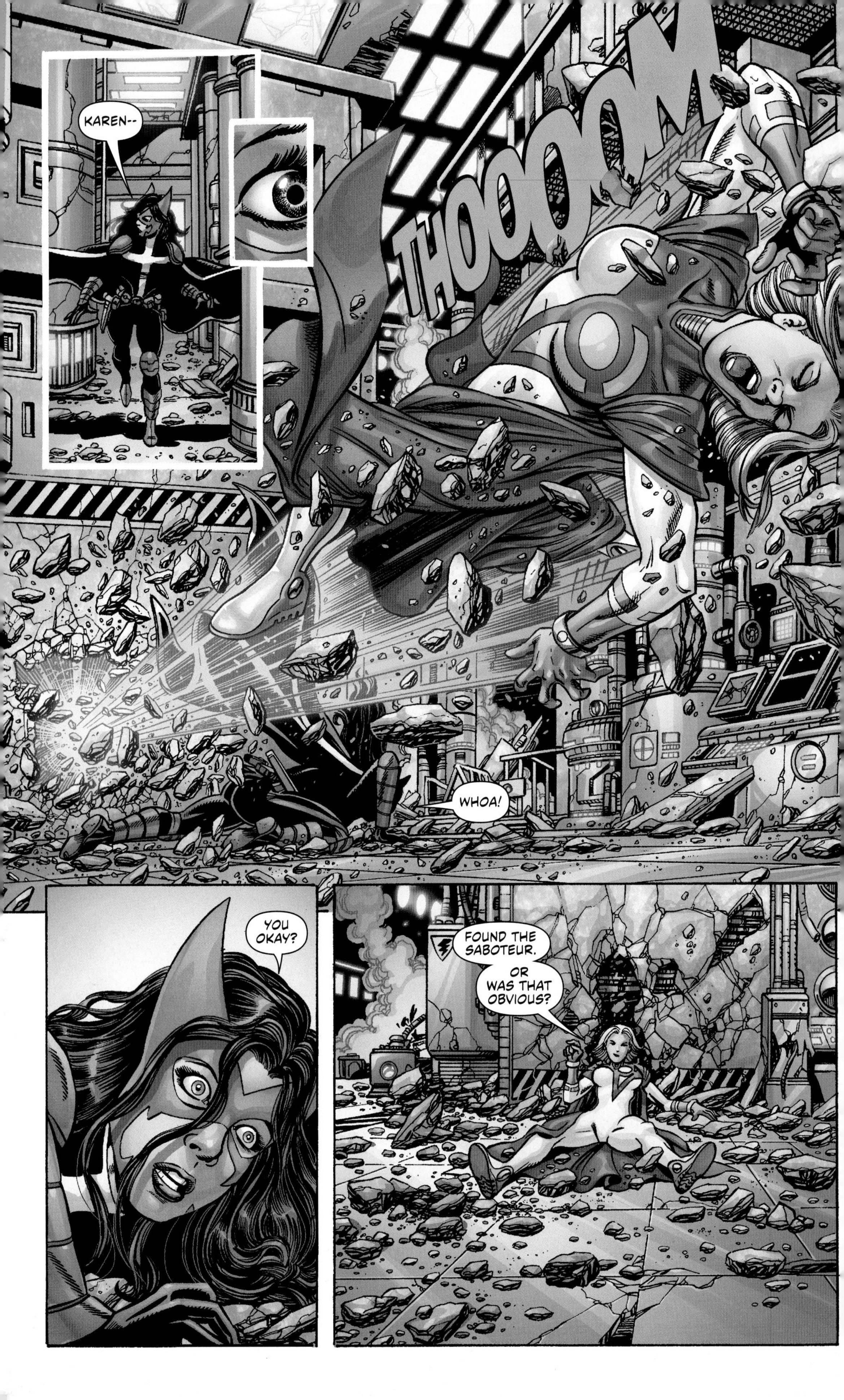
KAREN--
THOOOOM
WHOA!
YOU OKAY?
FOUND THE SABOTEUR.
OR WAS THAT OBVIOUS?

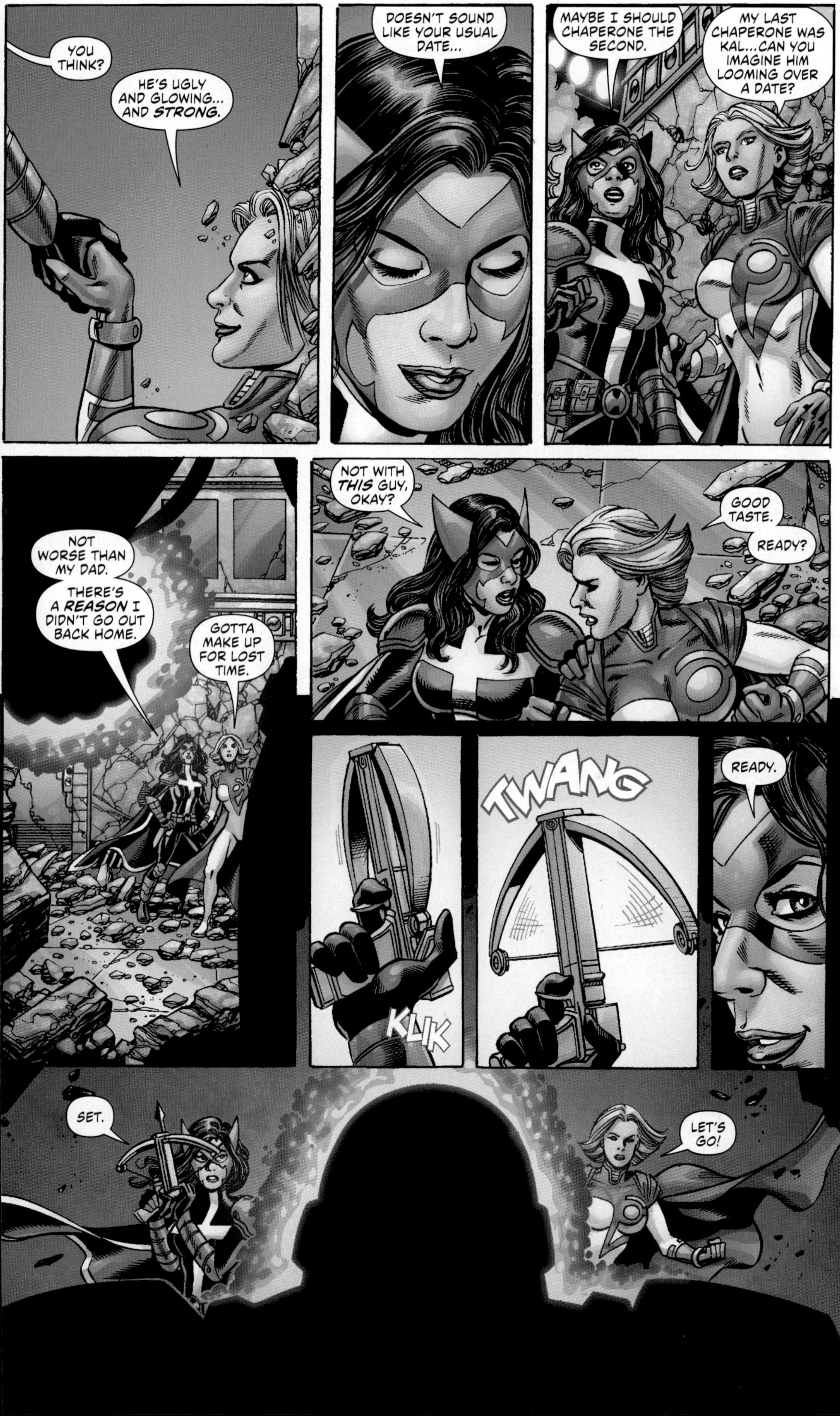
YOU THINK?
HE'S UGLY AND GLOWING... AND STRONG.
DOESN'T SOUND LIKE YOUR USUAL DATE...
MAYBE I SHOULD CHAPERONE THE SECOND.
MY LAST CHAPERONE WAS KAL...CAN YOU IMAGINE HIM LOOMING OVER A DATE?
NOT WORSE THAN MY DAD.
THERE'S A REASON I DIDN'T GO OUT BACK HOME.
GOTTA MAKE UP FOR LOST TIME.
NOT WITH THIS GUY, OKAY?
GOOD TASTE.
READY?
KLIK
TWANG
READY.
SET.
LET'S GO!

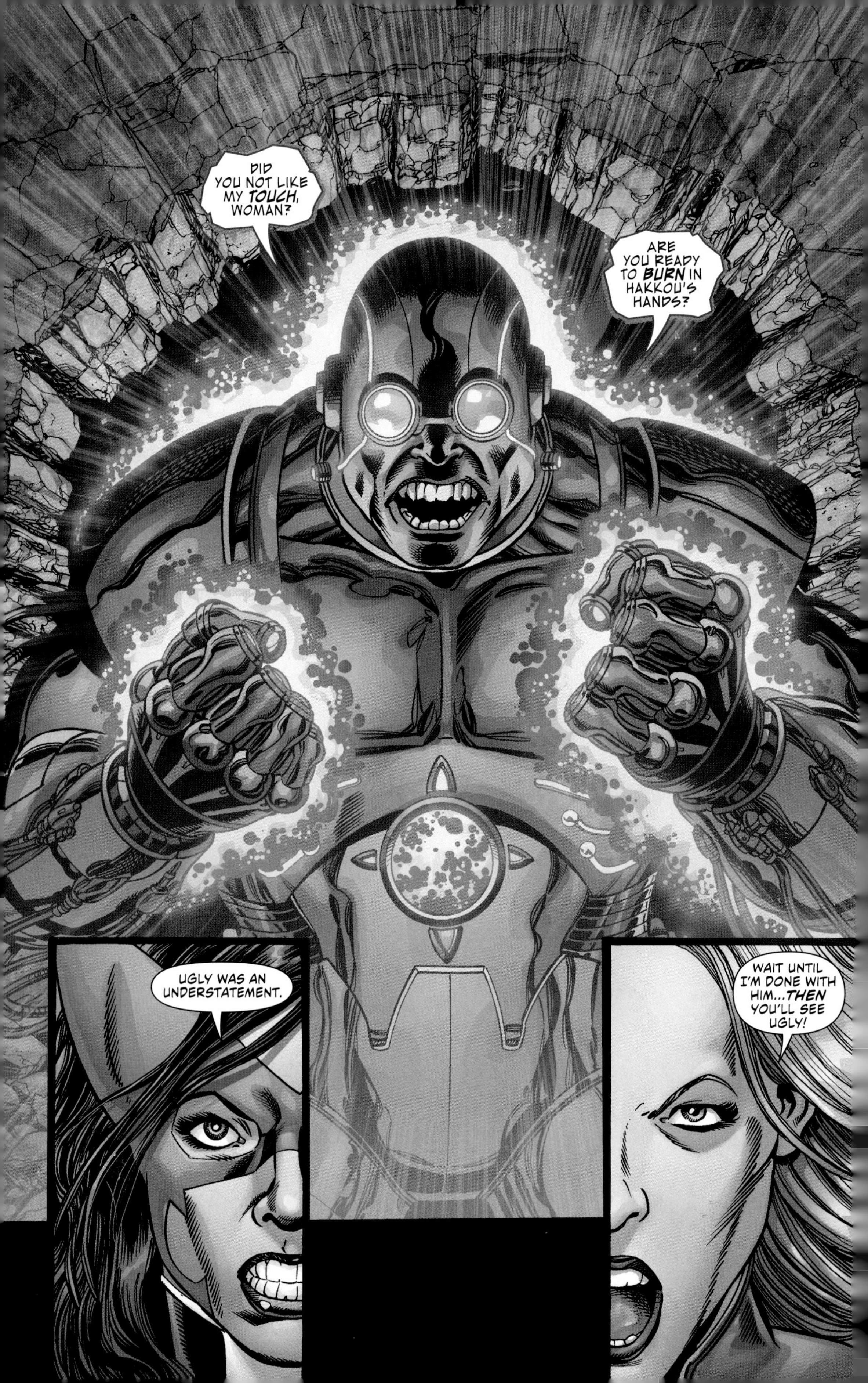
DID YOU NOT LIKE MY TOUCH, WOMAN?
ARE YOU READY TO BURN IN HAKKOU'S HANDS?
UGLY WAS AN UNDERSTATEMENT.
WAIT UNTIL I'M DONE WITH HIM...THEN YOU'LL SEE UGLY!

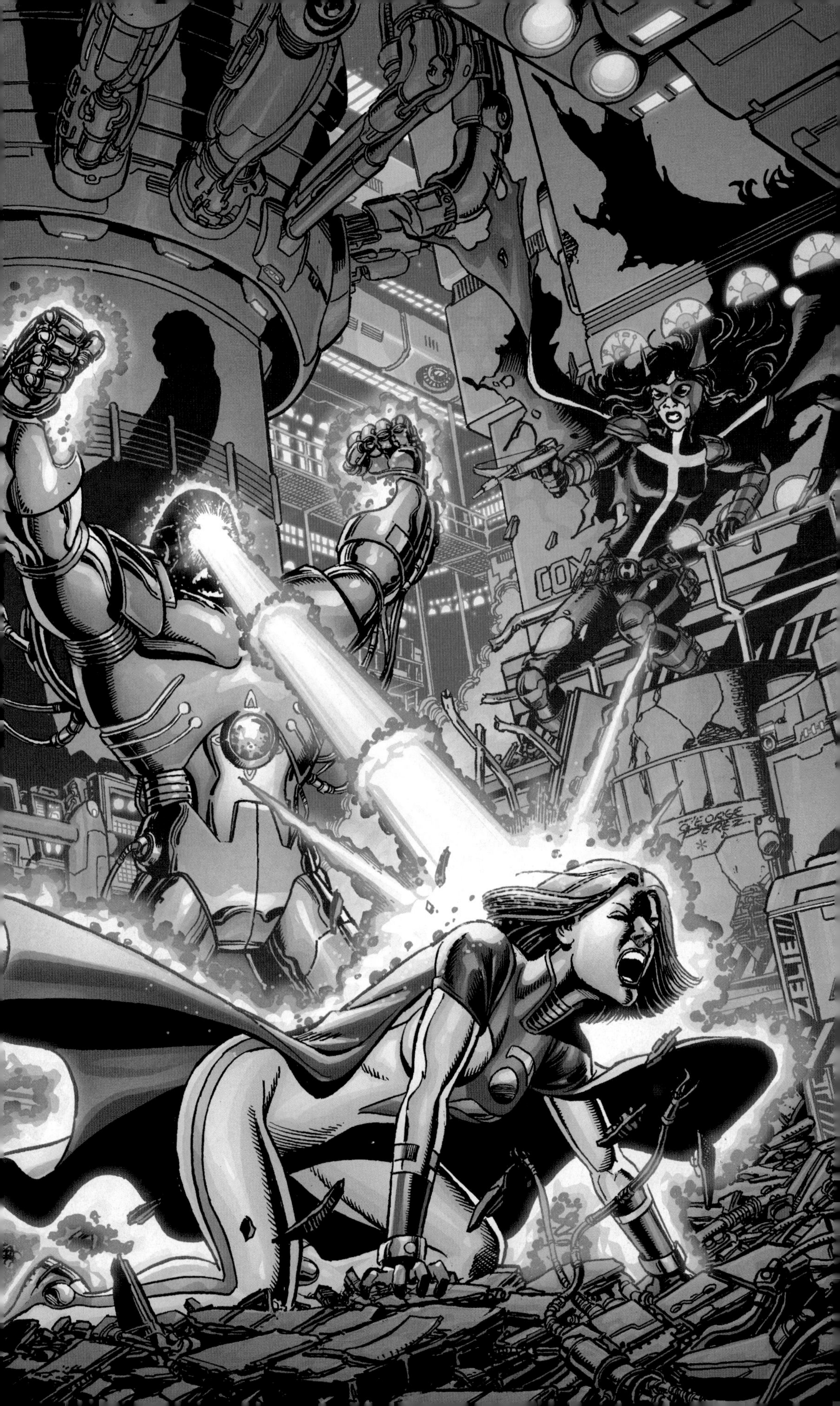

**PAUL LEVITZ** writer **GEORGE PEREZ** penciller (present-day sequence)
**SCOTT KOBLISH** inker (present-day sequence) **KEVIN MAGUIRE** artist (flashback sequence)

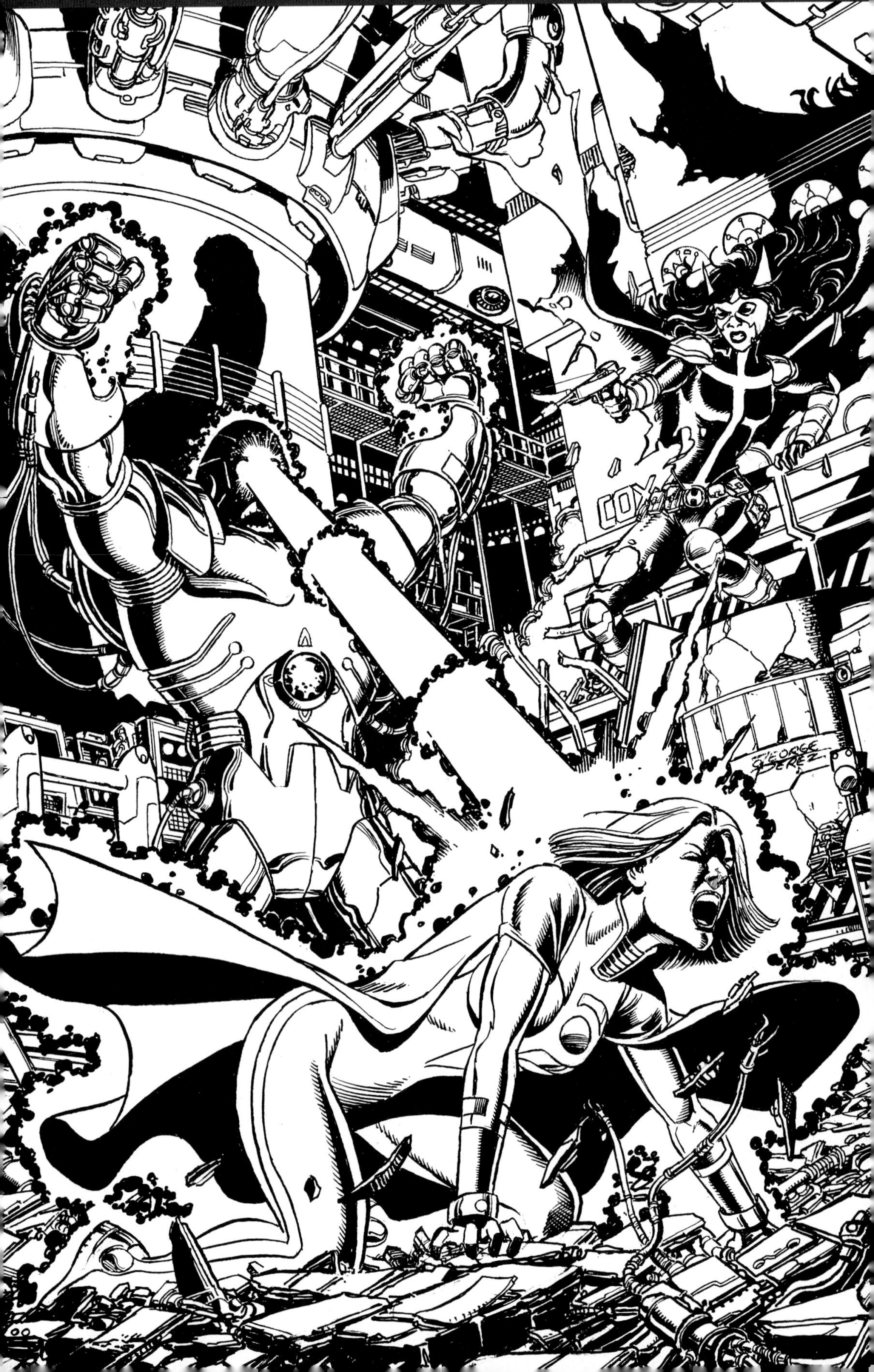
GEORGE PEREZ

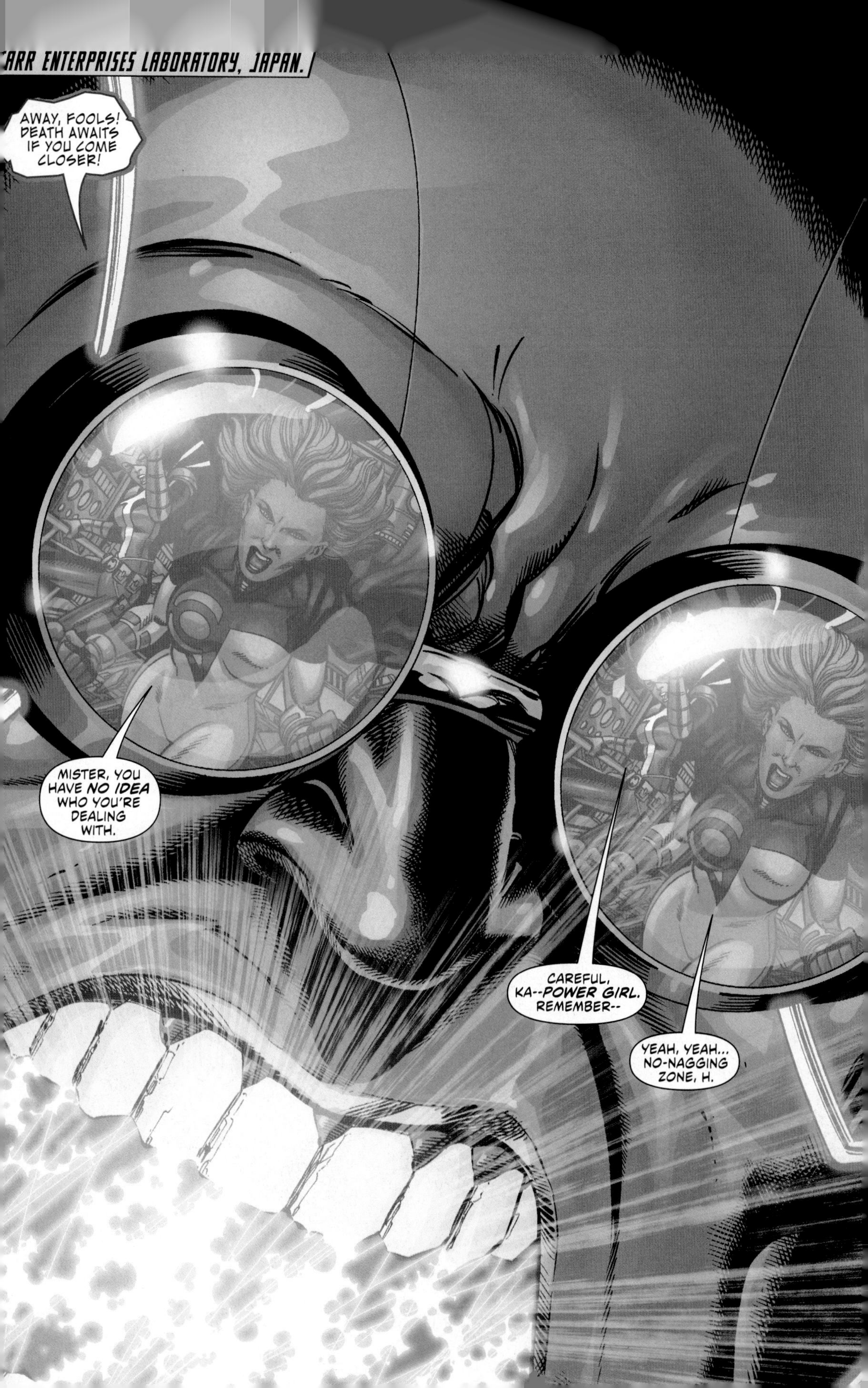

ARR ENTERPRISES LABORATORY, JAPAN.
AWAY, FOOLS! DEATH AWAITS IF YOU COME CLOSER!
MISTER, YOU HAVE NO IDEA WHO YOU'RE DEALING WITH.
CAREFUL, KA--POWER GIRL. REMEMBER--
YEAH, YEAH... NO-NAGGING ZONE, H.

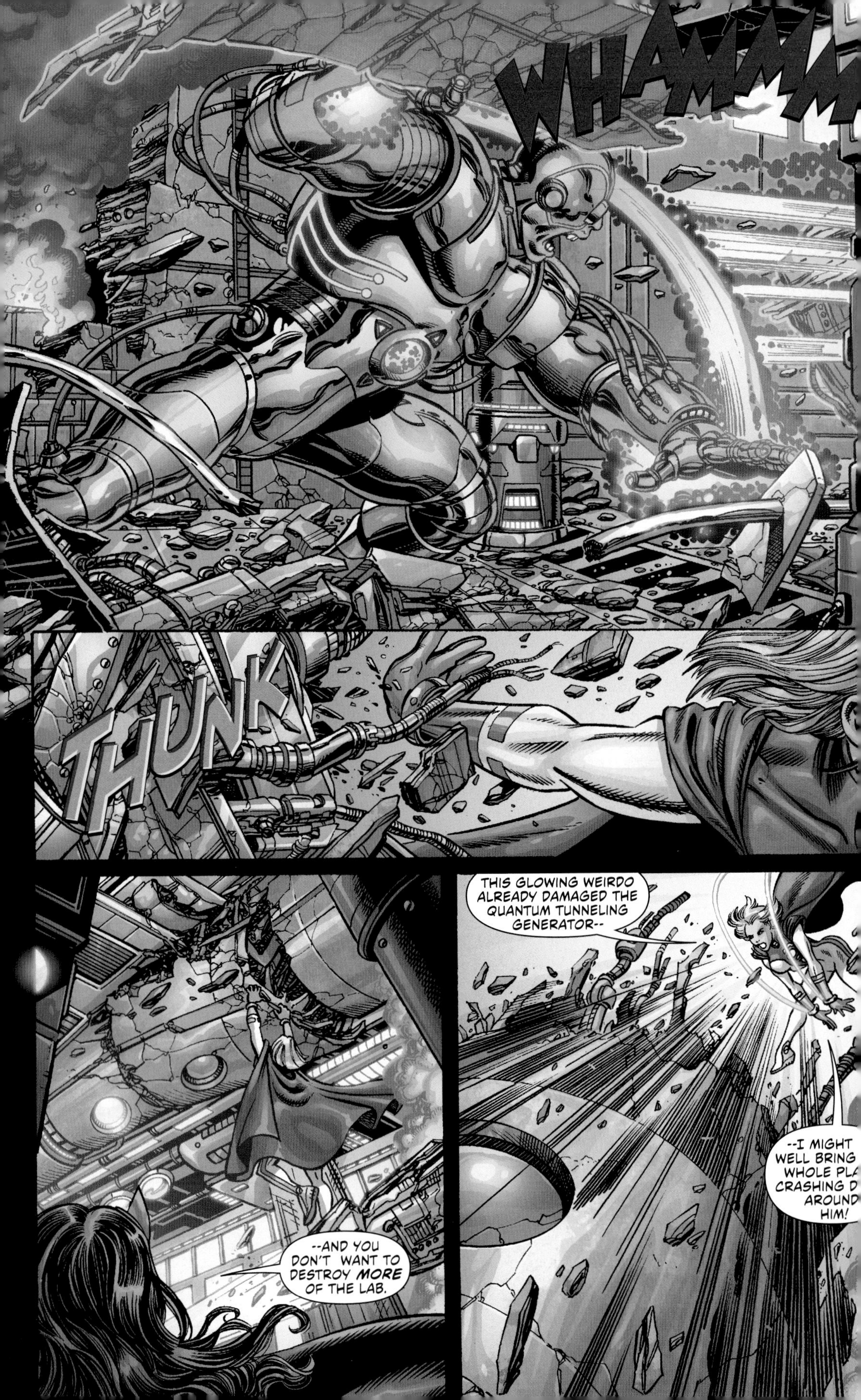
WHAMMM
THUNK
THIS GLOWING WEIRDO ALREADY DAMAGED THE QUANTUM TUNNELING GENERATOR--
--AND YOU DON'T WANT TO DESTROY MORE OF THE LAB.
--I MIGHT WELL BRING WHOLE PLA CRASHING D AROUND HIM!

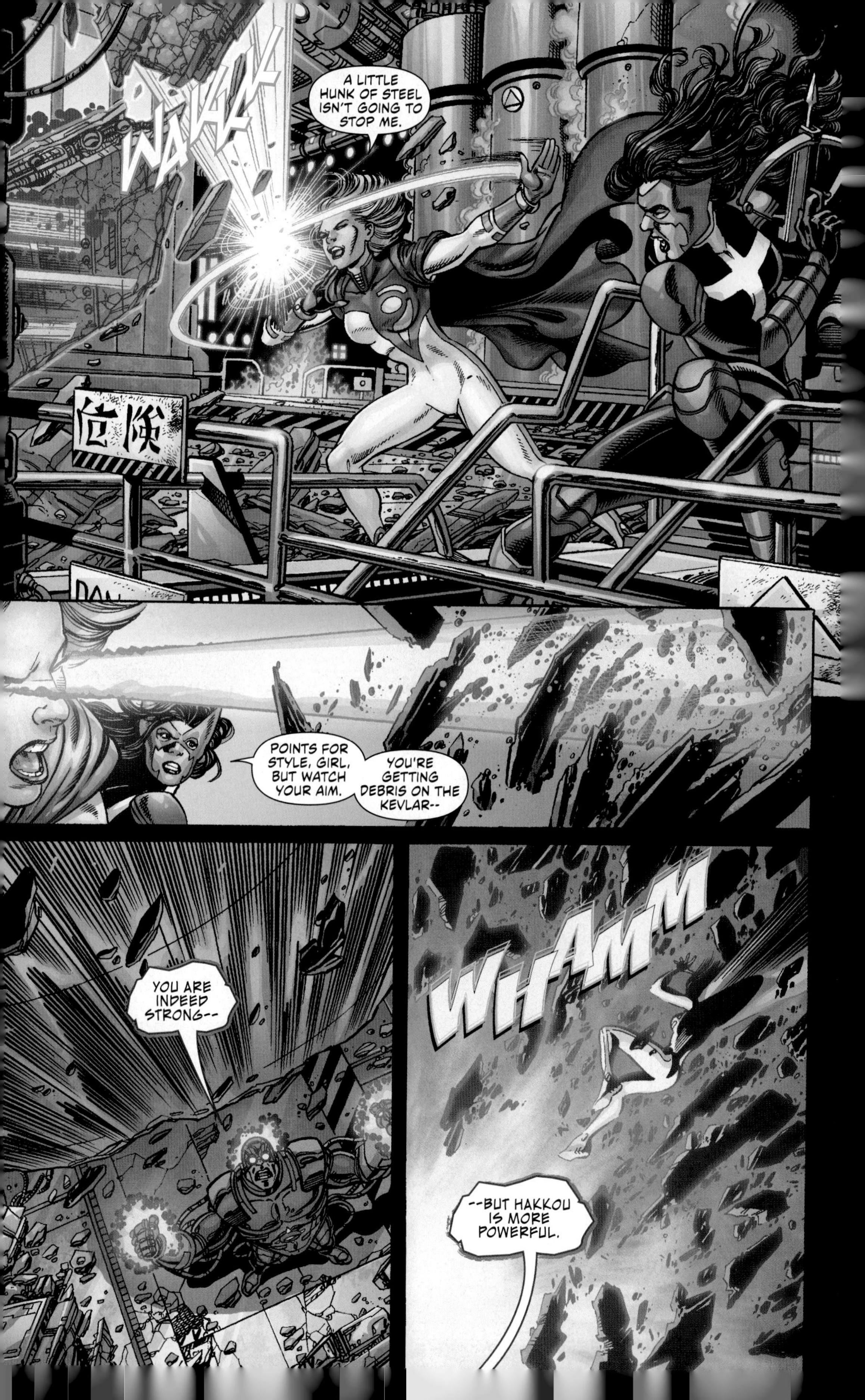
WAKK
A LITTLE HUNK OF STEEL ISN'T GOING TO STOP ME.
危険
POINTS FOR STYLE, GIRL, BUT WATCH YOUR AIM.
YOU'RE GETTING DEBRIS ON THE KEVLAR--
YOU ARE INDEED STRONG--
WHAMM
--BUT HAKKOU IS MORE POWERFUL.

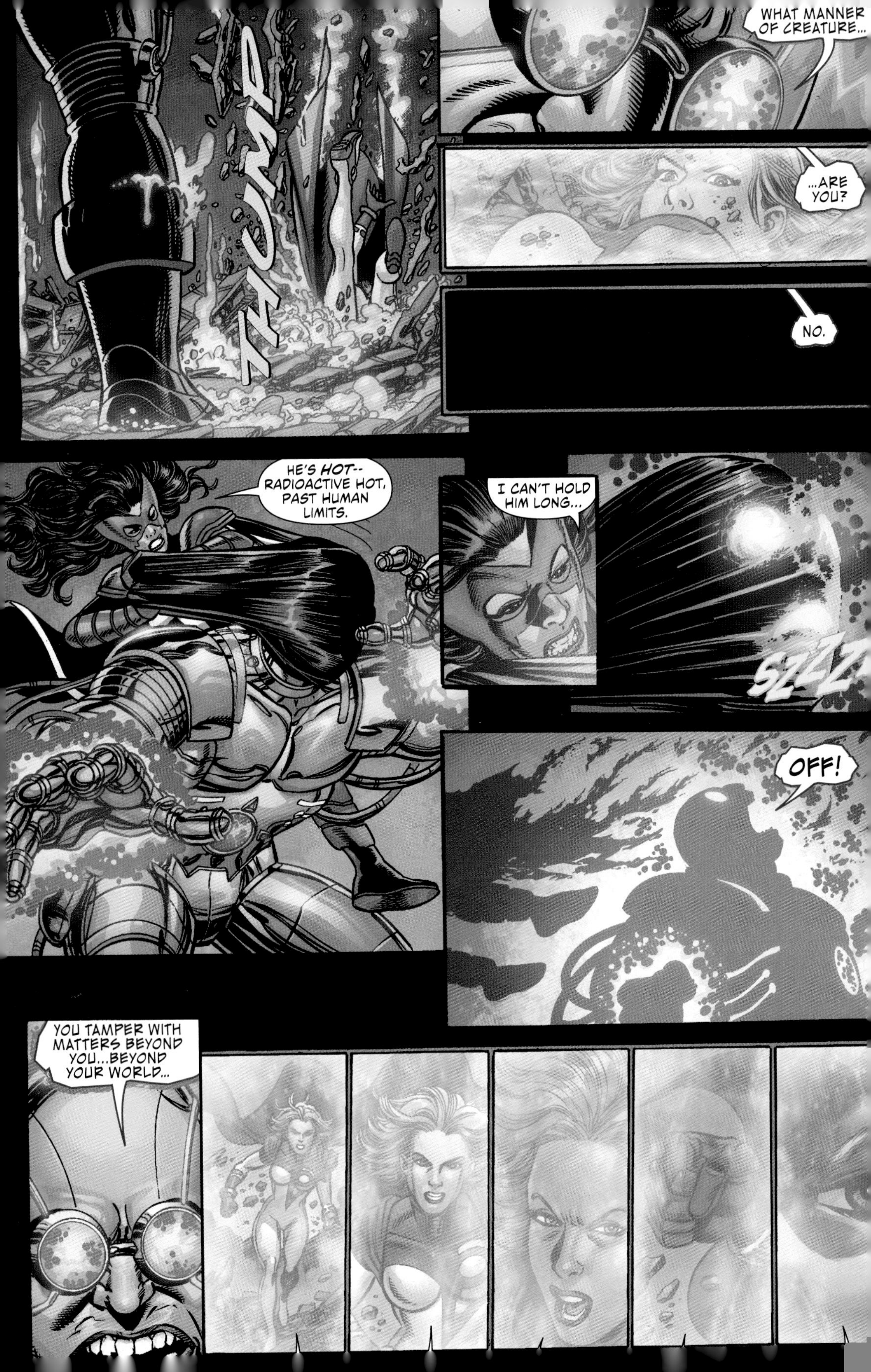
THUMP
WHAT MANNER OF CREATURE...
...ARE YOU?
NO.
HE'S HOT-- RADIOACTIVE HOT, PAST HUMAN LIMITS.
I CAN'T HOLD HIM LONG...
SZZZ
OFF!
YOU TAMPER WITH MATTERS BEYOND YOU...BEYOND YOUR WORLD...

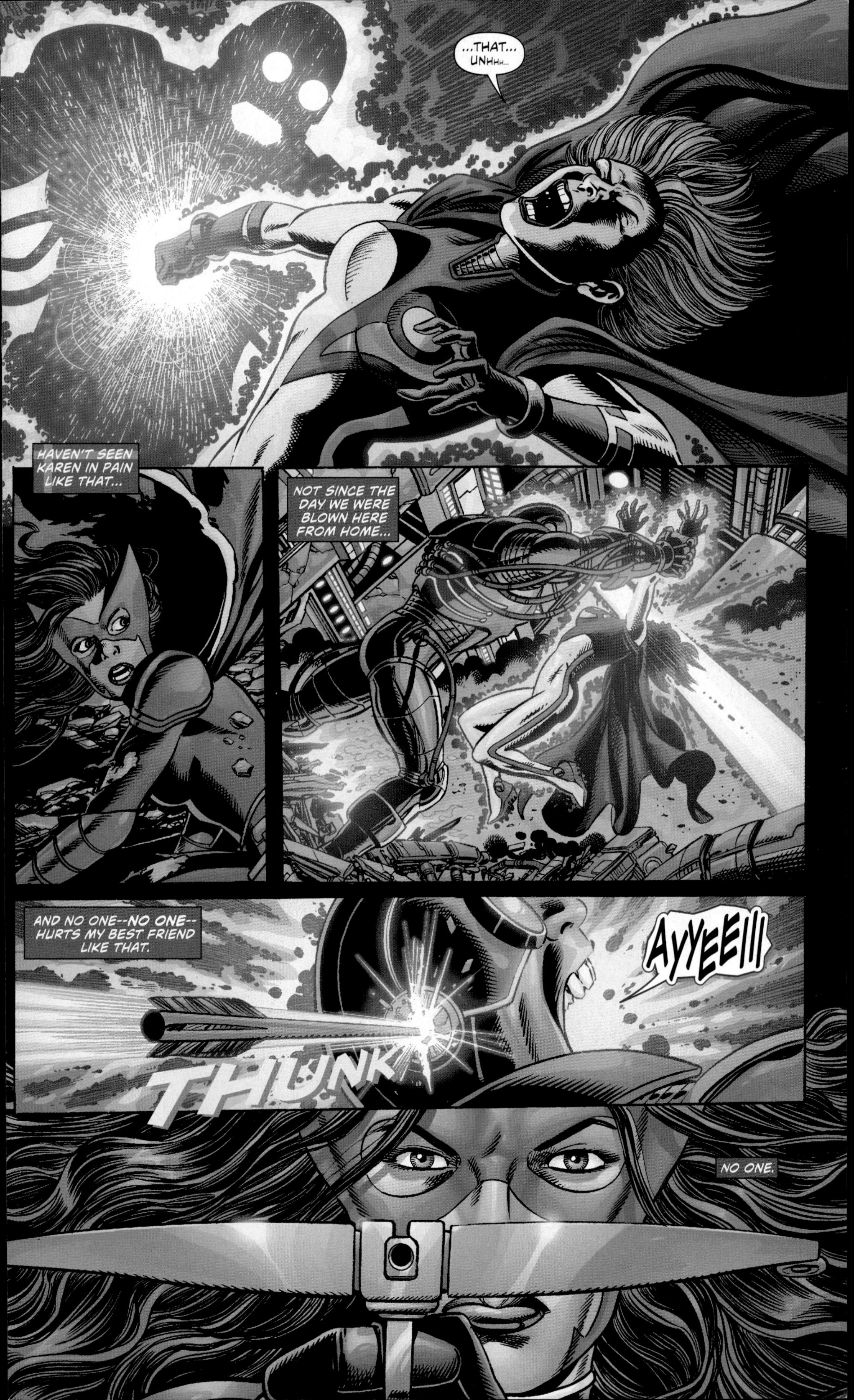
...THAT... UNHHH...
HAVEN'T SEEN KAREN IN PAIN LIKE THAT...
NOT SINCE THE DAY WE WERE BLOWN HERE FROM HOME...
AND NO ONE--NO ONE--HURTS MY BEST FRIEND LIKE THAT.
AYYEE!!!
THUNK
NO ONE.

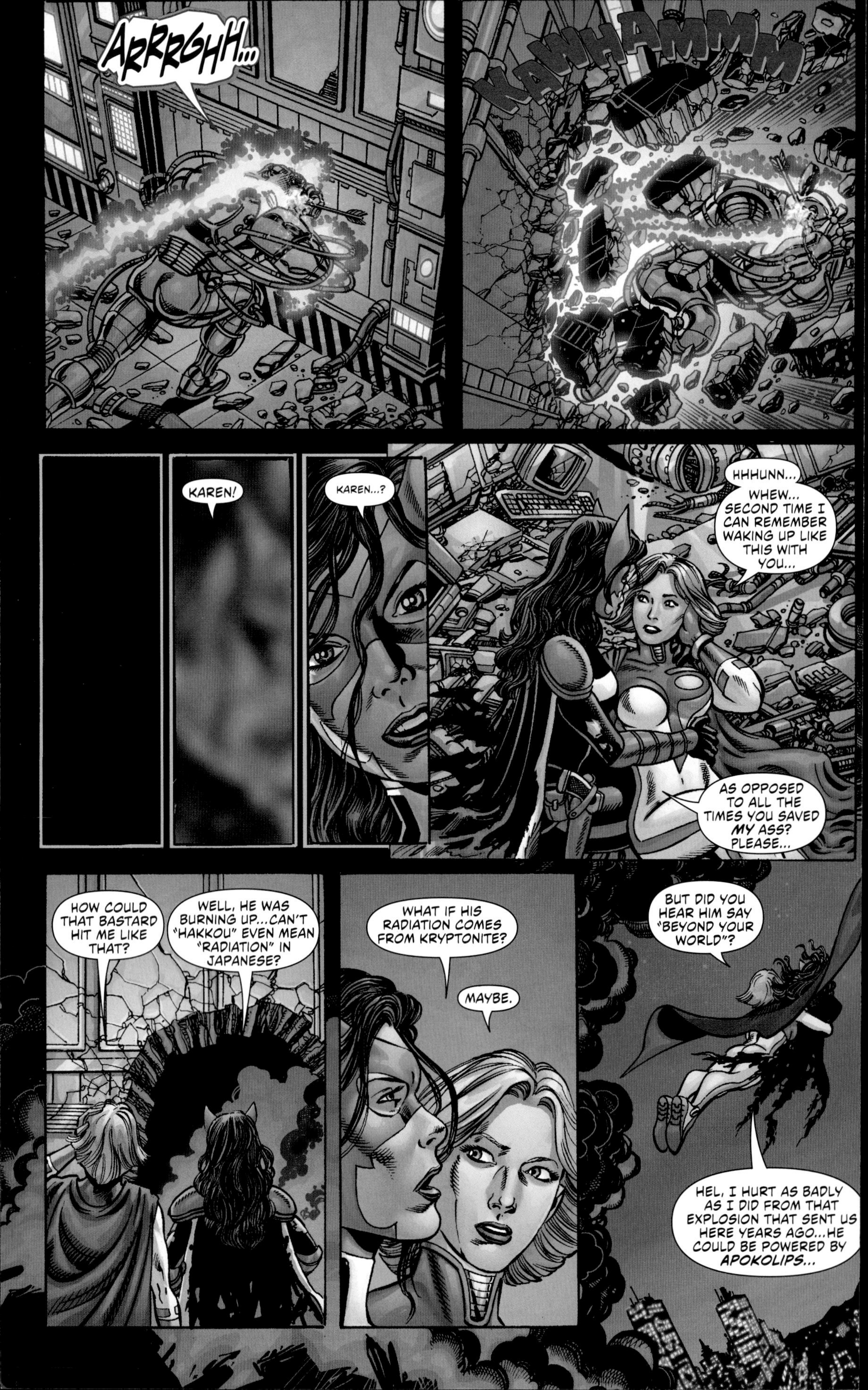
ARRRGHH...
KAWHAMMM
KAREN!
KAREN...?
HHHUNN... WHEW... SECOND TIME I CAN REMEMBER WAKING UP LIKE THIS WITH YOU...
AS OPPOSED TO ALL THE TIMES YOU SAVED MY ASS? PLEASE...
HOW COULD THAT BASTARD HIT ME LIKE THAT?
WELL, HE WAS BURNING UP...CAN'T "HAKKOU" EVEN MEAN "RADIATION" IN JAPANESE?
WHAT IF HIS RADIATION COMES FROM KRYPTONITE?
MAYBE.
BUT DID YOU HEAR HIM SAY "BEYOND YOUR WORLD"?
HEL, I HURT AS BADLY AS I DID FROM THAT EXPLOSION THAT SENT US HERE YEARS AGO...HE COULD BE POWERED BY APOKOLIPS...

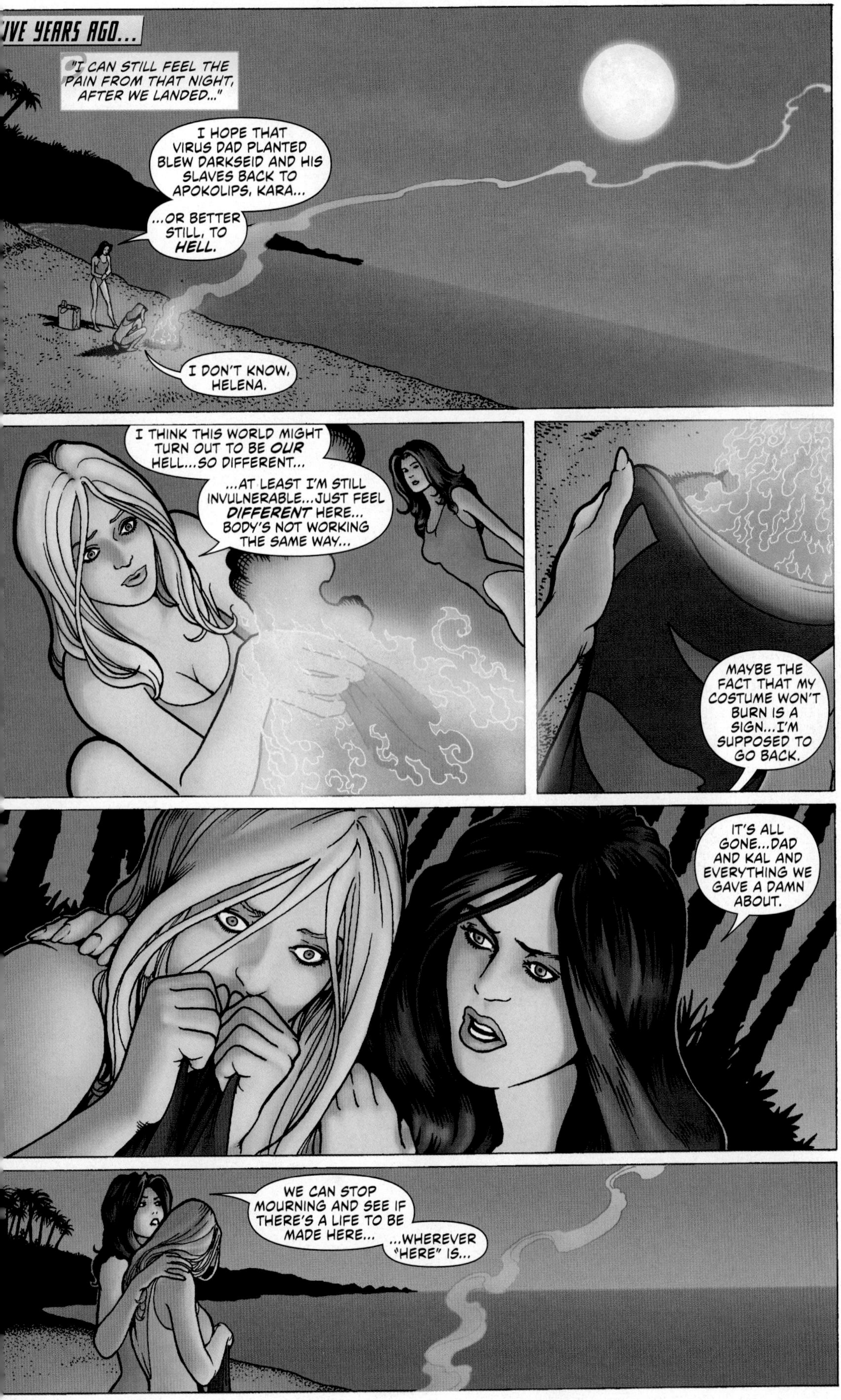

IVE YEARS AGO...
"I CAN STILL FEEL THE PAIN FROM THAT NIGHT, AFTER WE LANDED..."
I HOPE THAT VIRUS DAD PLANTED BLEW DARKSEID AND HIS SLAVES BACK TO APOKOLIPS, KARA...
...OR BETTER STILL, TO **HELL.**
I DON'T KNOW, HELENA.
I THINK THIS WORLD MIGHT TURN OUT TO BE ***OUR*** HELL...SO DIFFERENT...
...AT LEAST I'M STILL INVULNERABLE...JUST FEEL ***DIFFERENT*** HERE... BODY'S NOT WORKING THE SAME WAY...
MAYBE THE FACT THAT MY COSTUME WON'T BURN IS A SIGN...I'M SUPPOSED TO GO BACK.
IT'S ALL GONE...DAD AND KAL AND EVERYTHING WE GAVE A DAMN ABOUT.
WE CAN STOP MOURNING AND SEE IF THERE'S A LIFE TO BE MADE HERE...
...WHEREVER "HERE" IS...

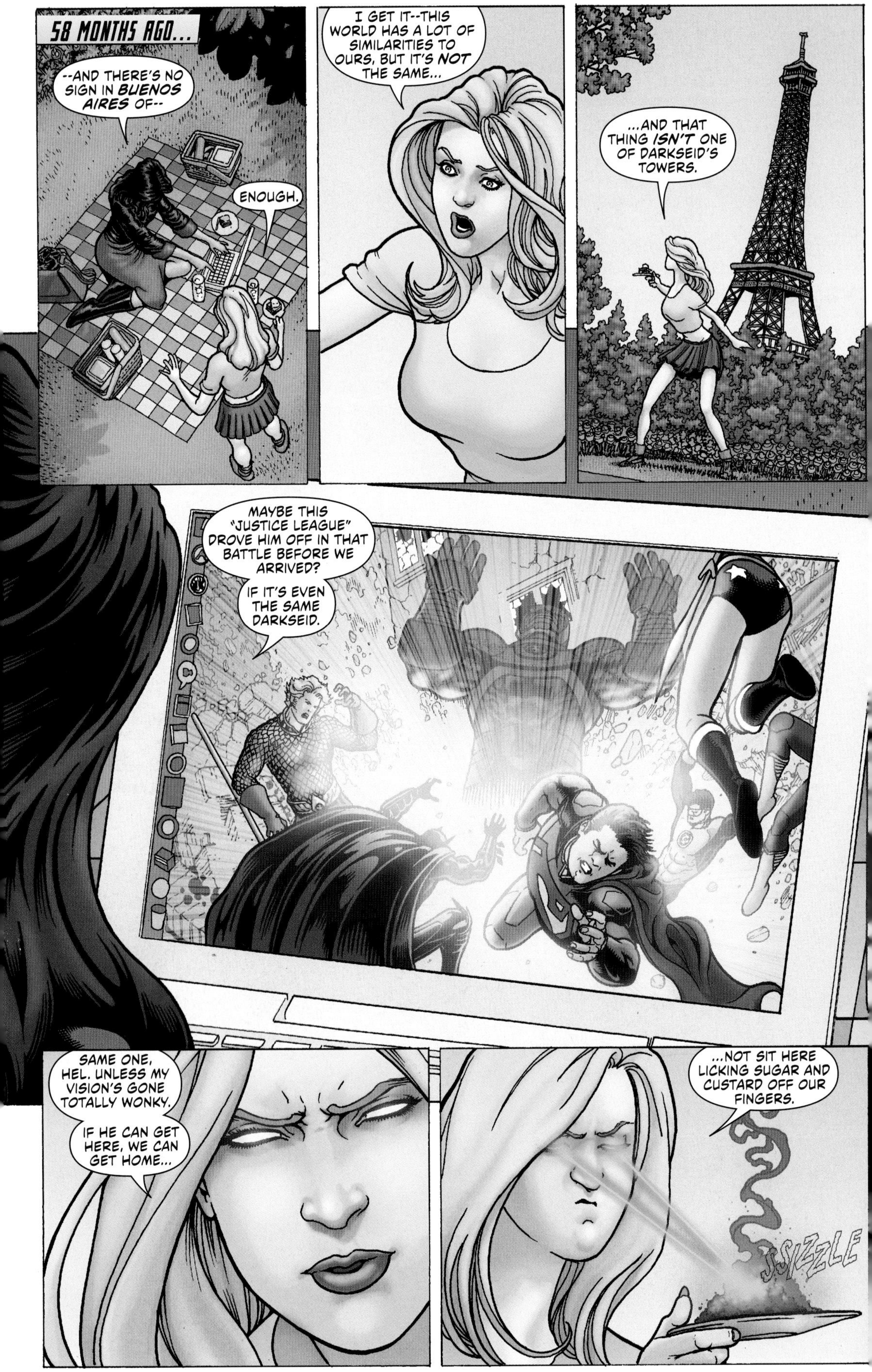
58 MONTHS AGO...
--AND THERE'S NO SIGN IN BUENOS AIRES OF--
ENOUGH.
I GET IT--THIS WORLD HAS A LOT OF SIMILARITIES TO OURS, BUT IT'S NOT THE SAME...
...AND THAT THING ISN'T ONE OF DARKSEID'S TOWERS.
MAYBE THIS "JUSTICE LEAGUE" DROVE HIM OFF IN THAT BATTLE BEFORE WE ARRIVED?
IF IT'S EVEN THE SAME DARKSEID.
SAME ONE, HEL. UNLESS MY VISION'S GONE TOTALLY WONKY.
IF HE CAN GET HERE, WE CAN GET HOME...
...NOT SIT HERE LICKING SUGAR AND CUSTARD OFF OUR FINGERS.
SSIZZLE

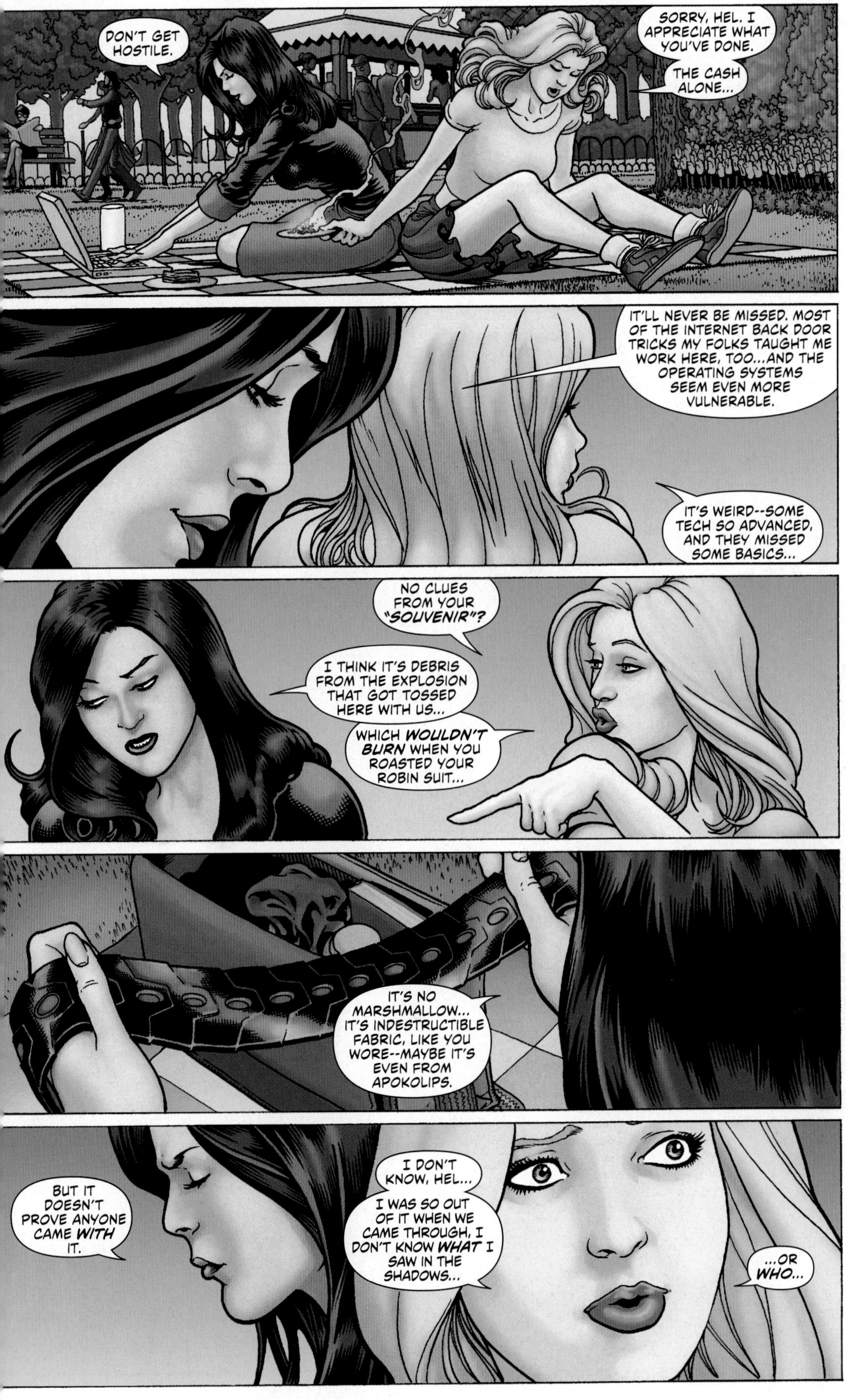
DON'T GET HOSTILE.
SORRY, HEL. I APPRECIATE WHAT YOU'VE DONE.
THE CASH ALONE...
IT'LL NEVER BE MISSED. MOST OF THE INTERNET BACK DOOR TRICKS MY FOLKS TAUGHT ME WORK HERE, TOO...AND THE OPERATING SYSTEMS SEEM EVEN MORE VULNERABLE.
IT'S WEIRD--SOME TECH SO ADVANCED, AND THEY MISSED SOME BASICS...
NO CLUES FROM YOUR "SOUVENIR"?
I THINK IT'S DEBRIS FROM THE EXPLOSION THAT GOT TOSSED HERE WITH US...
WHICH WOULDN'T BURN WHEN YOU ROASTED YOUR ROBIN SUIT...
IT'S NO MARSHMALLOW... IT'S INDESTRUCTIBLE FABRIC, LIKE YOU WORE--MAYBE IT'S EVEN FROM APOKOLIPS.
BUT IT DOESN'T PROVE ANYONE CAME WITH IT.
I DON'T KNOW, HEL...
I WAS SO OUT OF IT WHEN WE CAME THROUGH, I DON'T KNOW WHAT I SAW IN THE SHADOWS...
...OR WHO...

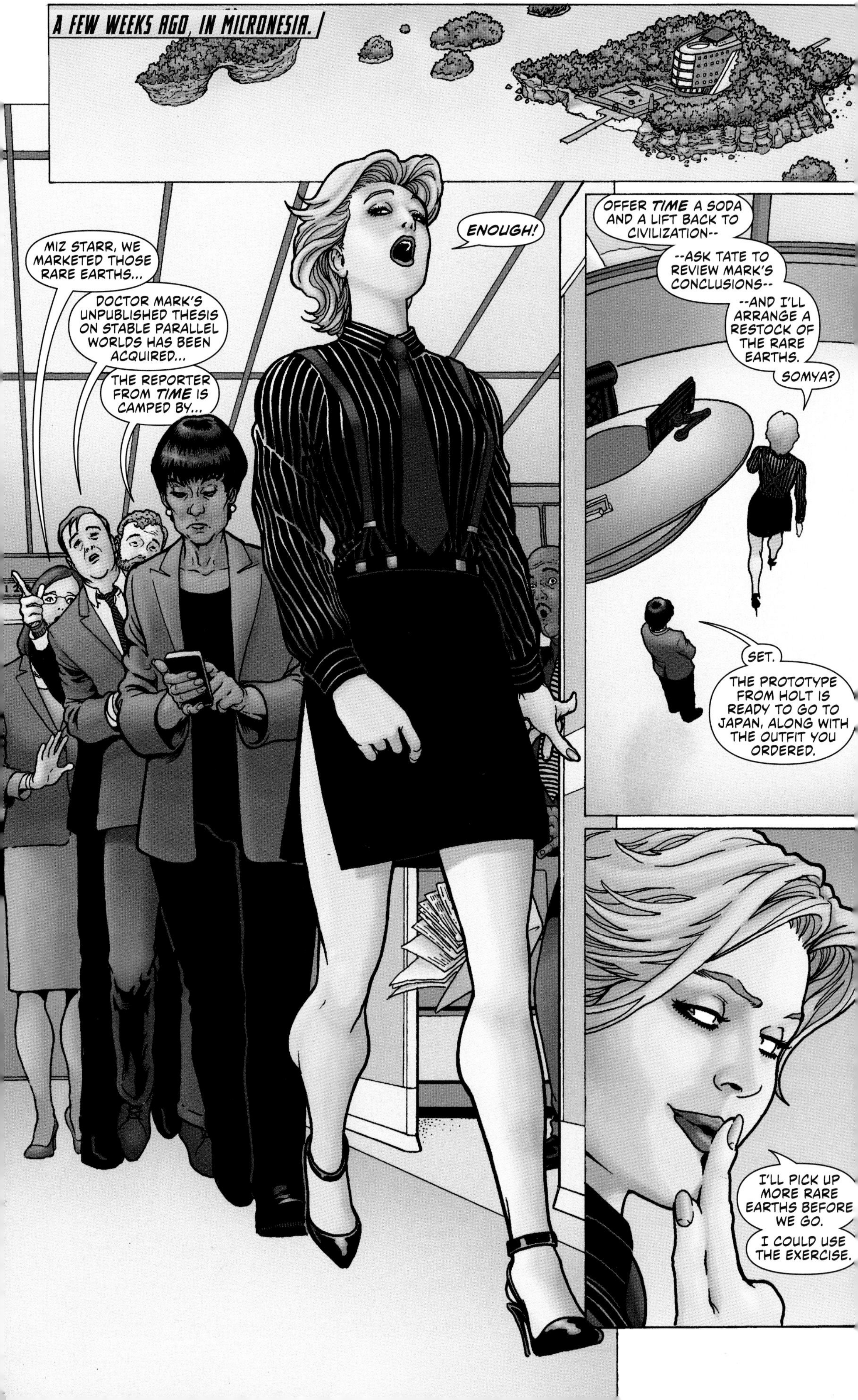
A FEW WEEKS AGO, IN MICRONESIA.
MIZ STARR, WE MARKETED THOSE RARE EARTHS...
DOCTOR MARK'S UNPUBLISHED THESIS ON STABLE PARALLEL WORLDS HAS BEEN ACQUIRED...
THE REPORTER FROM TIME IS CAMPED BY...
ENOUGH!
OFFER TIME A SODA AND A LIFT BACK TO CIVILIZATION--
--ASK TATE TO REVIEW MARK'S CONCLUSIONS--
--AND I'LL ARRANGE A RESTOCK OF THE RARE EARTHS.
SOMYA?
SET.
THE PROTOTYPE FROM HOLT IS READY TO GO TO JAPAN, ALONG WITH THE OUTFIT YOU ORDERED.
I'LL PICK UP MORE RARE EARTHS BEFORE WE GO.
I COULD USE THE EXERCISE.

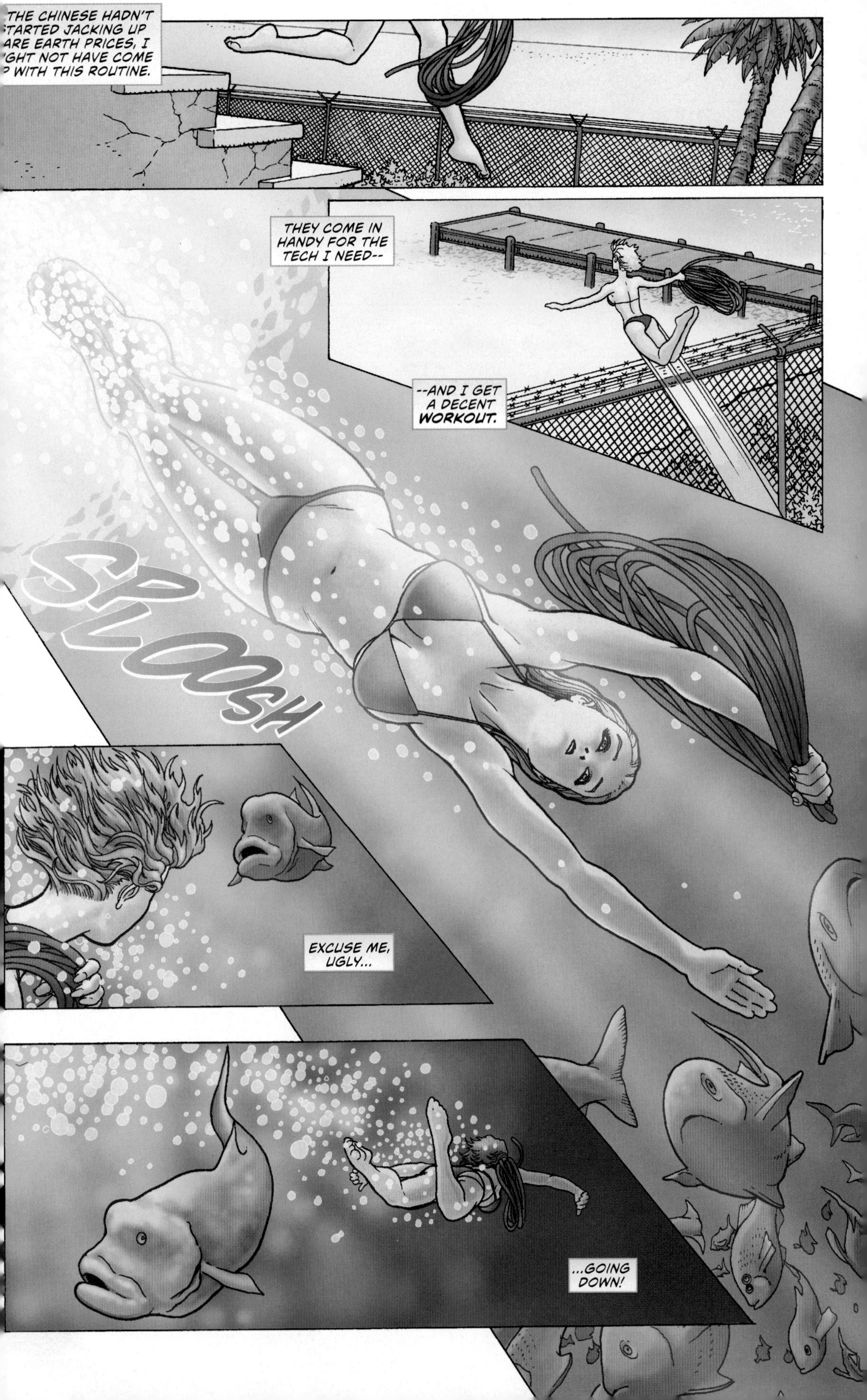
THE CHINESE HADN'T STARTED JACKING UP ARE EARTH PRICES, I GHT NOT HAVE COME P WITH THIS ROUTINE.
THEY COME IN HANDY FOR THE TECH I NEED--
--AND I GET A DECENT WORKOUT.
SPLOOSH
EXCUSE ME, UGLY...
...GOING DOWN!

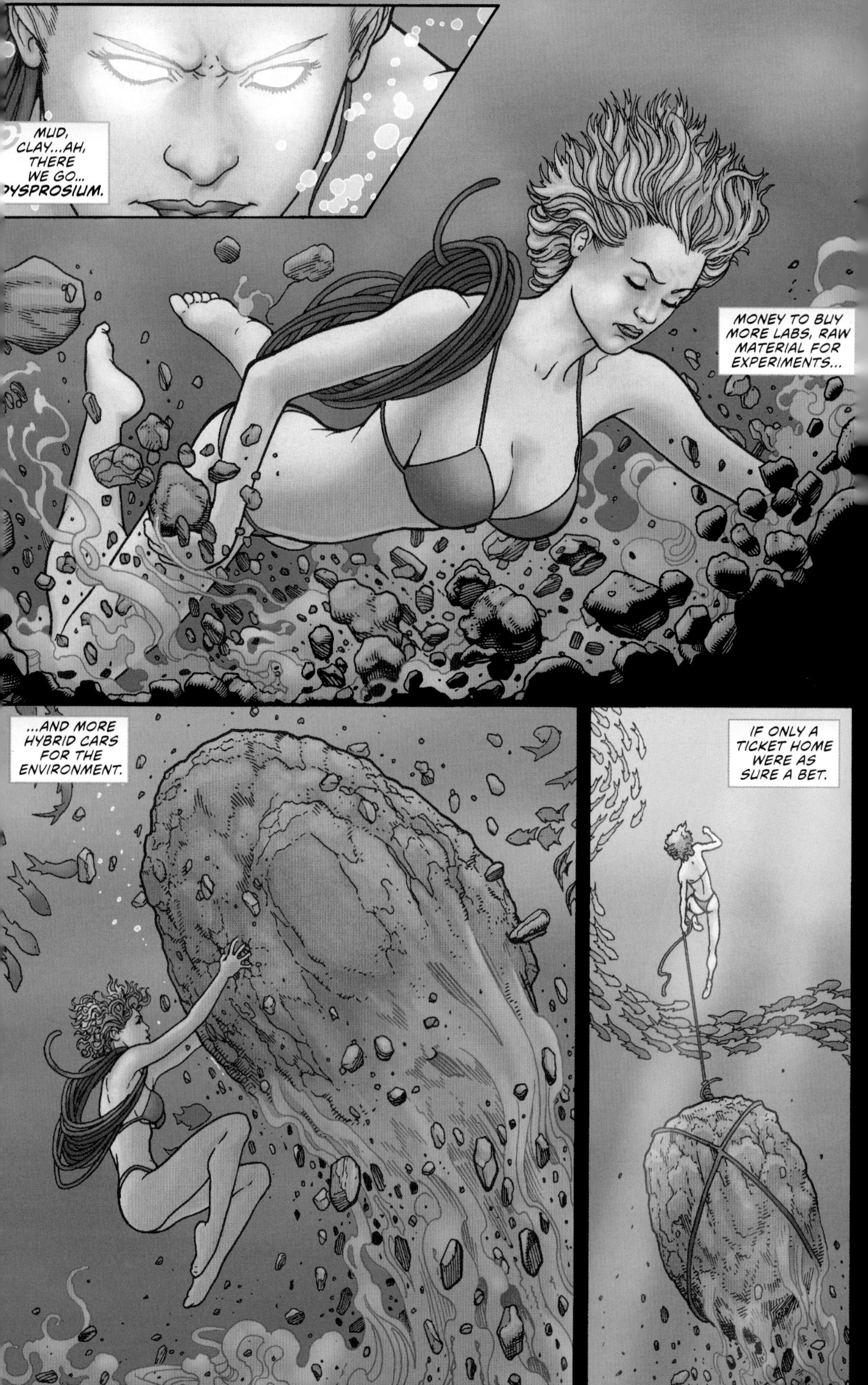
MUD, CLAY...AH, THERE WE GO... DYSPROSIUM.
MONEY TO BUY MORE LABS, RAW MATERIAL FOR EXPERIMENTS...
...AND MORE HYBRID CARS FOR THE ENVIRONMENT.
IF ONLY A TICKET HOME WERE AS SURE A BET.

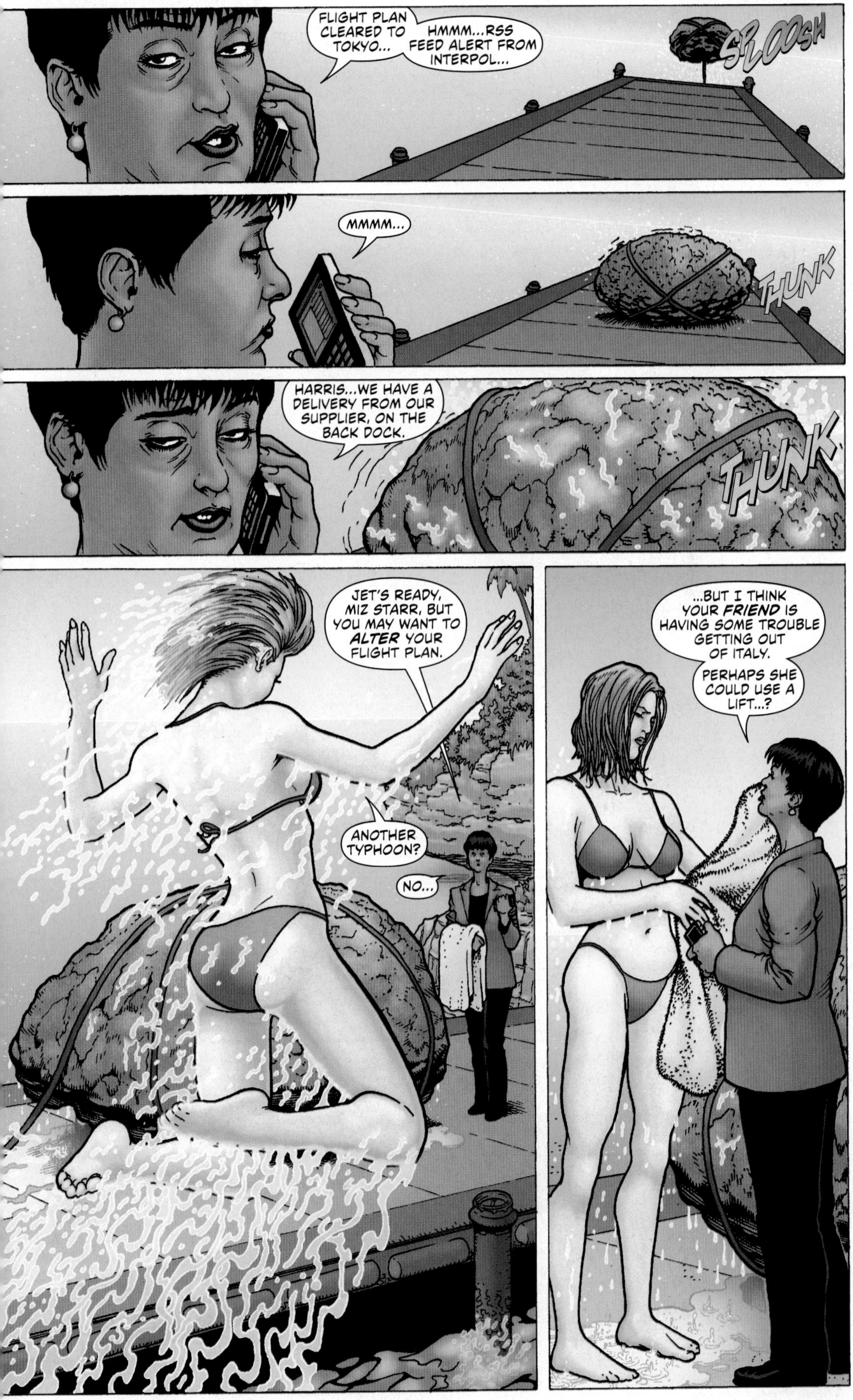
FLIGHT PLAN CLEARED TO TOKYO...
HMMM...RSS FEED ALERT FROM INTERPOL...
SPLOOSH
MMMM...
THUNK
HARRIS...WE HAVE A DELIVERY FROM OUR SUPPLIER, ON THE BACK DOCK.
THUNK
JET'S READY, MIZ STARR, BUT YOU MAY WANT TO ALTER YOUR FLIGHT PLAN.
ANOTHER TYPHOON?
NO...
...BUT I THINK YOUR FRIEND IS HAVING SOME TROUBLE GETTING OUT OF ITALY.
PERHAPS SHE COULD USE A LIFT...?

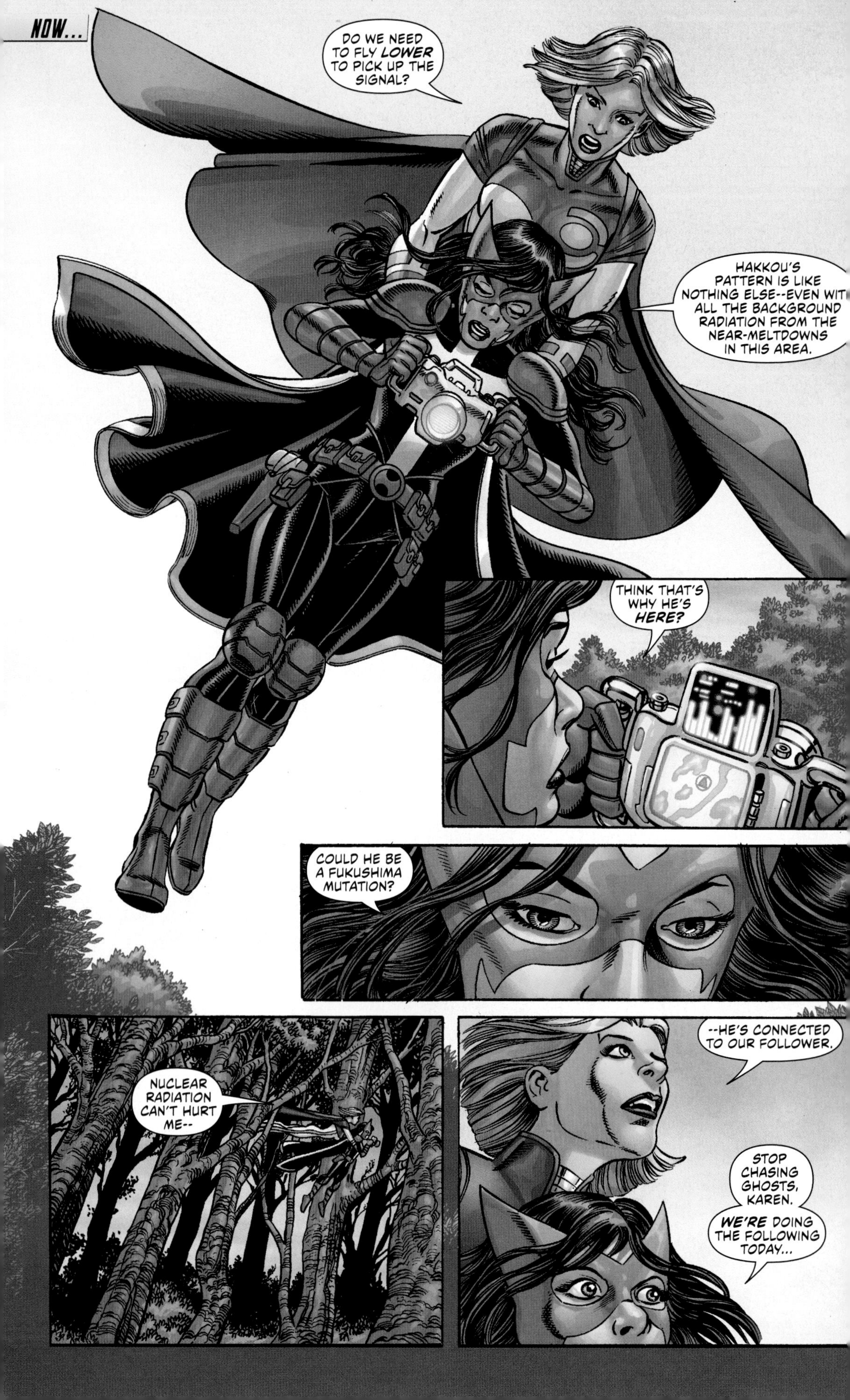
NOW...
DO WE NEED TO FLY LOWER TO PICK UP THE SIGNAL?
HAKKOU'S PATTERN IS LIKE NOTHING ELSE--EVEN WIT ALL THE BACKGROUND RADIATION FROM THE NEAR-MELTDOWNS IN THIS AREA.
THINK THAT'S WHY HE'S HERE?
COULD HE BE A FUKUSHIMA MUTATION?
NUCLEAR RADIATION CAN'T HURT ME--
--HE'S CONNECTED TO OUR FOLLOWER.
STOP CHASING GHOSTS, KAREN.
WE'RE DOING THE FOLLOWING TODAY...

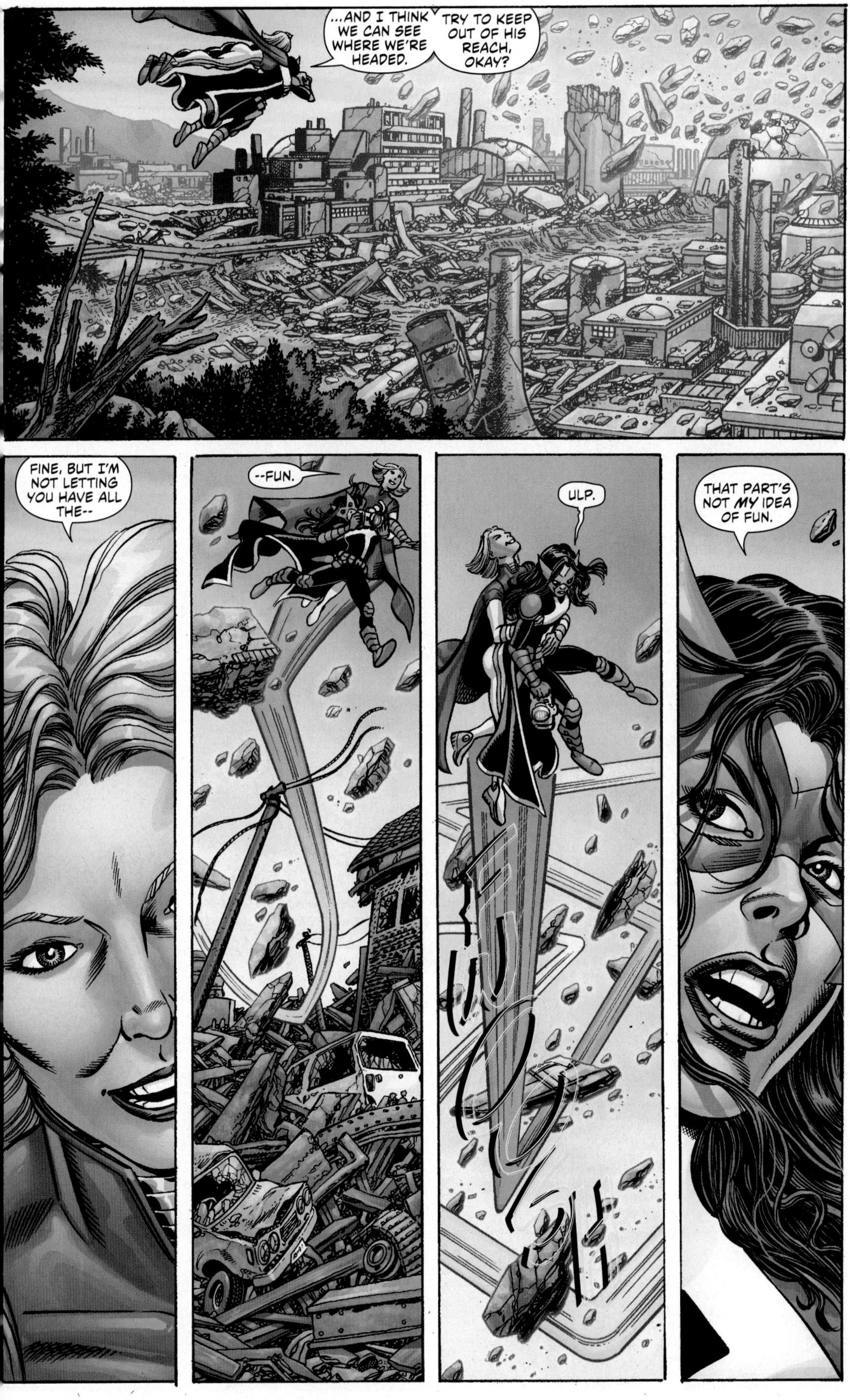
...AND I THINK WE CAN SEE WHERE WE'RE HEADED.
TRY TO KEEP OUT OF HIS REACH, OKAY?
FINE, BUT I'M NOT LETTING YOU HAVE ALL THE--
--FUN.
ULP.
THAT PART'S NOT MY IDEA OF FUN.

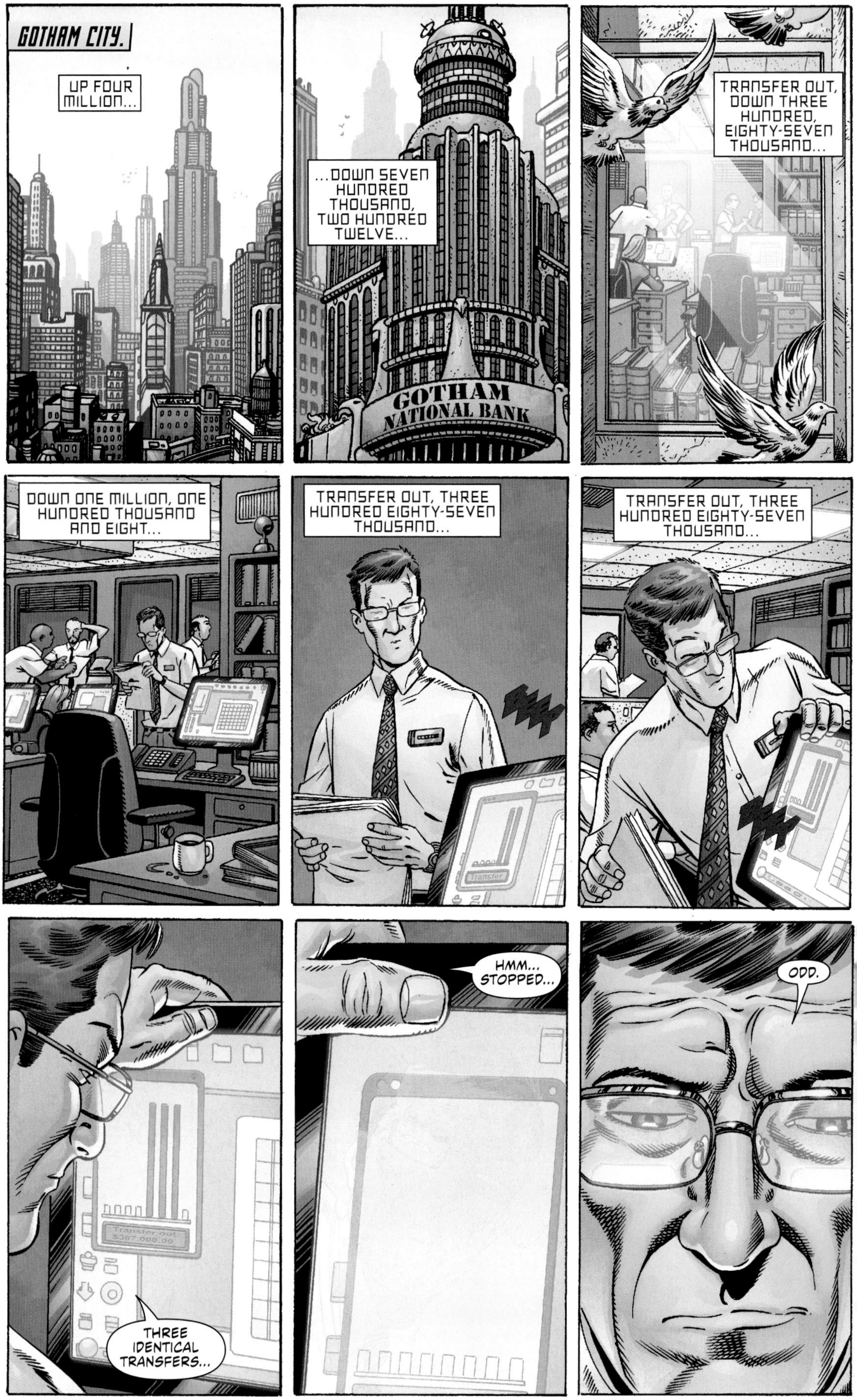
GOTHAM CITY.
UP FOUR MILLION...
...DOWN SEVEN HUNDRED THOUSAND, TWO HUNDRED TWELVE...
GOTHAM NATIONAL BANK
TRANSFER OUT, DOWN THREE HUNDRED, EIGHTY-SEVEN THOUSAND...
DOWN ONE MILLION, ONE HUNDRED THOUSAND AND EIGHT...
TRANSFER OUT, THREE HUNDRED EIGHTY-SEVEN THOUSAND...
Transfer
TRANSFER OUT, THREE HUNDRED EIGHTY-SEVEN THOUSAND...
Transfer out
$387,000.00
THREE IDENTICAL TRANSFERS...
HMM... STOPPED...
ODD.

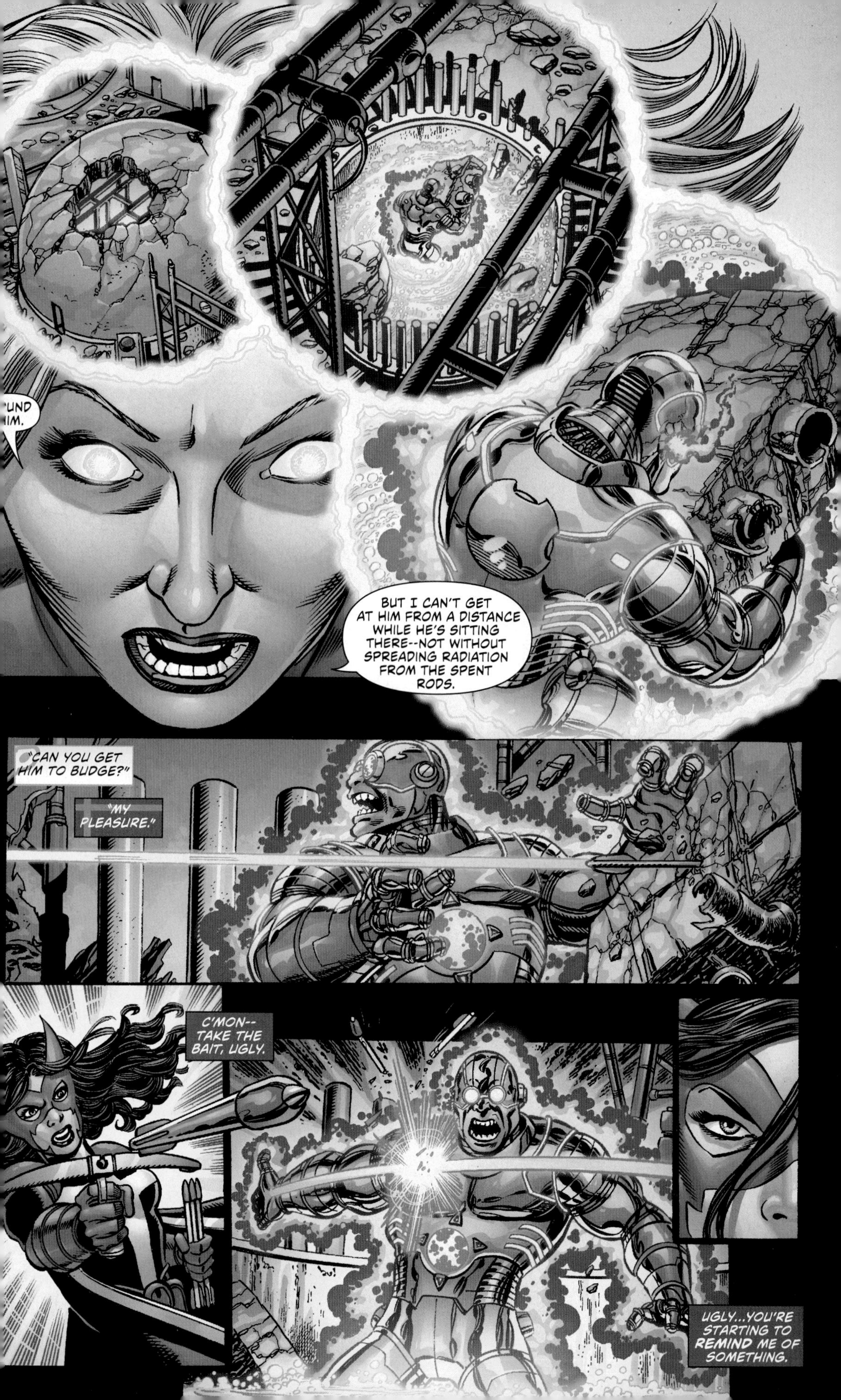
BUT I CAN'T GET AT HIM FROM A DISTANCE WHILE HE'S SITTING THERE--NOT WITHOUT SPREADING RADIATION FROM THE SPENT RODS.
"CAN YOU GET HIM TO BUDGE?"
"MY PLEASURE."
C'MON-- TAKE THE BAIT, UGLY.
UGLY...YOU'RE STARTING TO REMIND ME OF SOMETHING.

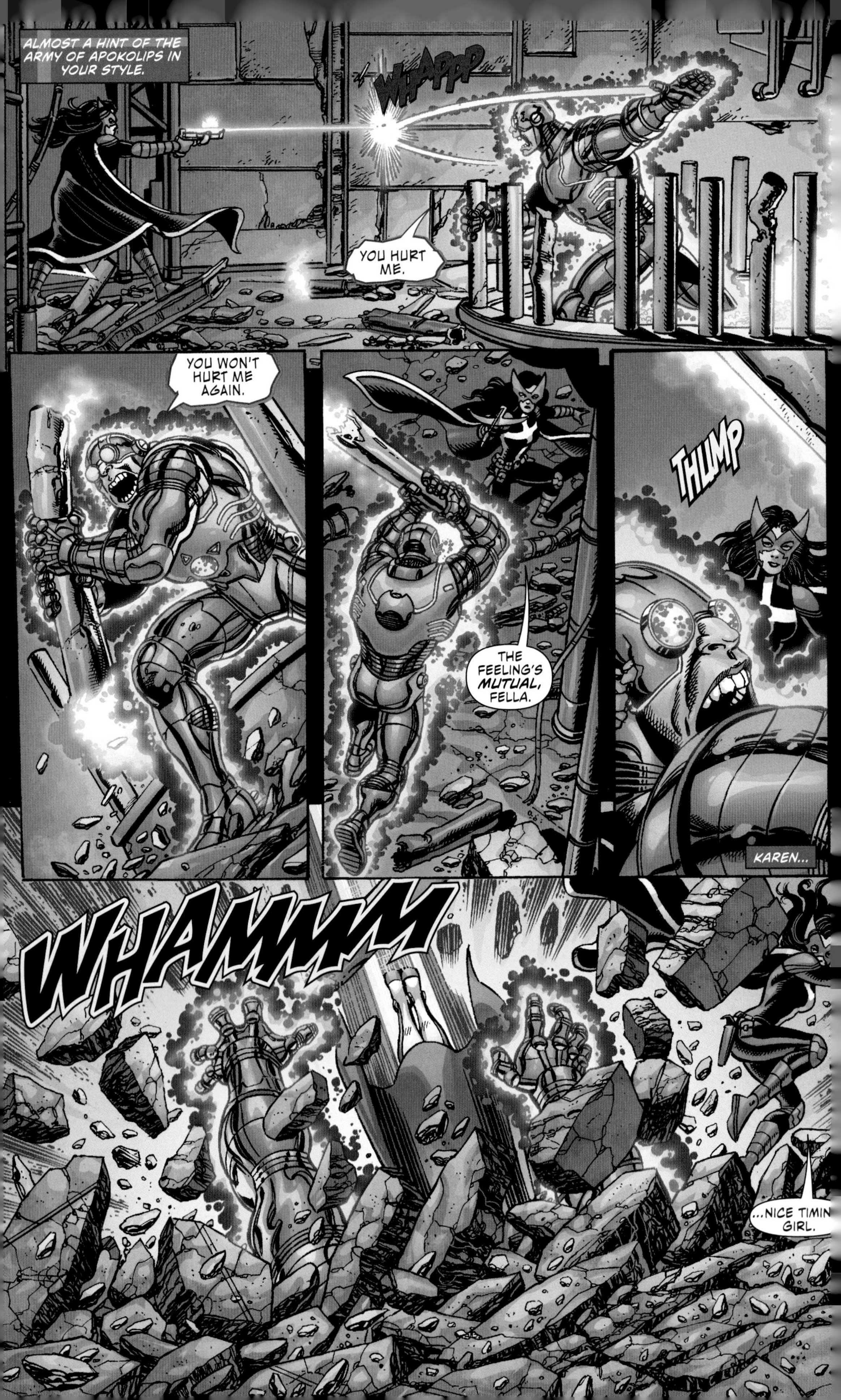

ALMOST A HINT OF THE ARMY OF APOKOLIPS IN YOUR STYLE.
WHAPPP
YOU HURT ME.
YOU WON'T HURT ME AGAIN.
THE FEELING'S MUTUAL, FELLA.
THUMP
KAREN...
WHAMMM
...NICE TIMIN GIRL.

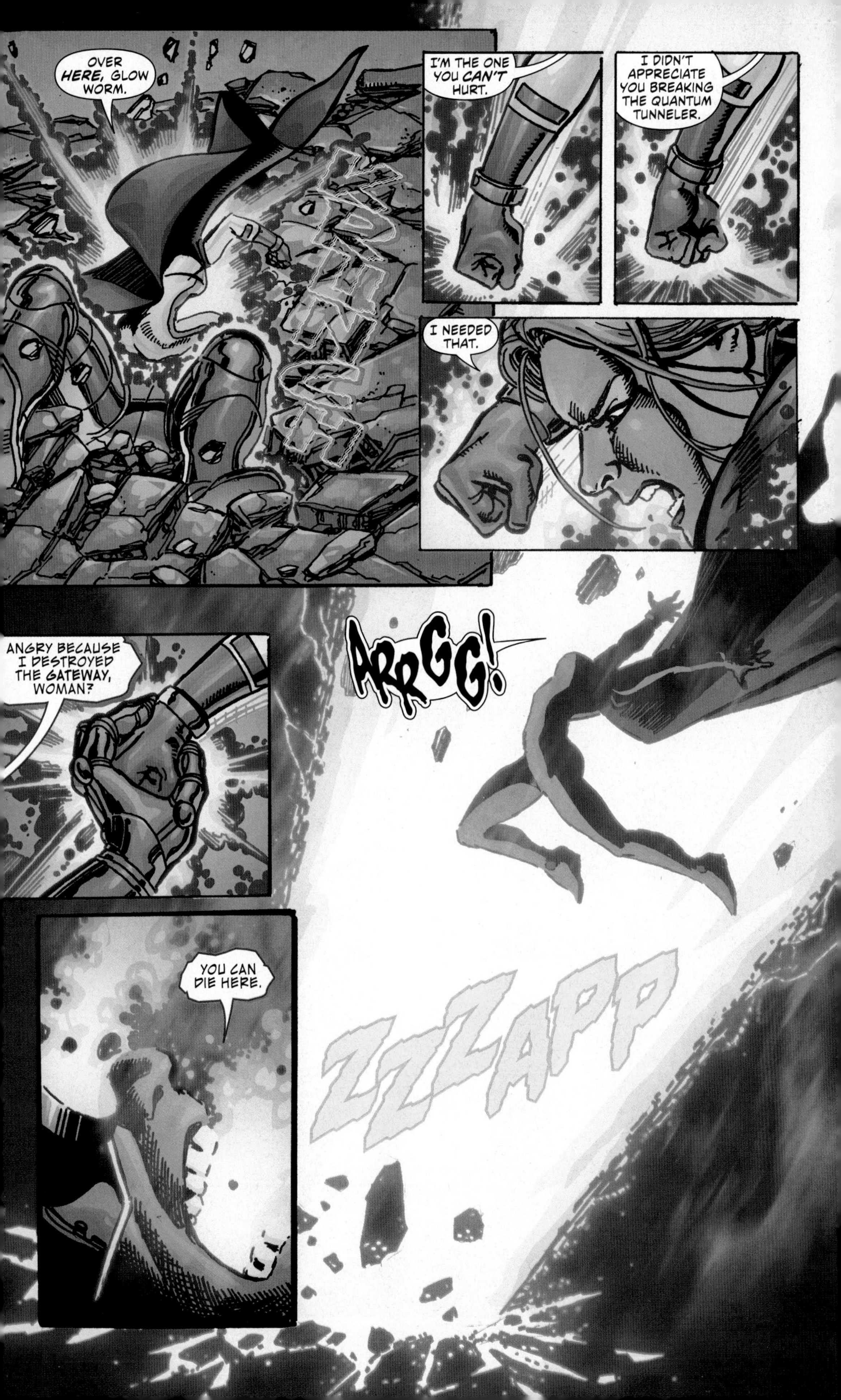
OVER HERE, GLOW WORM.
I'M THE ONE YOU CAN'T HURT.
I DIDN'T APPRECIATE YOU BREAKING THE QUANTUM TUNNELER.
I NEEDED THAT.
ANGRY BECAUSE I DESTROYED THE GATEWAY, WOMAN?
ARRGG!
YOU CAN DIE HERE.
ZZZAPP

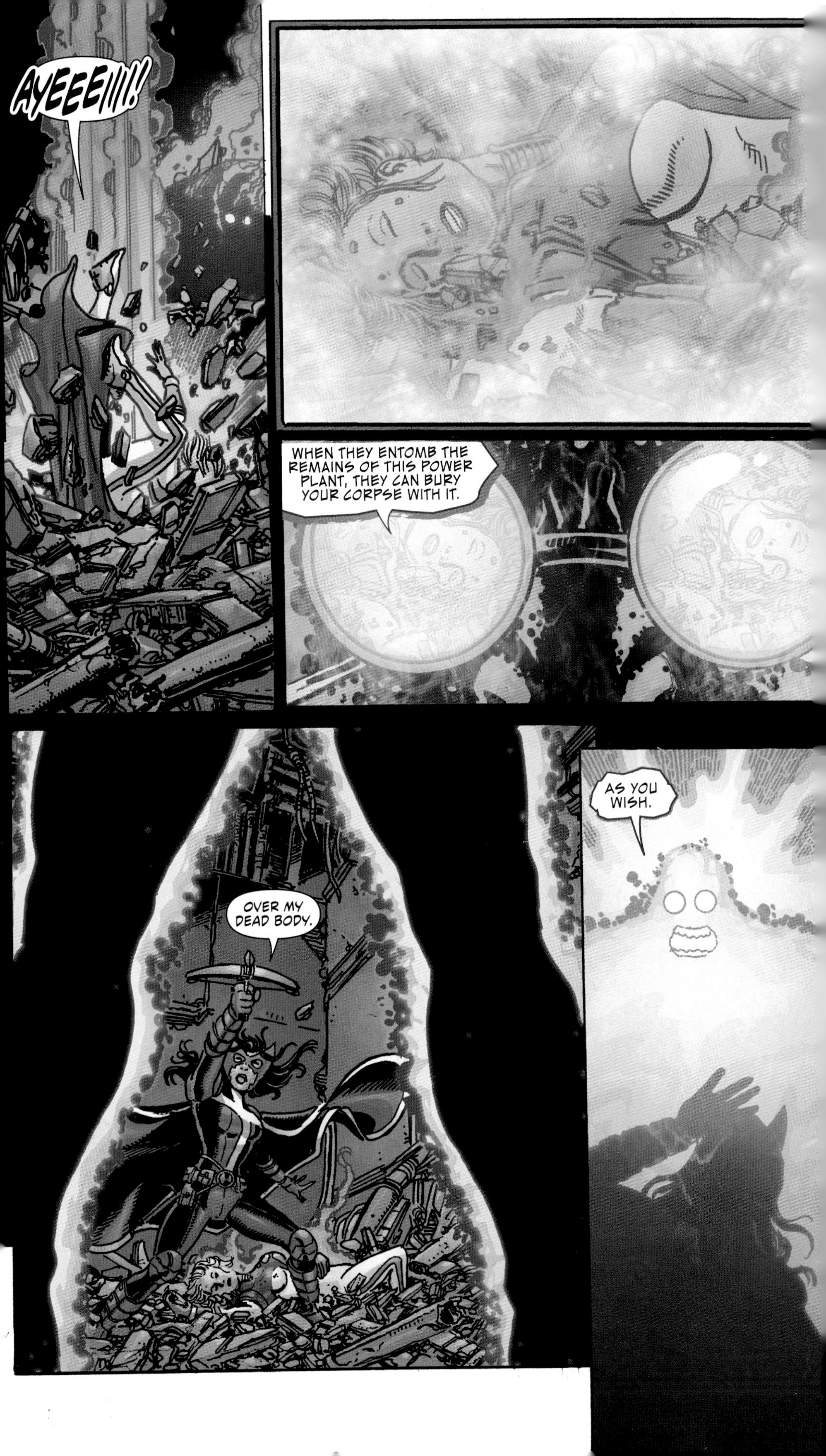
AYEEE!!!!!
WHEN THEY ENTOMB THE REMAINS OF THIS POWER PLANT, THEY CAN BURY YOUR CORPSE WITH IT.
OVER MY DEAD BODY.
AS YOU WISH.

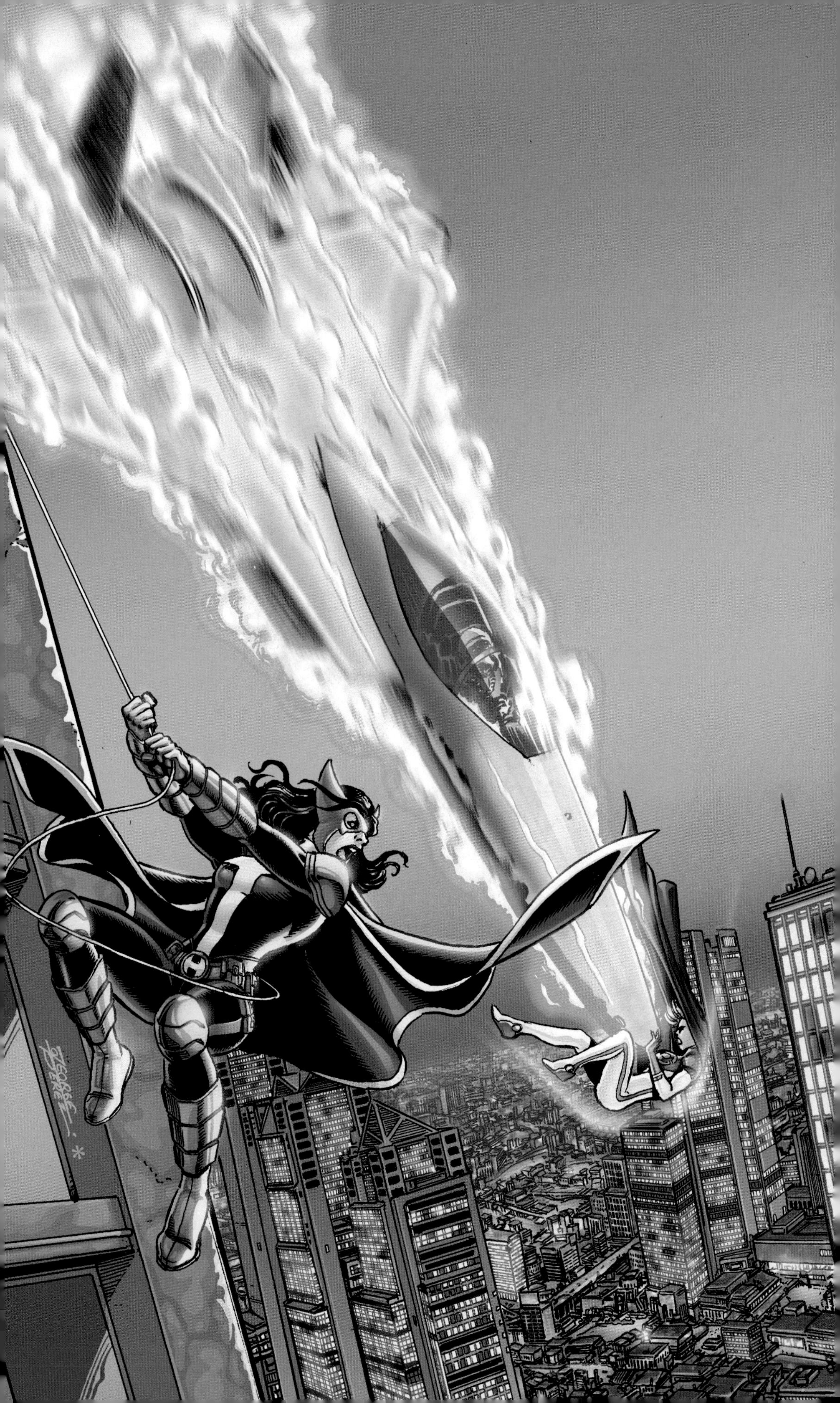

PAUL LEVITZ writer GEORGE PEREZ penciller (present-day sequence)
SCOTT KOBLISH inker (present-day sequence) KEVIN MAGUIRE artist (flashback sequence)

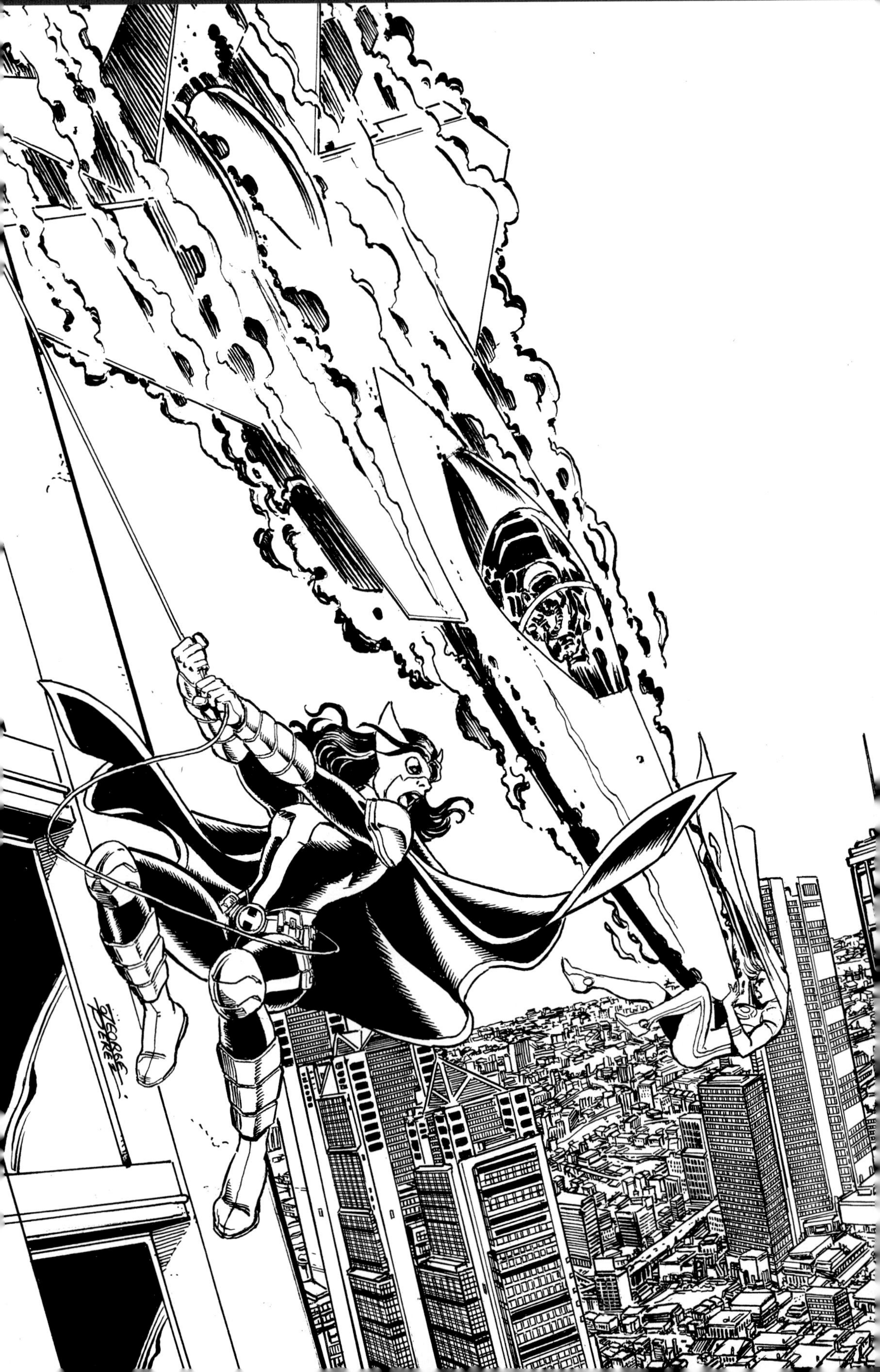

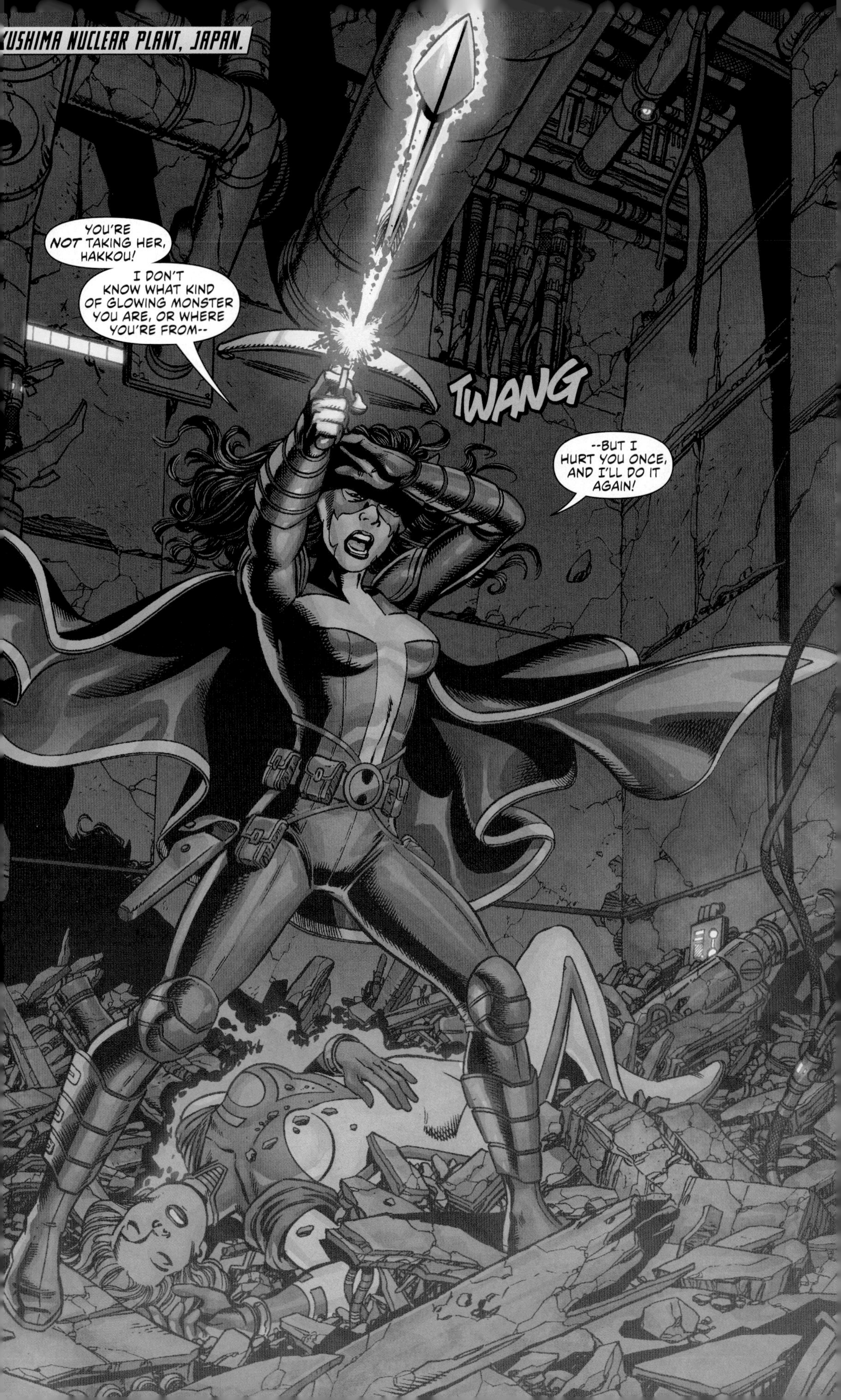

KUSHIMA NUCLEAR PLANT, JAPAN.
YOU'RE NOT TAKING HER, HAKKOU!
I DON'T KNOW WHAT KIND OF GLOWING MONSTER YOU ARE, OR WHERE YOU'RE FROM--
TWANG
--BUT I HURT YOU ONCE, AND I'LL DO IT AGAIN!

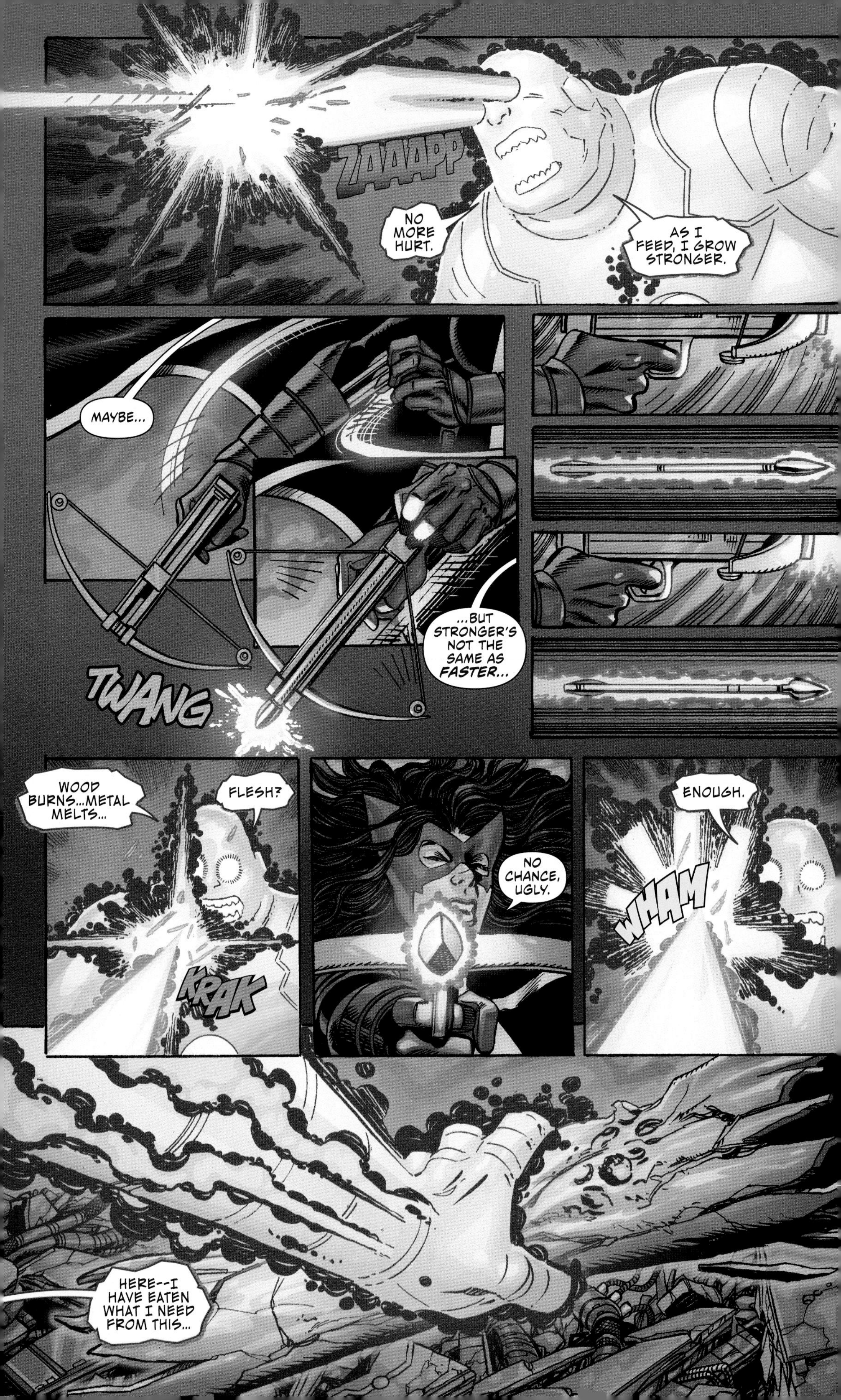
ZAAAPP
NO MORE HURT.
AS I FEED, I GROW STRONGER.
MAYBE...
TWANG
...BUT STRONGER'S NOT THE SAME AS *FASTER*...
WOOD BURNS...METAL MELTS...
FLESH?
KRAK
NO CHANCE, UGLY.
ENOUGH.
WHAM
HERE--I HAVE EATEN WHAT I NEED FROM THIS...

THUNK

YOU MAY HAVE IT.

YOU HAVE TRAVELED FAR TO END YOUR JOURNEY IN THIS BROKEN PLACE ON A DOOMED WORLD...

KEEP TALKING...

...BUT YOU HAVE NO FARTHER TO GO.

THUNK

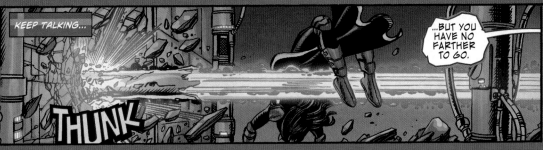

...BREATH PAUSES TELEGRAPH YOUR MOVES...

THUNK

...A LITTLE TOO CLOSE...

THUNK

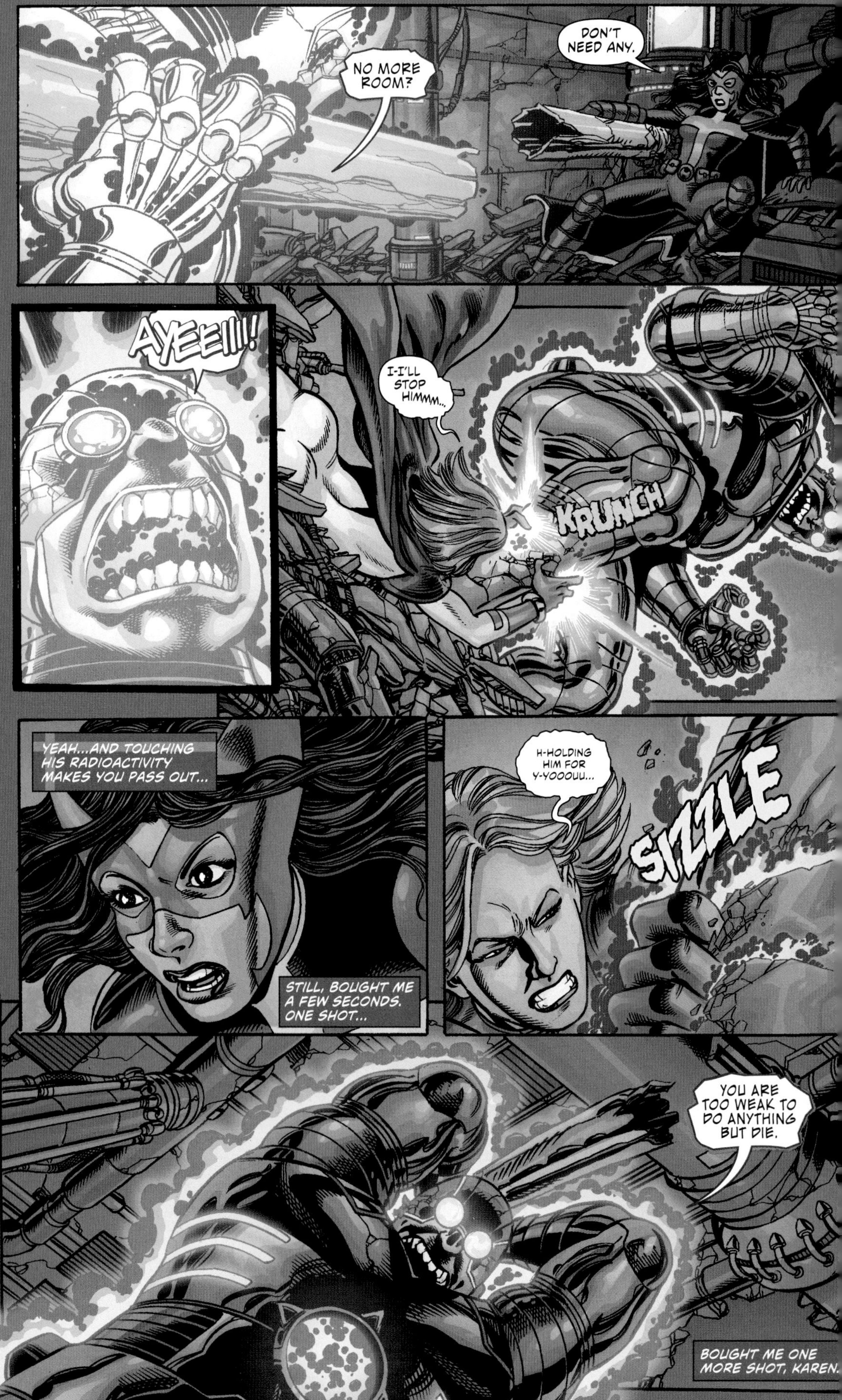
NO MORE ROOM?
DON'T NEED ANY.
AYEEIIII!
I-I'LL STOP HIMMM...
KRUNCH
YEAH...AND TOUCHING HIS RADIOACTIVITY MAKES YOU PASS OUT...
STILL, BOUGHT ME A FEW SECONDS. ONE SHOT...
H-HOLDING HIM FOR Y-YOOOUU...
SIZZLE
YOU ARE TOO WEAK TO DO ANYTHING BUT DIE.
BOUGHT ME ONE MORE SHOT, KAREN.

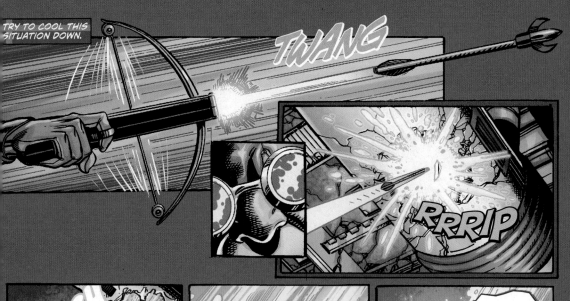

TRY TO COOL THIS SITUATION DOWN.

TWANG

RRRIP

FWOOOSH

MORE?

I HAVE FED ENOUGH...

ENOUGH!!!

NO MORE!!!

UGLY, RADIOACTIVE AND OVERSTUFFED-- WHAT A GREAT COMBINATION.

DIDN'T REALIZE THE COOLANT WAS CONTAMINATED WITH RADIOACTIVE WASTE. THIS PLANT'S A TOTAL DISASTER.

BUT IT GOT HIM OFF KAREN.

KRASH

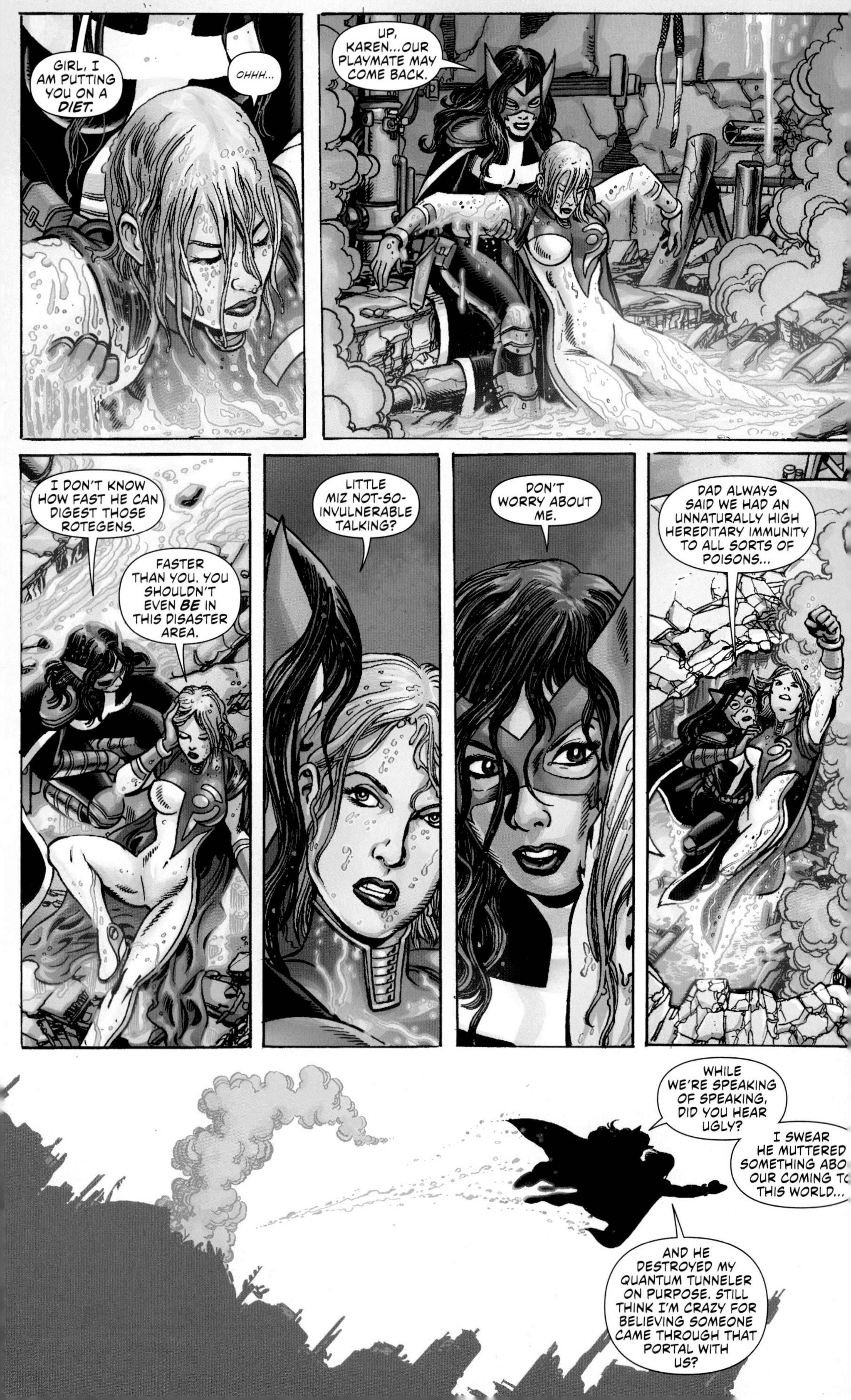
GIRL, I AM PUTTING YOU ON A *DIET.*
OHHH...
UP, KAREN...OUR PLAYMATE MAY COME BACK.
I DON'T KNOW HOW FAST HE CAN DIGEST THOSE ROTEGENS.
FASTER THAN YOU. YOU SHOULDN'T EVEN *BE* IN THIS DISASTER AREA.
LITTLE MIZ NOT-SO-INVULNERABLE TALKING?
DON'T WORRY ABOUT ME.
DAD ALWAYS SAID WE HAD AN UNNATURALLY HIGH HEREDITARY IMMUNITY TO ALL SORTS OF POISONS...
WHILE WE'RE SPEAKING OF SPEAKING, DID YOU HEAR UGLY?
I SWEAR HE MUTTERED SOMETHING ABO OUR COMING T THIS WORLD...
AND HE DESTROYED MY QUANTUM TUNNELER ON PURPOSE. STILL THINK I'M CRAZY FOR BELIEVING SOMEONE CAME THROUGH THAT PORTAL WITH US?

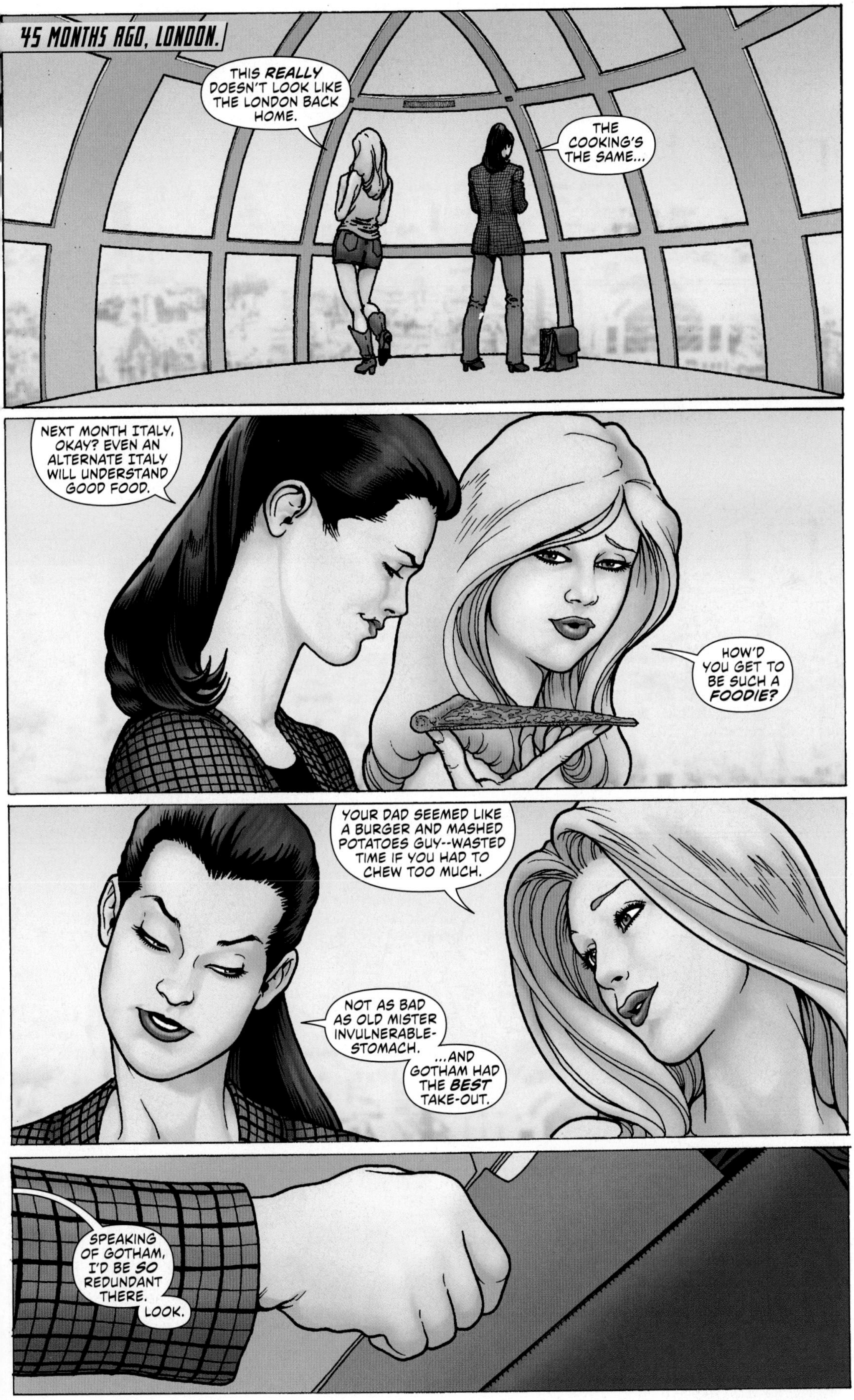
45 MONTHS AGO, LONDON.
THIS REALLY DOESN'T LOOK LIKE THE LONDON BACK HOME.
THE COOKING'S THE SAME...
NEXT MONTH ITALY, OKAY? EVEN AN ALTERNATE ITALY WILL UNDERSTAND GOOD FOOD.
HOW'D YOU GET TO BE SUCH A FOODIE?
YOUR DAD SEEMED LIKE A BURGER AND MASHED POTATOES GUY--WASTED TIME IF YOU HAD TO CHEW TOO MUCH.
NOT AS BAD AS OLD MISTER INVULNERABLE-STOMACH.
...AND GOTHAM HAD THE BEST TAKE-OUT.
SPEAKING OF GOTHAM, I'D BE SO REDUNDANT THERE.
LOOK.

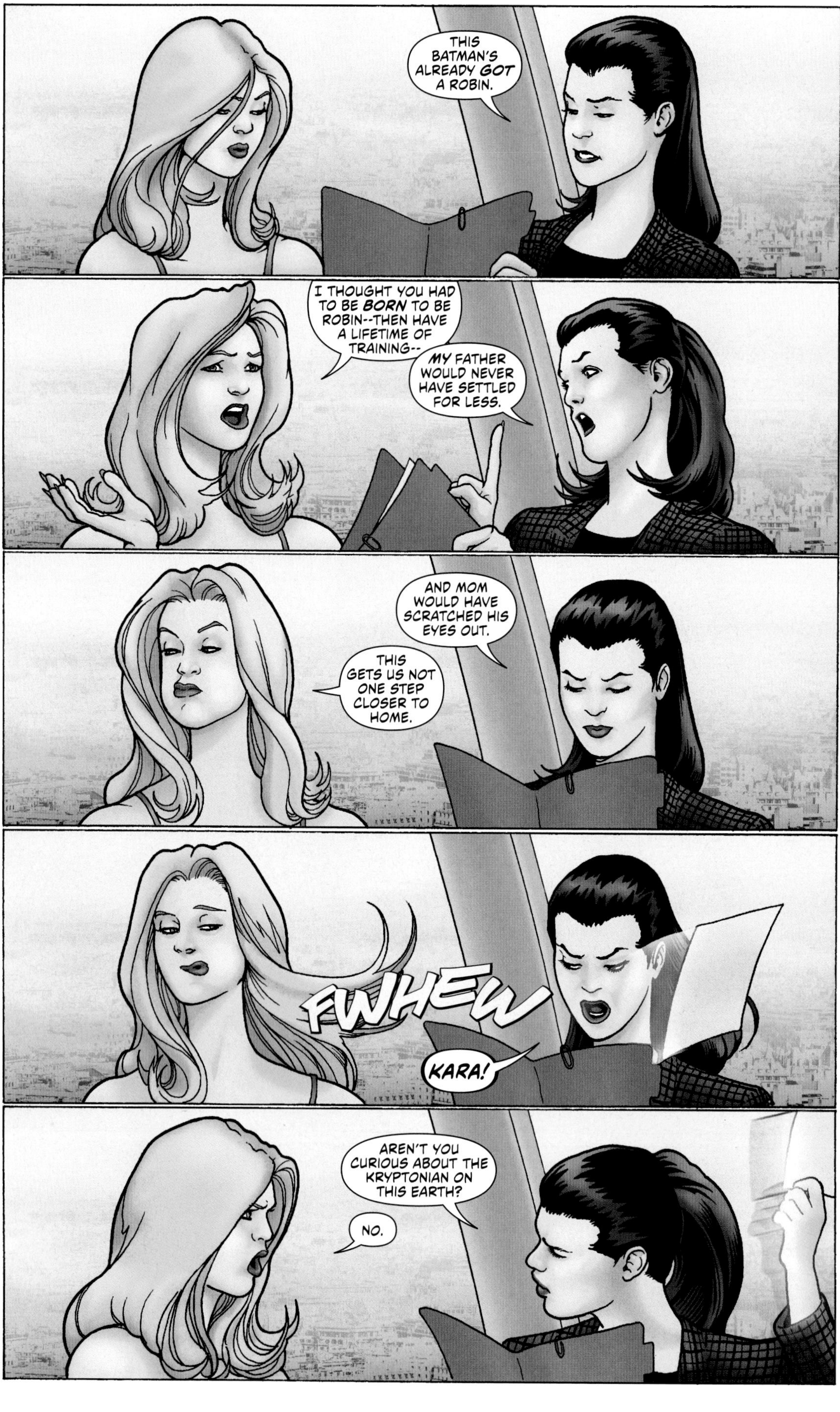
THIS BATMAN'S ALREADY GOT A ROBIN.
I THOUGHT YOU HAD TO BE BORN TO BE ROBIN--THEN HAVE A LIFETIME OF TRAINING--
MY FATHER WOULD NEVER HAVE SETTLED FOR LESS.
AND MOM WOULD HAVE SCRATCHED HIS EYES OUT.
THIS GETS US NOT ONE STEP CLOSER TO HOME.
FWHEW
KARA!
AREN'T YOU CURIOUS ABOUT THE KRYPTONIAN ON THIS EARTH?
NO.

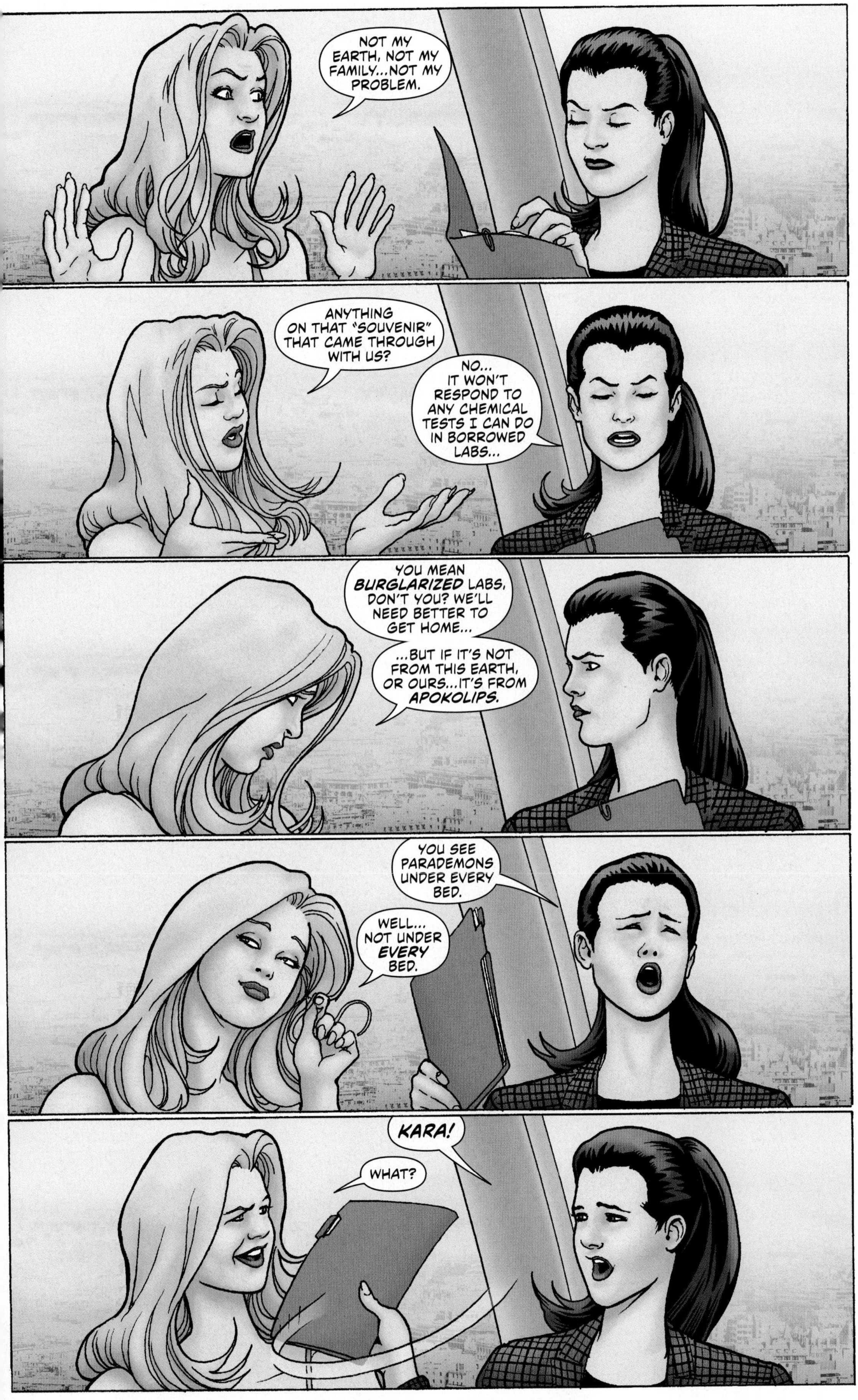

NOT MY EARTH, NOT MY FAMILY...NOT MY PROBLEM.
ANYTHING ON THAT "SOUVENIR" THAT CAME THROUGH WITH US?
NO... IT WON'T RESPOND TO ANY CHEMICAL TESTS I CAN DO IN BORROWED LABS...
YOU MEAN BURGLARIZED LABS, DON'T YOU? WE'LL NEED BETTER TO GET HOME...
...BUT IF IT'S NOT FROM THIS EARTH, OR OURS...IT'S FROM APOKOLIPS.
YOU SEE PARADEMONS UNDER EVERY BED.
WELL... NOT UNDER EVERY BED.
KARA!
WHAT?

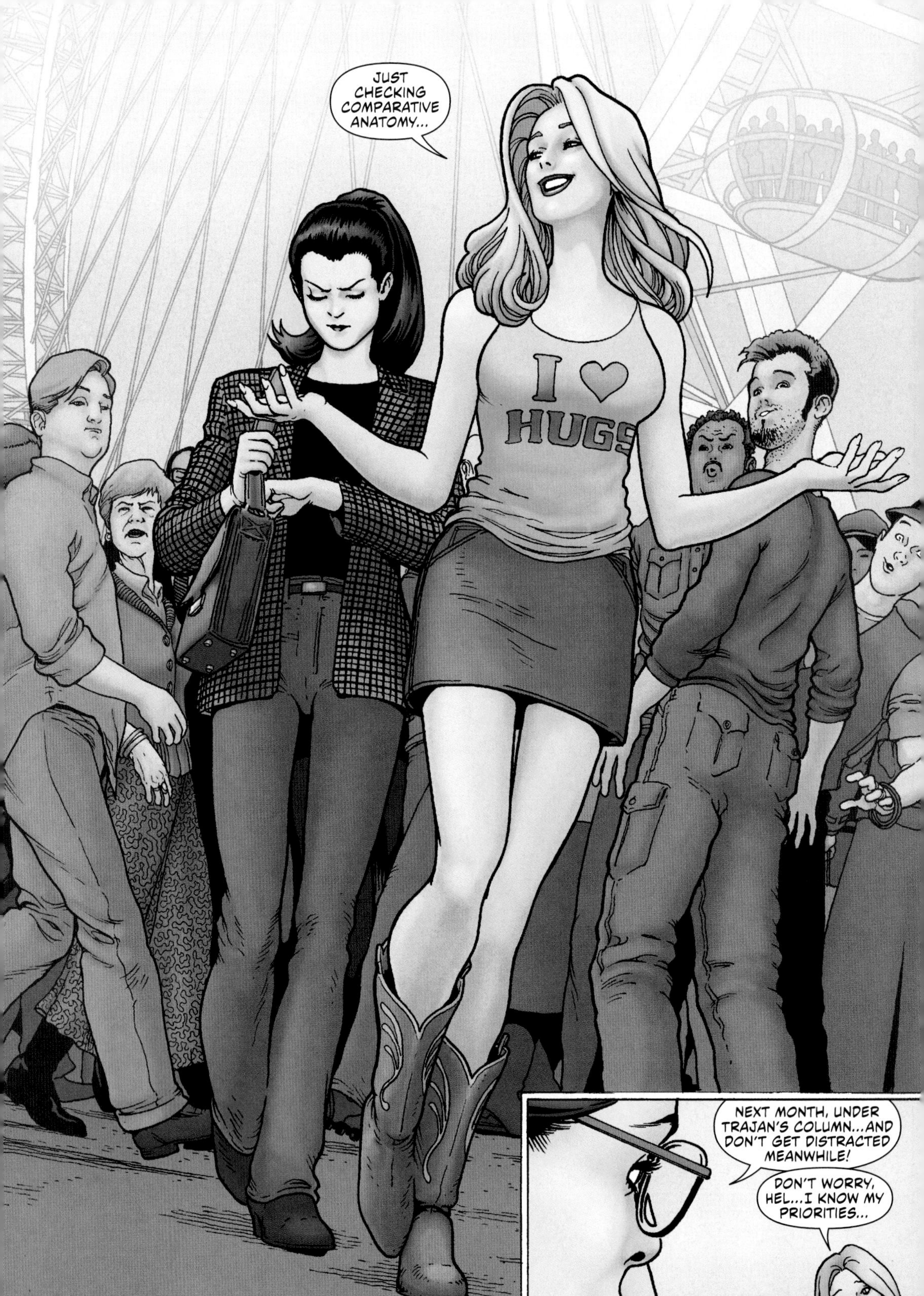
JUST CHECKING COMPARATIVE ANATOMY...
I ♥ HUGS

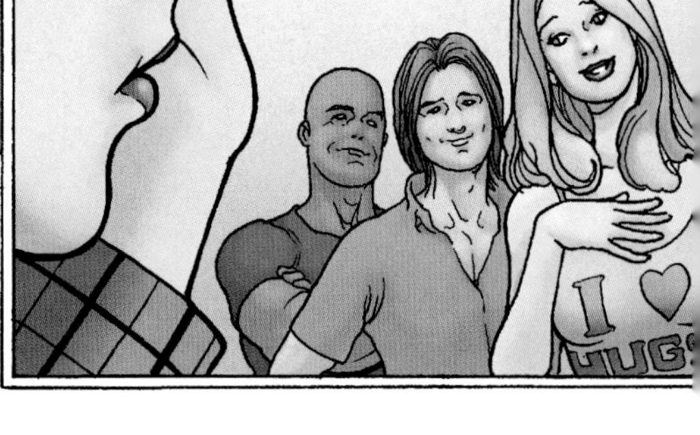
NEXT MONTH, UNDER TRAJAN'S COLUMN...AND DON'T GET DISTRACTED MEANWHILE!
DON'T WORRY, HEL...I KNOW MY PRIORITIES...

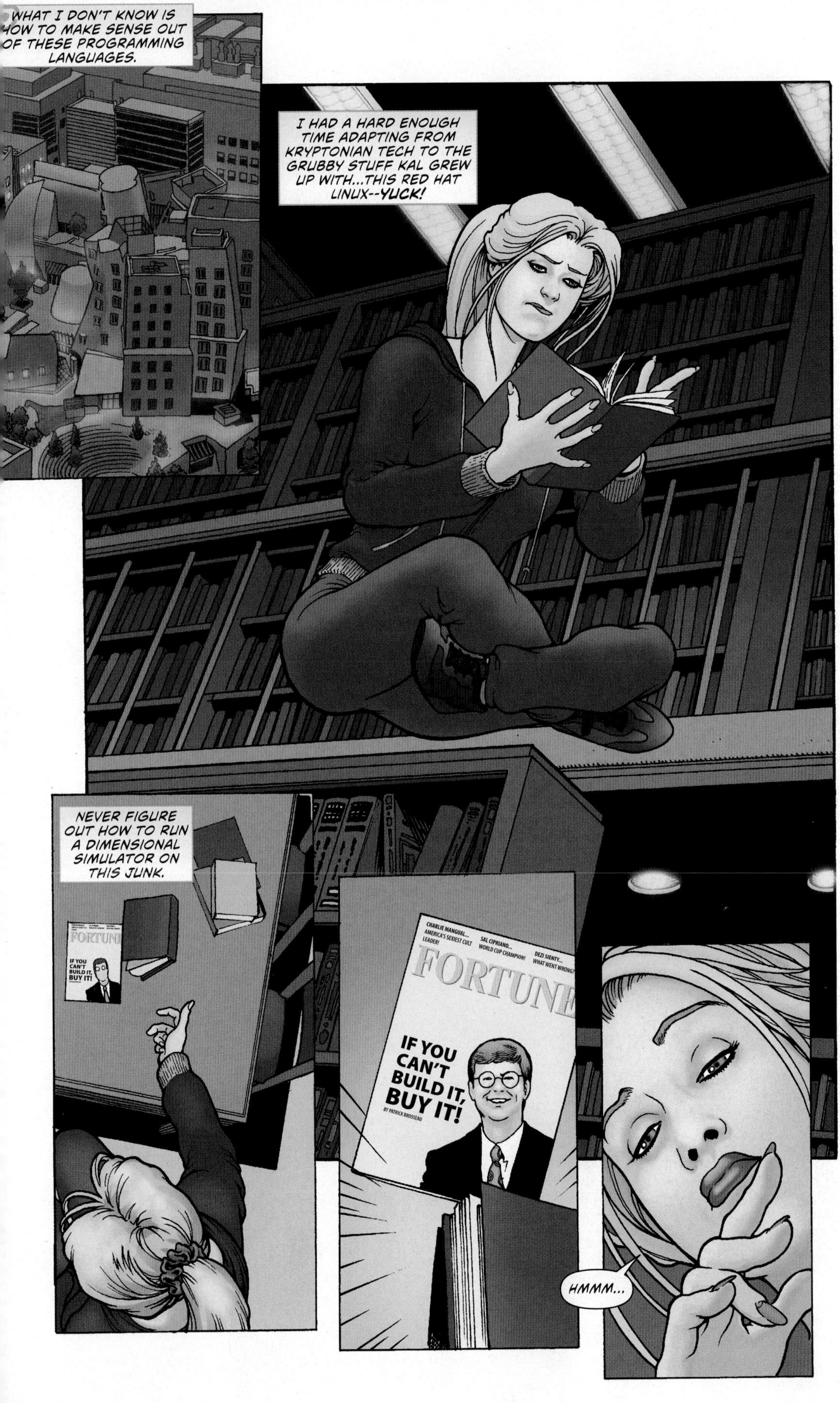
WHAT I DON'T KNOW IS HOW TO MAKE SENSE OUT OF THESE PROGRAMMING LANGUAGES.
I HAD A HARD ENOUGH TIME ADAPTING FROM KRYPTONIAN TECH TO THE GRUBBY STUFF KAL GREW UP WITH...THIS RED HAT LINUX--YUCK!
NEVER FIGURE OUT HOW TO RUN A DIMENSIONAL SIMULATOR ON THIS JUNK.
CHARLIE MANGUAL... AMERICA'S SEXIEST CULT LEADER!
SAL CIPRIANO... WORLD CUP CHAMPION!
DEZI SIENTY... WHAT WENT WRONG?
FORTUNE
IF YOU CAN'T BUILD IT, BUY IT!
BY PATRICK BROSSEAU
HMMM...

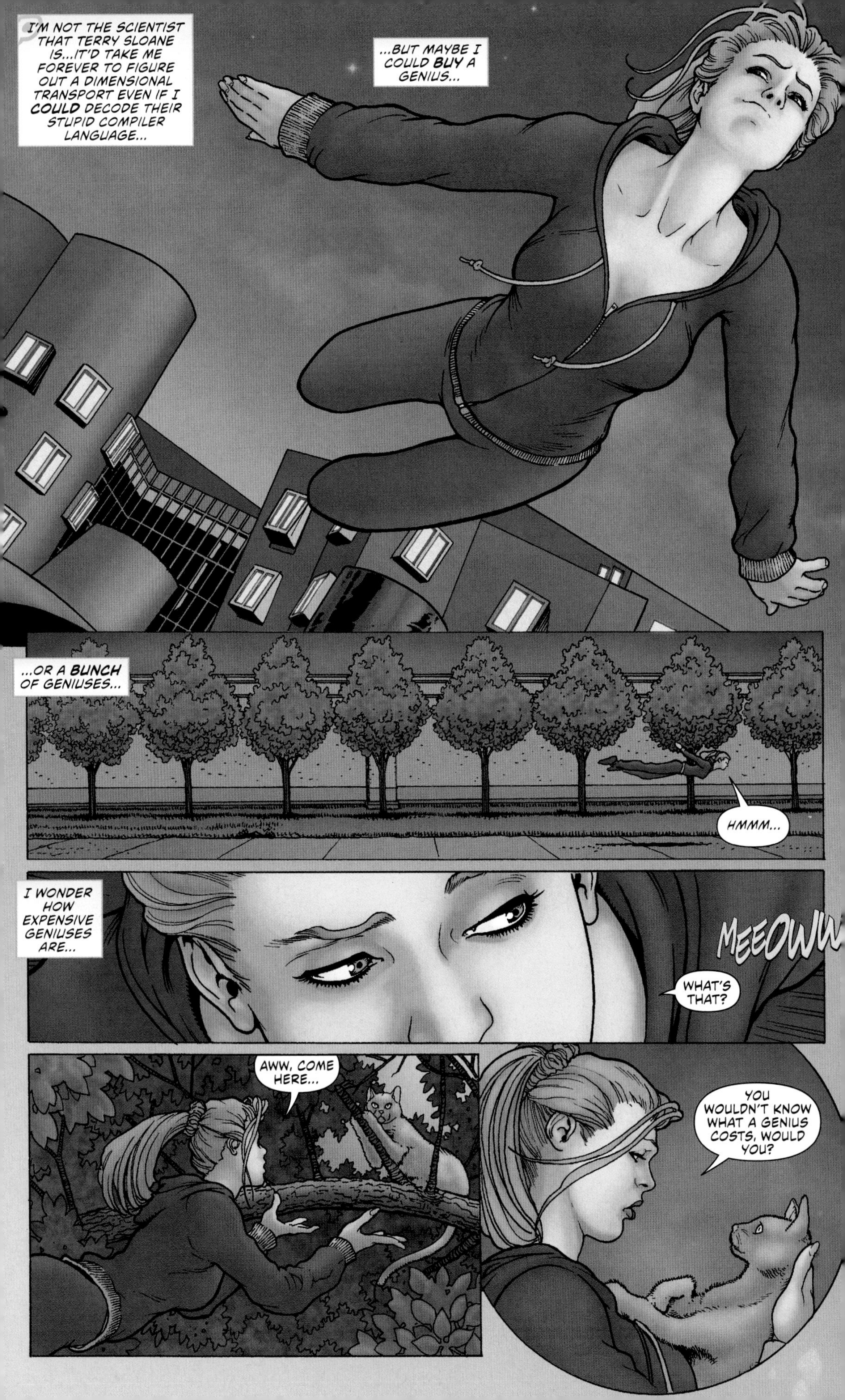
I'M NOT THE SCIENTIST THAT TERRY SLOANE IS...IT'D TAKE ME FOREVER TO FIGURE OUT A DIMENSIONAL TRANSPORT EVEN IF I **COULD** DECODE THEIR STUPID COMPILER LANGUAGE...
...BUT MAYBE I COULD **BUY** A GENIUS...
...OR A **BUNCH** OF GENIUSES...
HMMM...
I WONDER HOW EXPENSIVE GENIUSES ARE...
MEEOWW
WHAT'S THAT?
AWW, COME HERE...
YOU WOULDN'T KNOW WHAT A GENIUS COSTS, WOULD YOU?

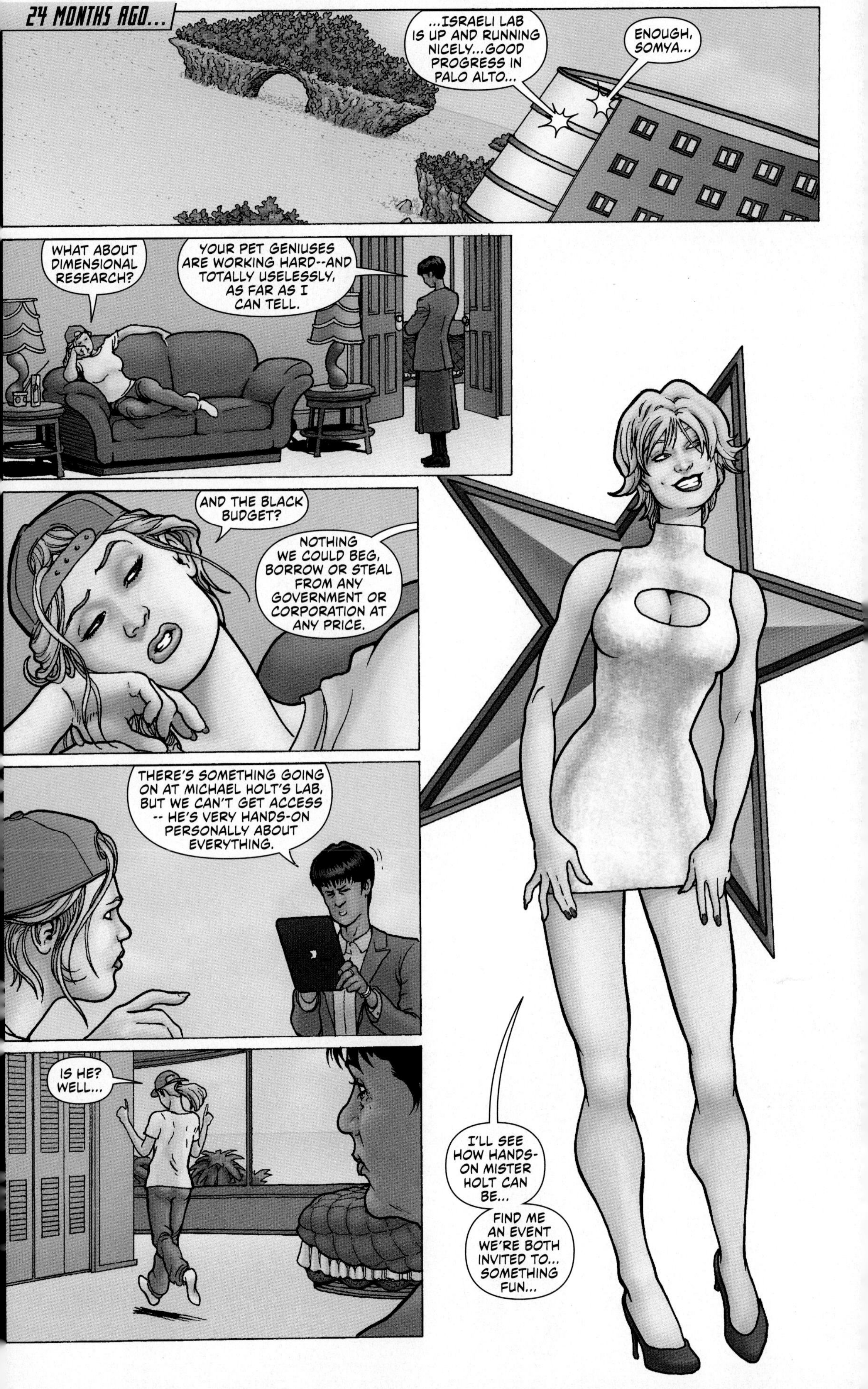
24 MONTHS AGO...
...ISRAELI LAB IS UP AND RUNNING NICELY...GOOD PROGRESS IN PALO ALTO...
ENOUGH, SOMYA...
WHAT ABOUT DIMENSIONAL RESEARCH?
YOUR PET GENIUSES ARE WORKING HARD--AND TOTALLY USELESSLY, AS FAR AS I CAN TELL.
AND THE BLACK BUDGET?
NOTHING WE COULD BEG, BORROW OR STEAL FROM ANY GOVERNMENT OR CORPORATION AT ANY PRICE.
THERE'S SOMETHING GOING ON AT MICHAEL HOLT'S LAB, BUT WE CAN'T GET ACCESS -- HE'S VERY HANDS-ON PERSONALLY ABOUT EVERYTHING.
IS HE? WELL...
I'LL SEE HOW HANDS-ON MISTER HOLT CAN BE...
FIND ME AN EVENT WE'RE BOTH INVITED TO... SOMETHING FUN...

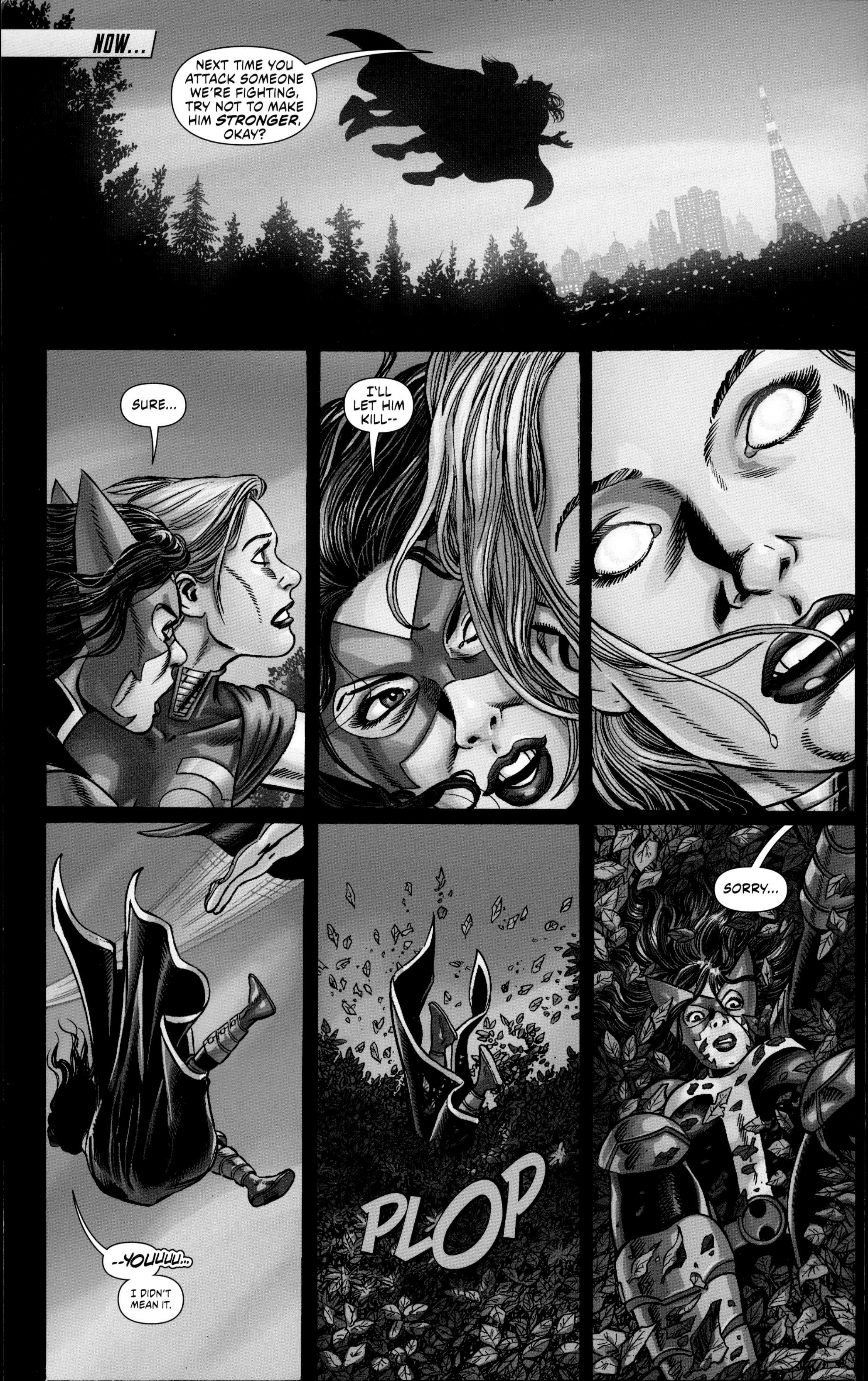
NOW...
NEXT TIME YOU ATTACK SOMEONE WE'RE FIGHTING, TRY NOT TO MAKE HIM STRONGER, OKAY?
SURE...
I'LL LET HIM KILL--
--YOUUUU...
I DIDN'T MEAN IT.
PLOP
SORRY...

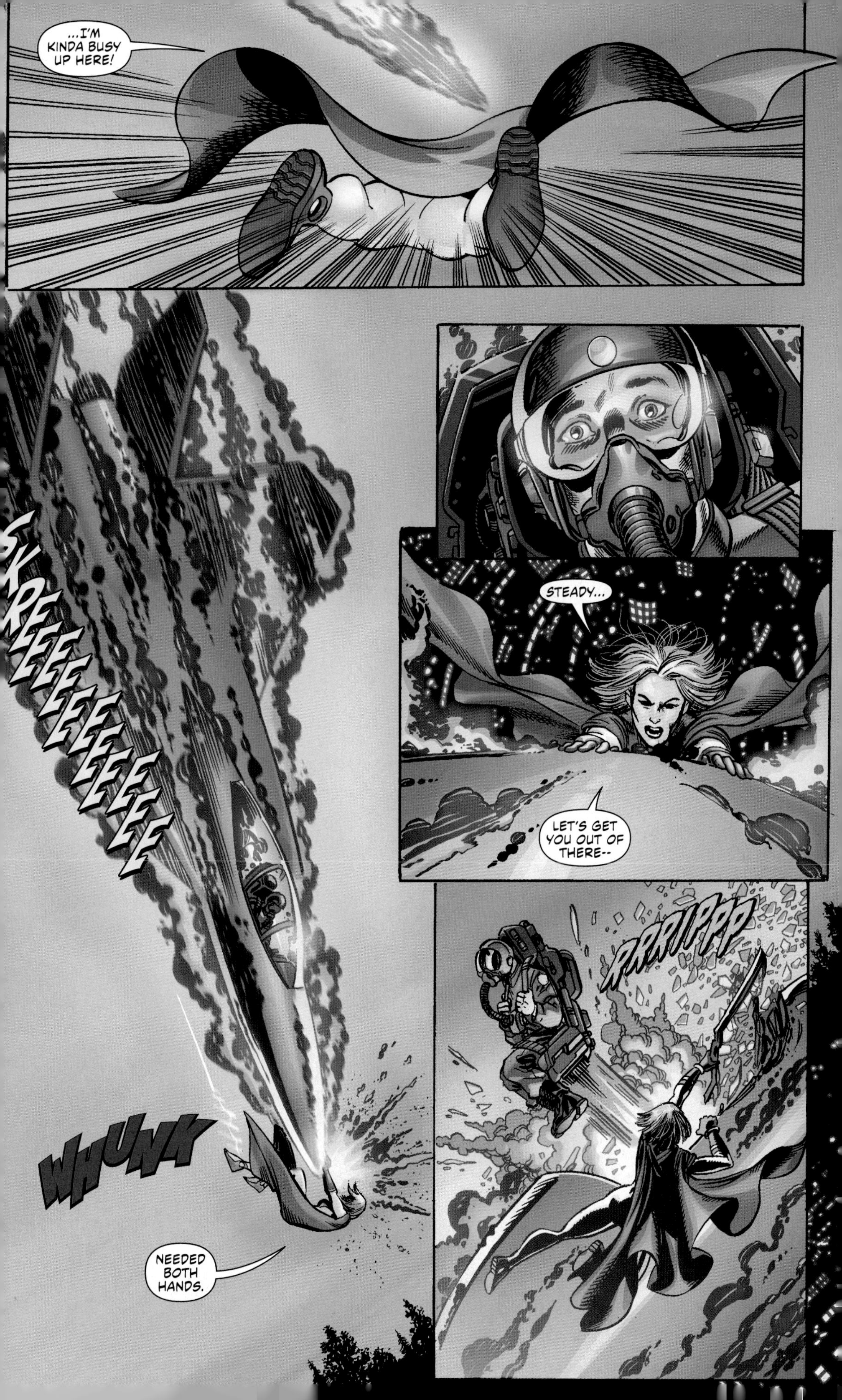
...I'M KINDA BUSY UP HERE!
SKREEEEEEEEEEEEE
STEADY...
LET'S GET YOU OUT OF THERE--
RRRIPPP
WHUNK
NEEDED BOTH HANDS.

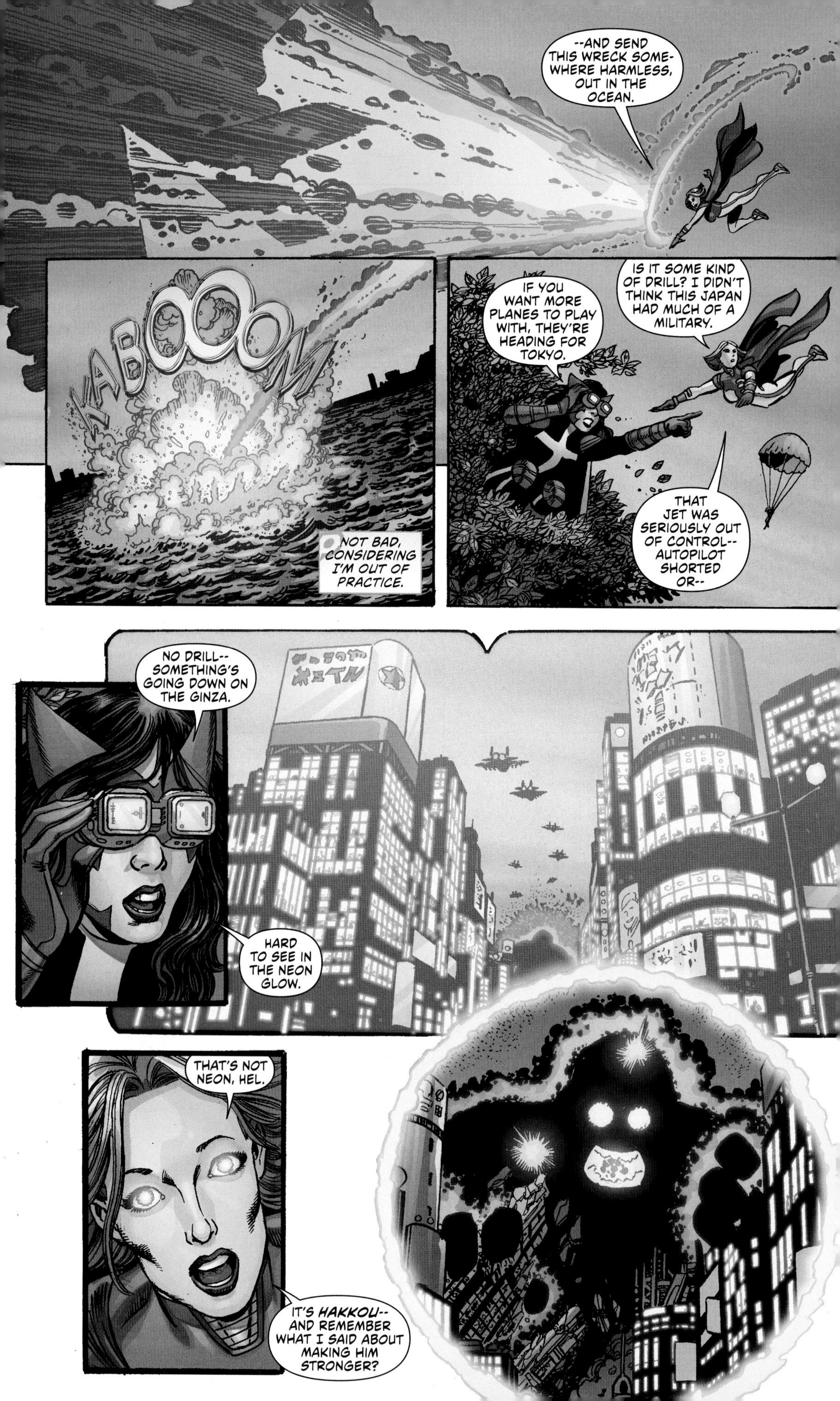
--AND SEND THIS WRECK SOME-WHERE HARMLESS, OUT IN THE OCEAN.
KABOOOM
NOT BAD, CONSIDERING I'M OUT OF PRACTICE.
IF YOU WANT MORE PLANES TO PLAY WITH, THEY'RE HEADING FOR TOKYO.
IS IT SOME KIND OF DRILL? I DIDN'T THINK THIS JAPAN HAD MUCH OF A MILITARY.
THAT JET WAS SERIOUSLY OUT OF CONTROL-- AUTOPILOT SHORTED OR--
NO DRILL-- SOMETHING'S GOING DOWN ON THE GINZA.
HARD TO SEE IN THE NEON GLOW.
THAT'S NOT NEON, HEL.
IT'S HAKKOU-- AND REMEMBER WHAT I SAID ABOUT MAKING HIM STRONGER?

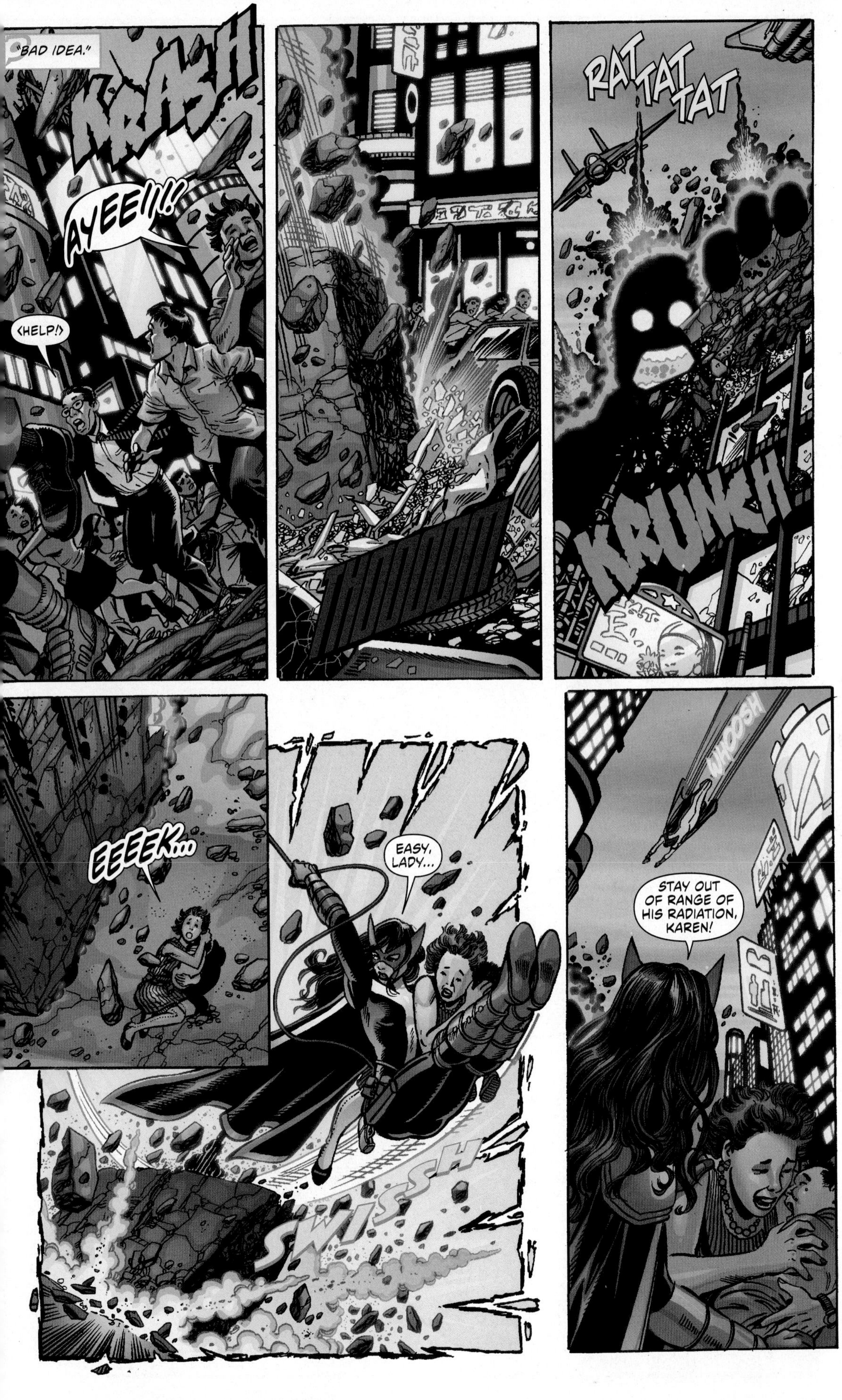

"BAD IDEA."
KRASH
AYEE!!!!
<HELP!>
THOOOM
RAT TAT TAT
KRUNKH
EEEEK...
EASY, LADY...
SWISSH
WHOOSH
STAY OUT OF RANGE OF HIS RADIATION, KAREN!

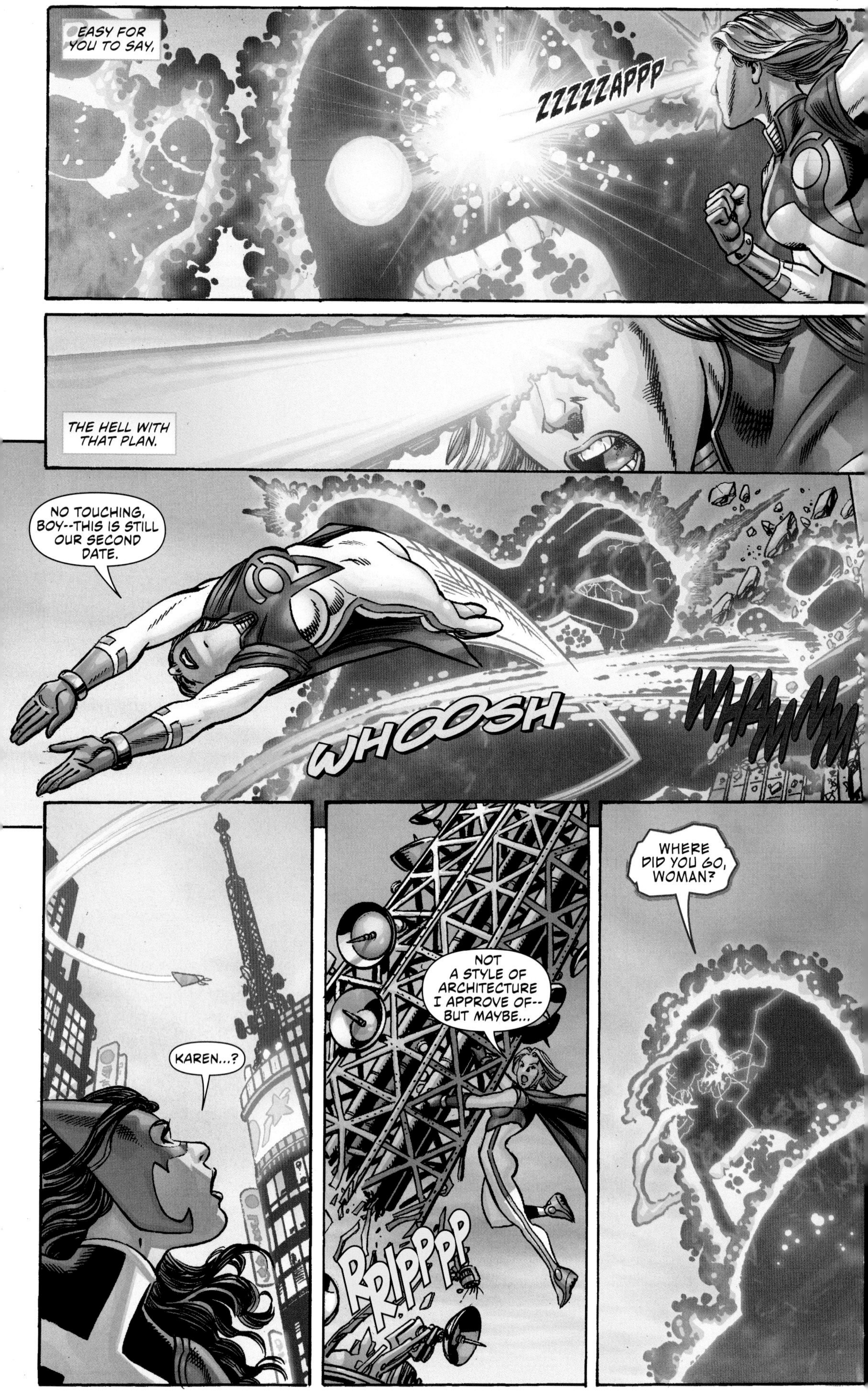
EASY FOR YOU TO SAY,
ZZZZZAPPP
THE HELL WITH THAT PLAN.
NO TOUCHING, BOY--THIS IS STILL OUR SECOND DATE.
WHOOSH
WHAMMM
KAREN...?
NOT A STYLE OF ARCHITECTURE I APPROVE OF--BUT MAYBE...
RRIPPPP
WHERE DID YOU GO, WOMAN?

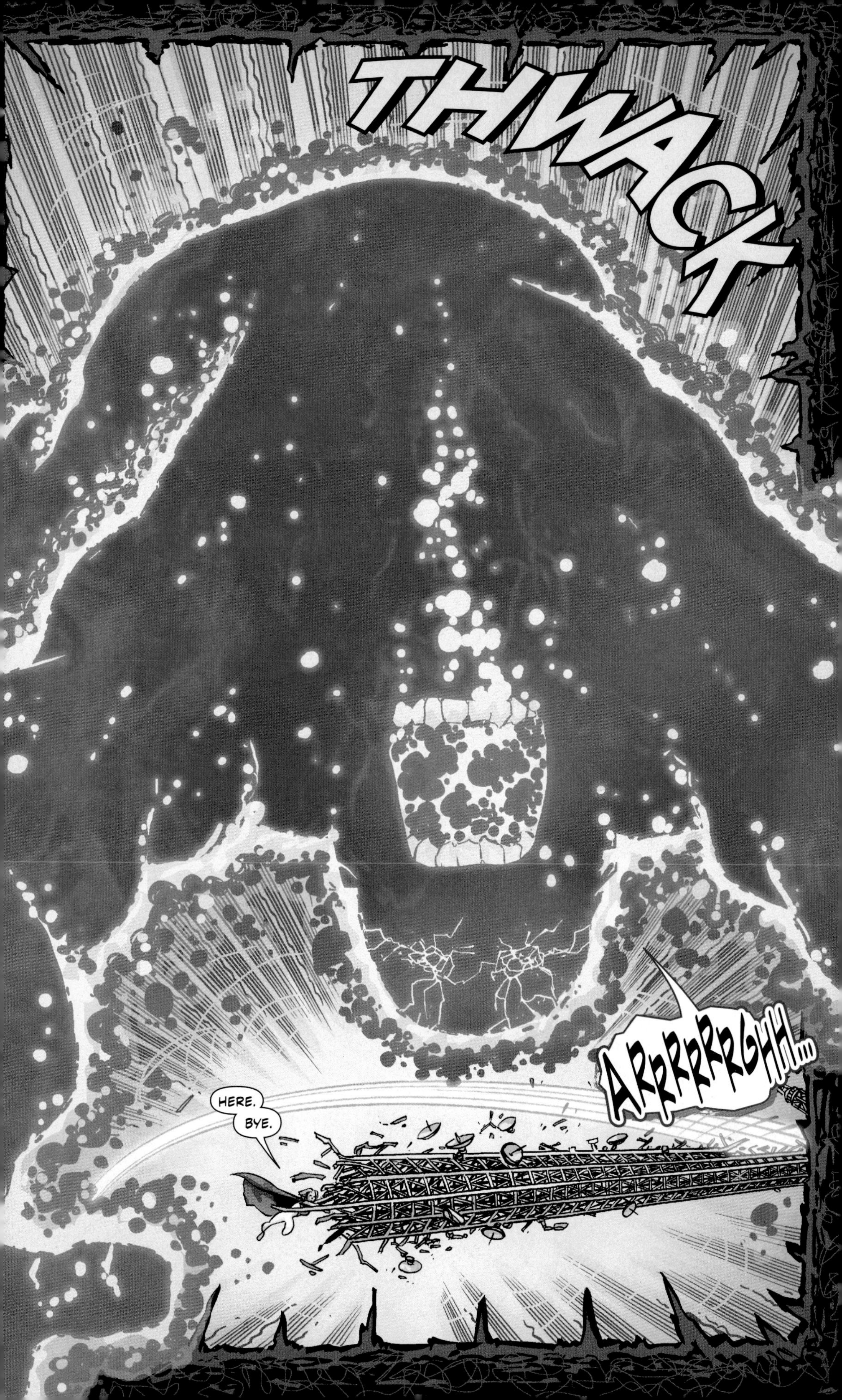
THWACK
ARRRRRRGHH...
HERE.
BYE.

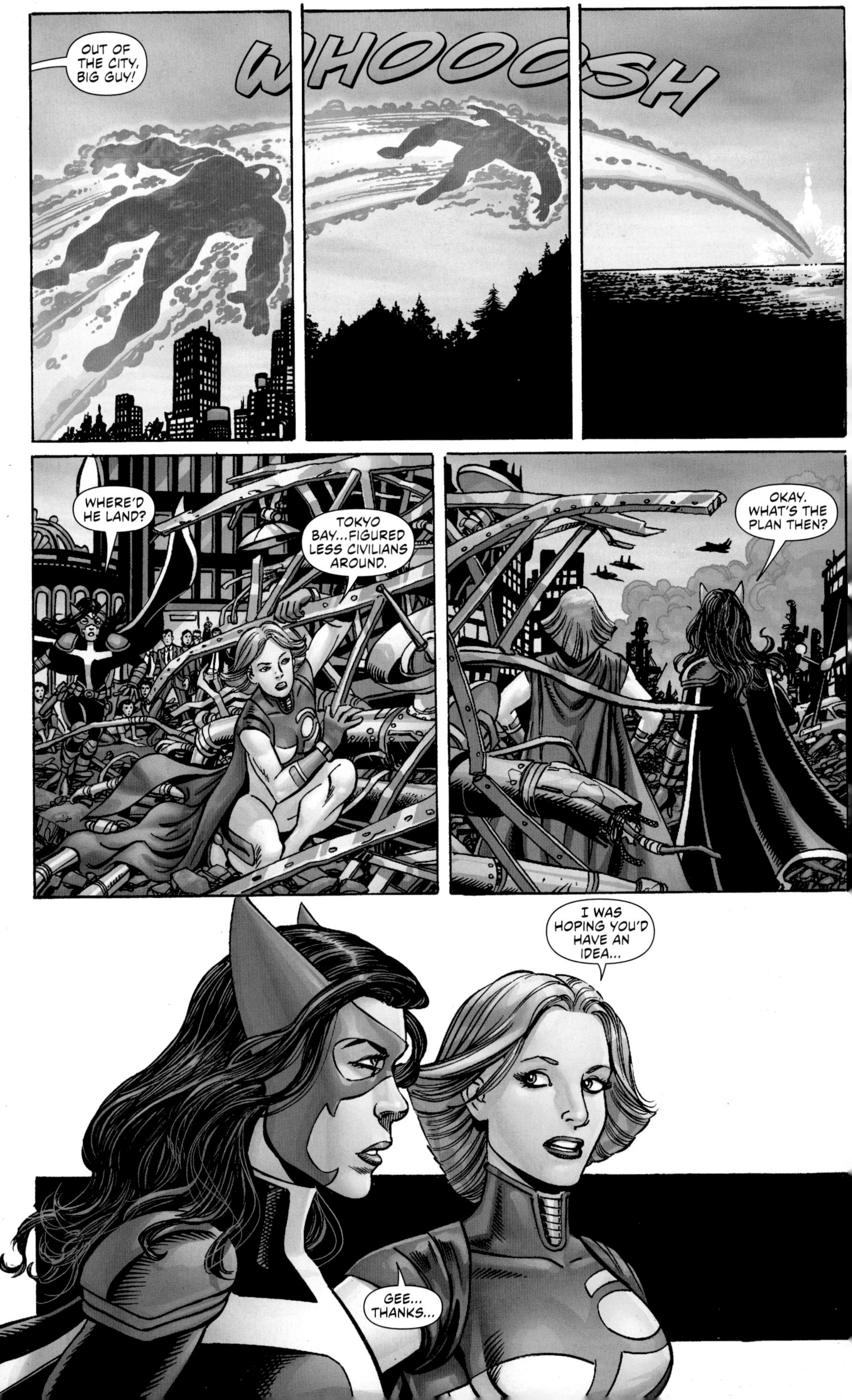
OUT OF THE CITY, BIG GUY!
WHOOOOSH
WHERE'D HE LAND?
TOKYO BAY...FIGURED LESS CIVILIANS AROUND.
OKAY. WHAT'S THE PLAN THEN?
I WAS HOPING YOU'D HAVE AN IDEA...
GEE... THANKS...

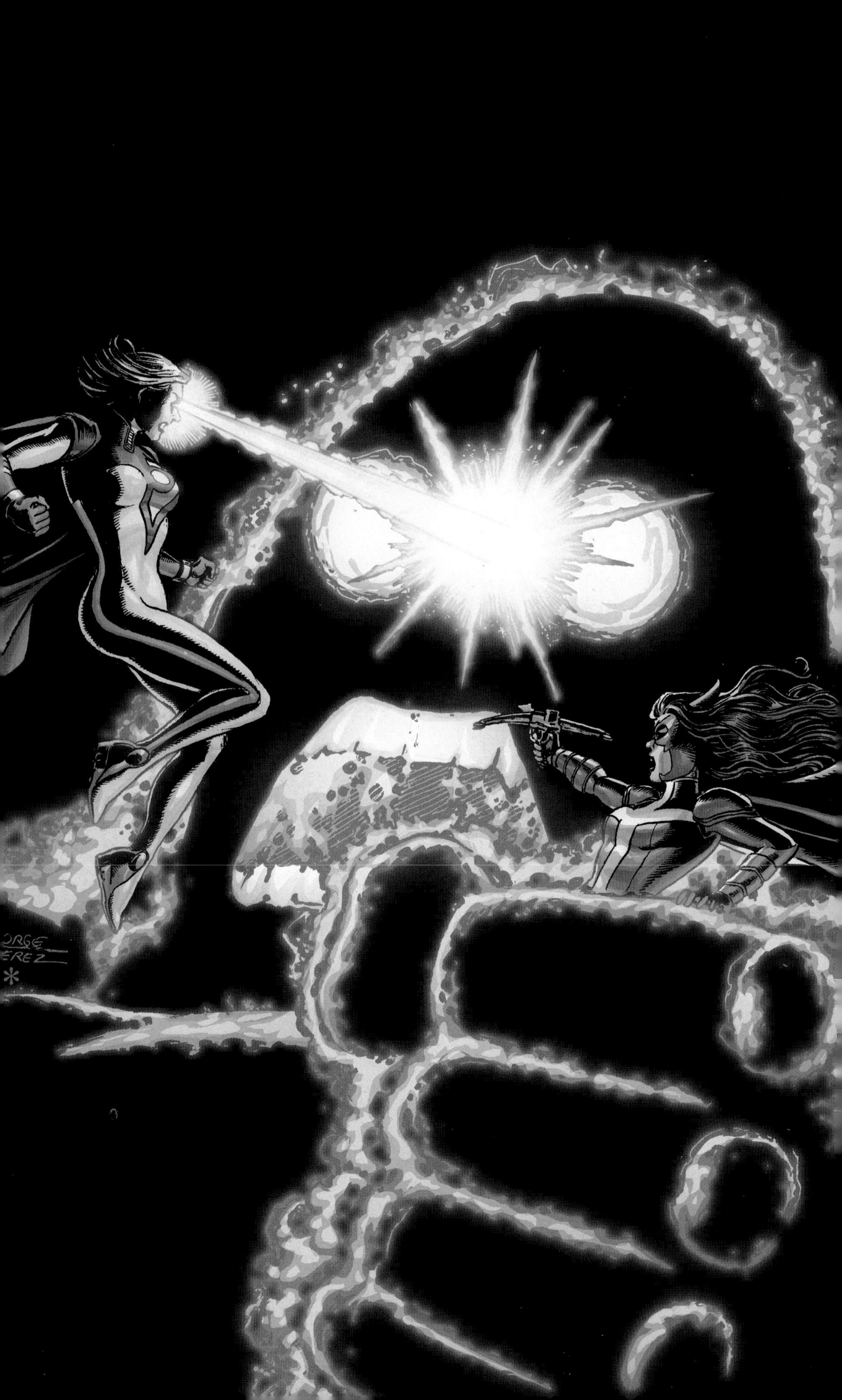

**PAUL LEVITZ** writer **GEORGE PÉREZ** penciller (present-day sequence)
**SCOTT KOBLISH** inker (present-day sequence) **KEVIN MAGUIRE** artist (flashback sequence)

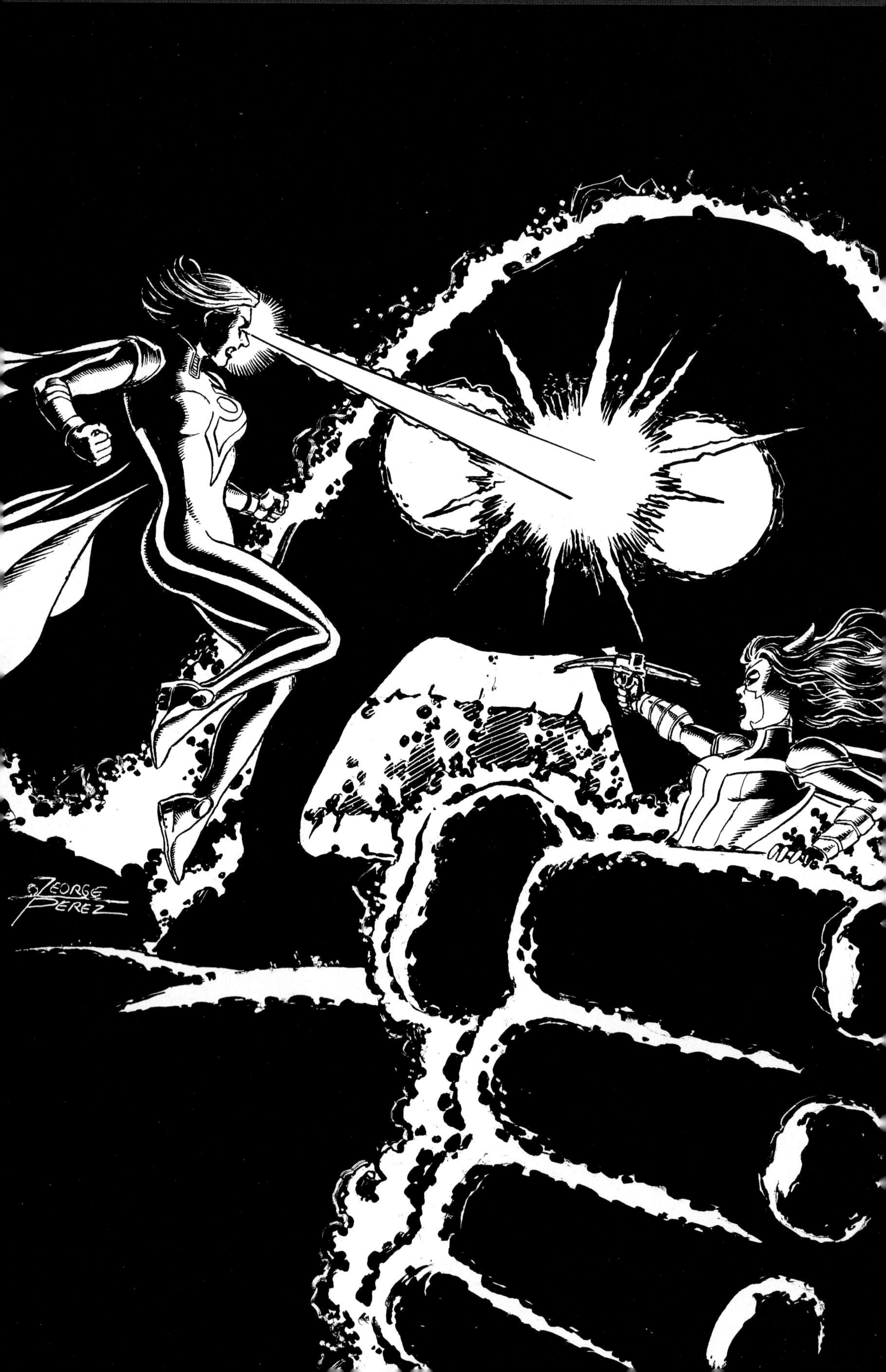
GEORGE PEREZ

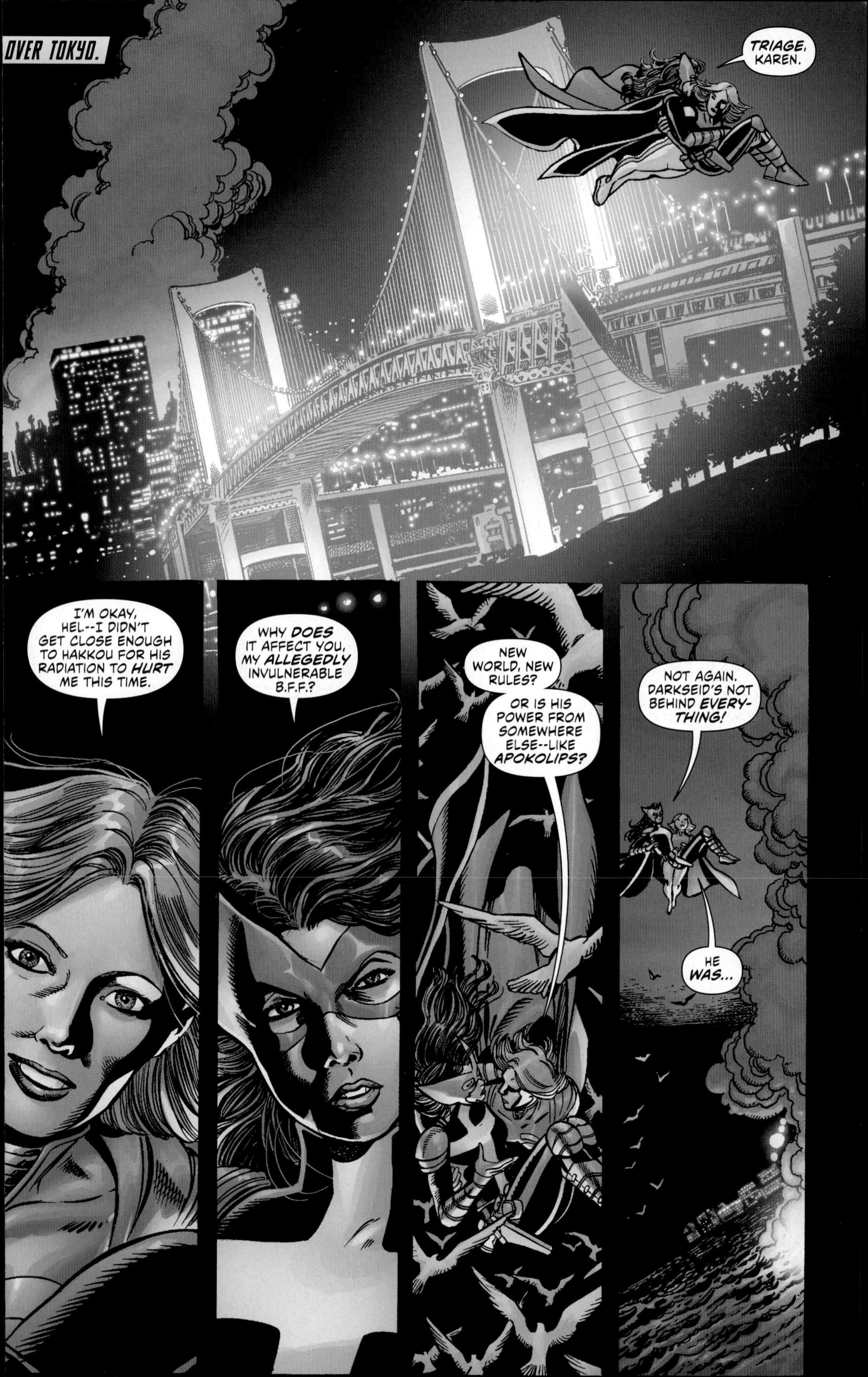
OVER TOKYO.
TRIAGE, KAREN.
I'M OKAY, HEL--I DIDN'T GET CLOSE ENOUGH TO HAKKOU FOR HIS RADIATION TO HURT ME THIS TIME.
WHY DOES IT AFFECT YOU, MY ALLEGEDLY INVULNERABLE B.F.F.?
NEW WORLD, NEW RULES?
OR IS HIS POWER FROM SOMEWHERE ELSE--LIKE APOKOLIPS?
NOT AGAIN. DARKSEID'S NOT BEHIND EVERY-THING!
HE WAS...

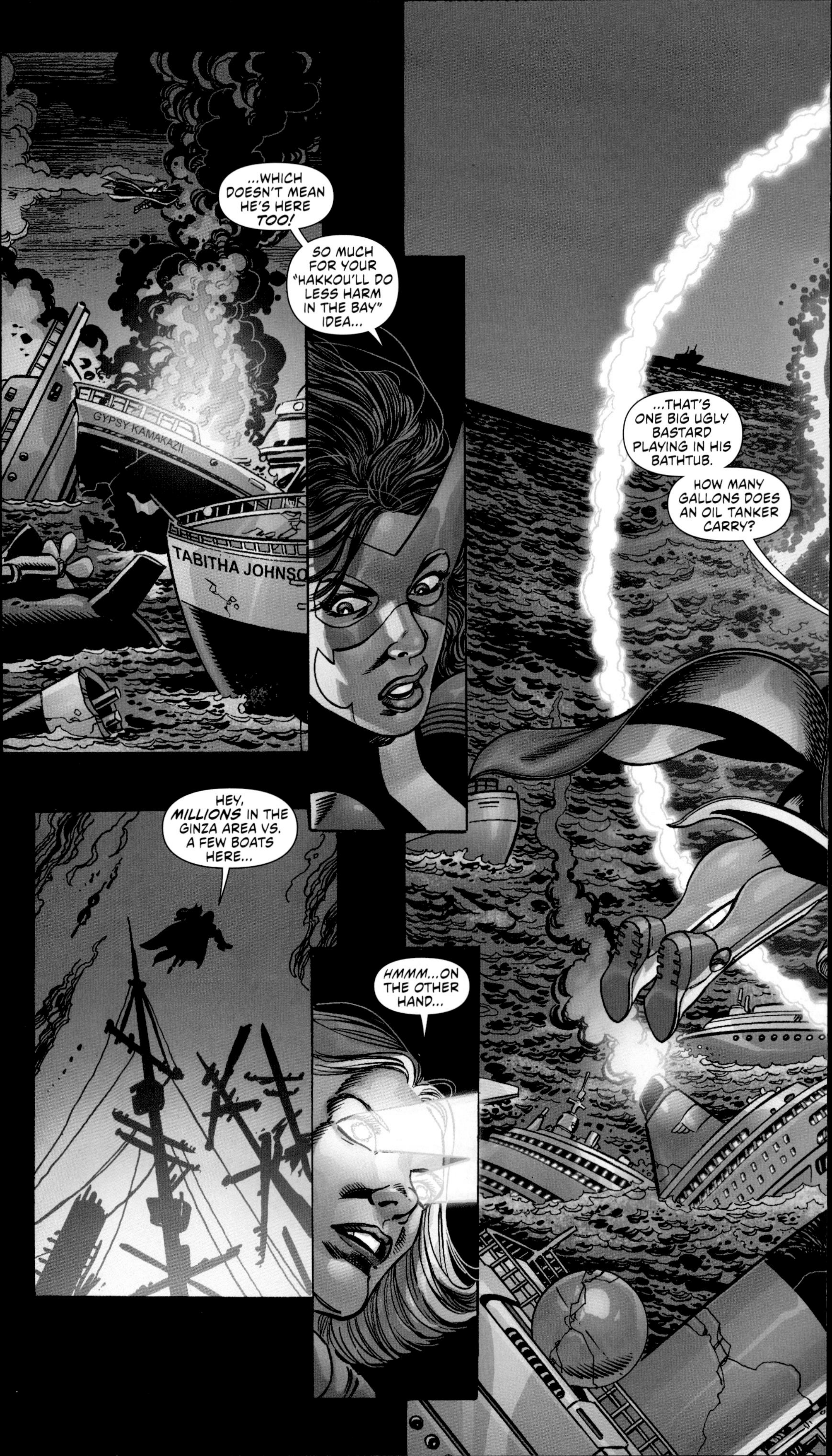
...WHICH DOESN'T MEAN HE'S HERE TOO!
SO MUCH FOR YOUR "HAKKOU'LL DO LESS HARM IN THE BAY" IDEA...
GYPSY KAMAKAZII
TABITHA JOHNSO
...THAT'S ONE BIG UGLY BASTARD PLAYING IN HIS BATHTUB.
HOW MANY GALLONS DOES AN OIL TANKER CARRY?
HEY, MILLIONS IN THE GINZA AREA VS. A FEW BOATS HERE...
HMMM...ON THE OTHER HAND...

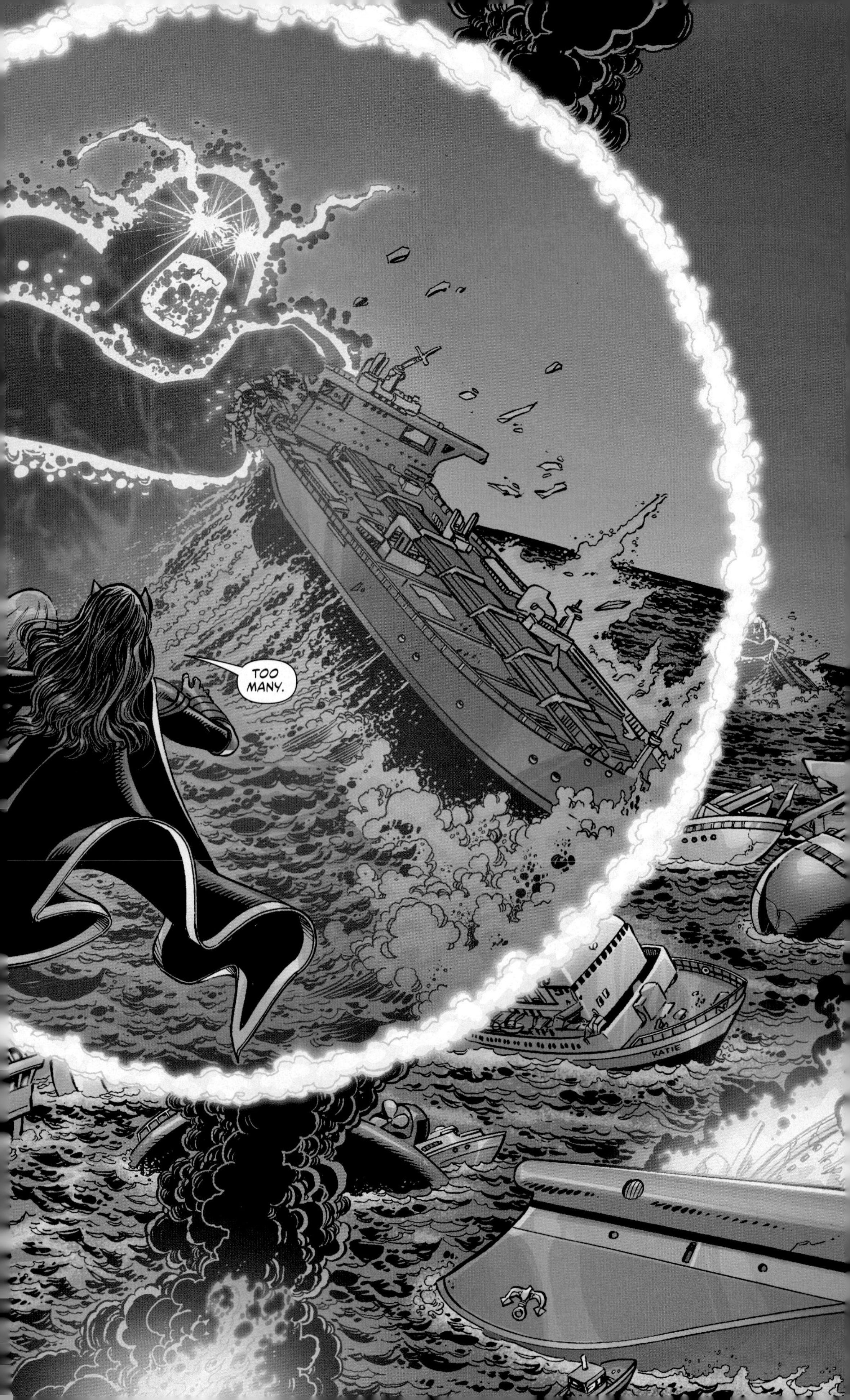
TOO MANY.
KATIE

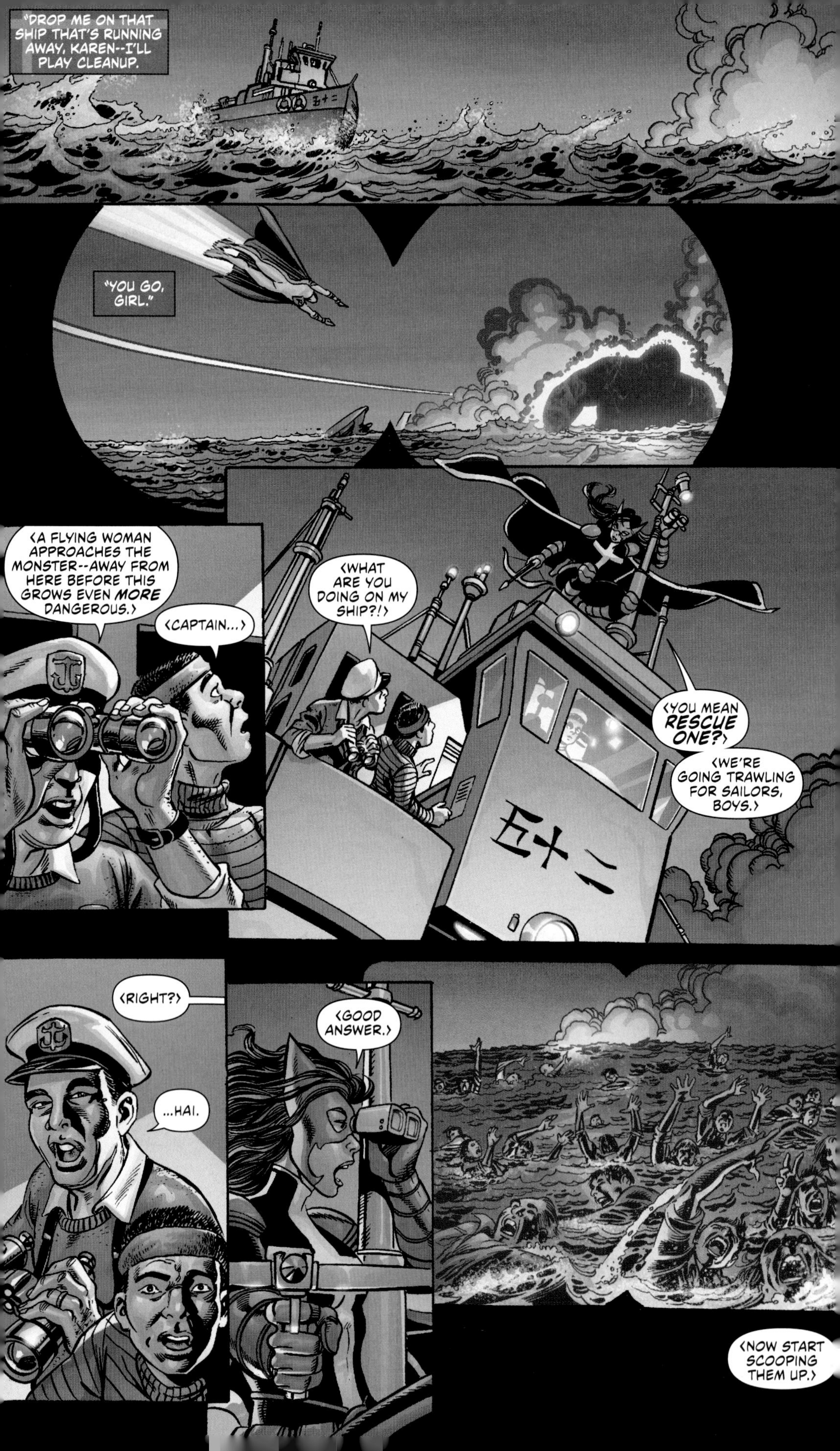
"DROP ME ON THAT SHIP THAT'S RUNNING AWAY, KAREN--I'LL PLAY CLEANUP.
"YOU GO, GIRL."
‹A FLYING WOMAN APPROACHES THE MONSTER--AWAY FROM HERE BEFORE THIS GROWS EVEN MORE DANGEROUS.›
‹CAPTAIN...›
‹WHAT ARE YOU DOING ON MY SHIP?!›
‹YOU MEAN RESCUE ONE?›
‹WE'RE GOING TRAWLING FOR SAILORS, BOYS.›
‹RIGHT?›
...HAI.
‹GOOD ANSWER.›
‹NOW START SCOOPING THEM UP.›

‹WE CAN ONLY HOLD...›

I'VE SEEN TOKYO SUBWAY CARS-- *SQUEEZE.*

‹WHAT'S THAT?›

‹Y-YOU ARE *RADIO-ACTIVE...*›

‹NOT *BIG* READING... NOT LIKE WHEN AMERICAN SHIPS GO BY WITH *NUCLEAR WEAPONS...*›

‹A LITTLE SPILL AT THE PLANT...›

‹...WE HAVE A BIGGER ONE TO DEAL WITH NOW.›

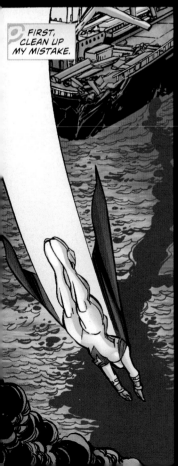

FIRST, CLEAN UP MY MISTAKE.

GROSS!!!!

SLIPPERY, TOO.

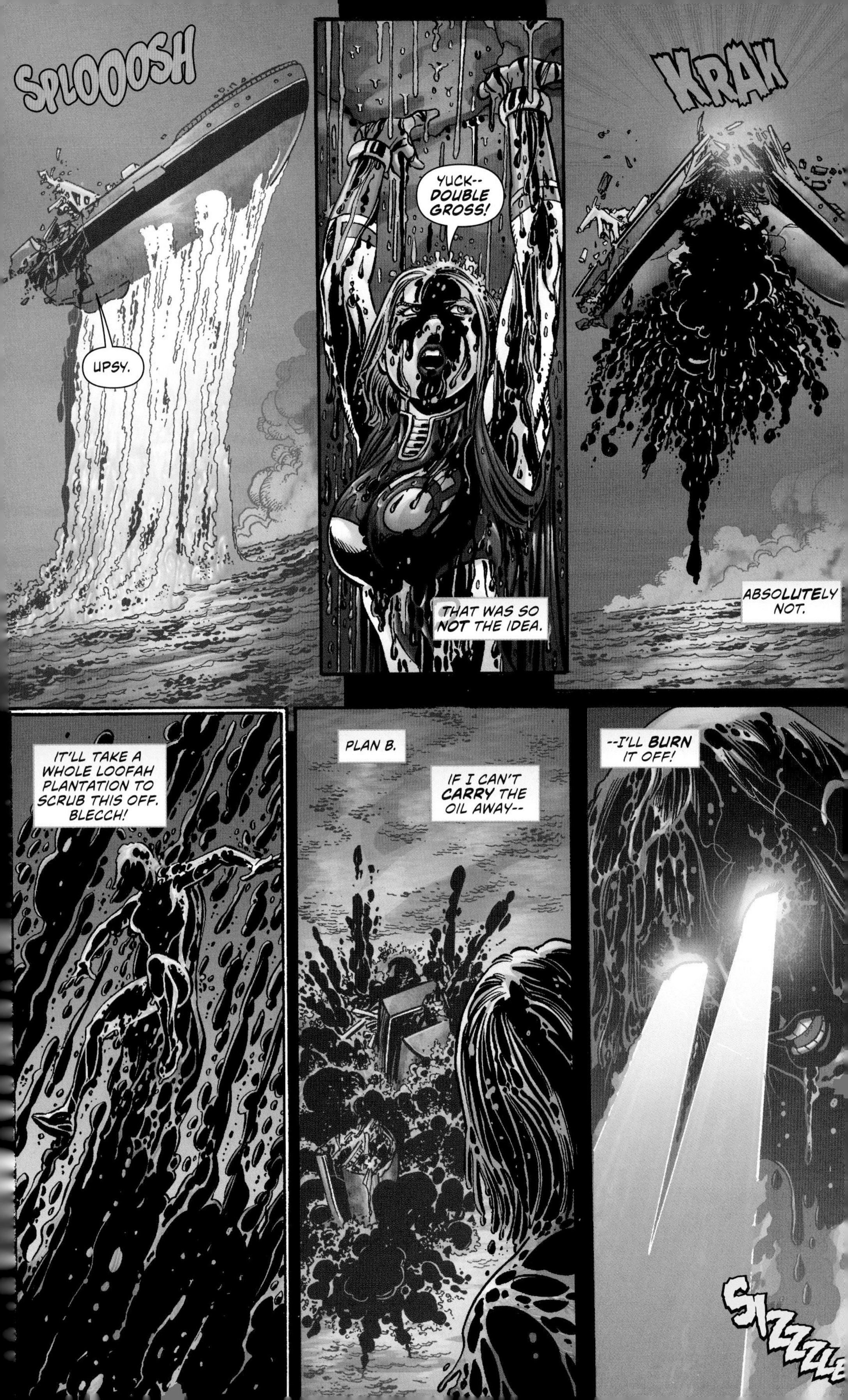
SPLOOOSH
UPSY.
YUCK--DOUBLE GROSS!
THAT WAS SO NOT THE IDEA.
KRAK
ABSOLUTELY NOT.
IT'LL TAKE A WHOLE LOOFAH PLANTATION TO SCRUB THIS OFF. BLECCH!
PLAN B.
IF I CAN'T CARRY THE OIL AWAY--
--I'LL BURN IT OFF!
SIZZZLE

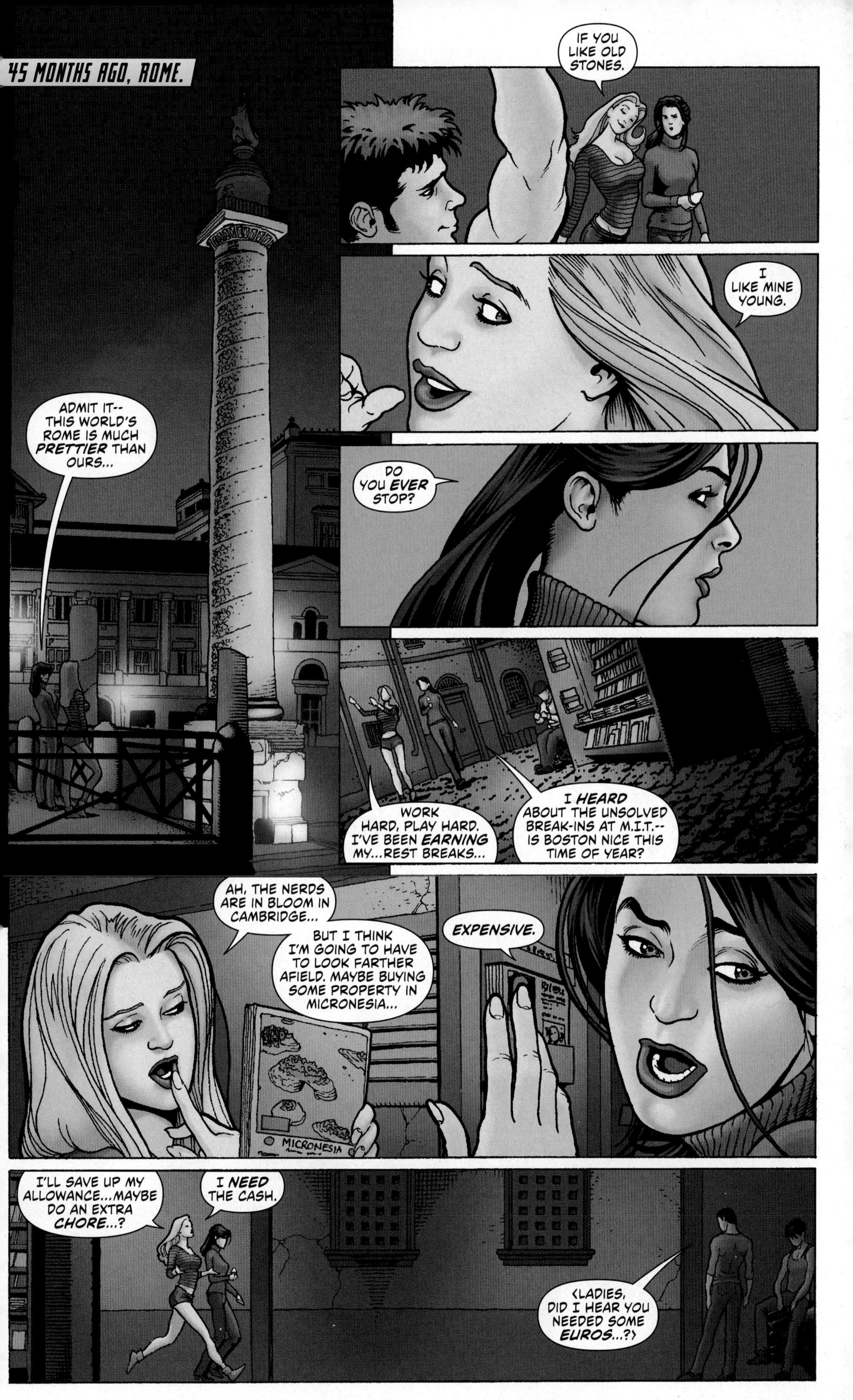
45 MONTHS AGO, ROME.
ADMIT IT-- THIS WORLD'S ROME IS MUCH PRETTIER THAN OURS...
IF YOU LIKE OLD STONES.
I LIKE MINE YOUNG.
DO YOU EVER STOP?
WORK HARD, PLAY HARD. I'VE BEEN EARNING MY...REST BREAKS...
I HEARD ABOUT THE UNSOLVED BREAK-INS AT M.I.T.-- IS BOSTON NICE THIS TIME OF YEAR?
AH, THE NERDS ARE IN BLOOM IN CAMBRIDGE...
BUT I THINK I'M GOING TO HAVE TO LOOK FARTHER AFIELD. MAYBE BUYING SOME PROPERTY IN MICRONESIA...
EXPENSIVE.
MICRONESIA
I'LL SAVE UP MY ALLOWANCE...MAYBE DO AN EXTRA CHORE...?
I NEED THE CASH.
<LADIES, DID I HEAR YOU NEEDED SOME EUROS...?>

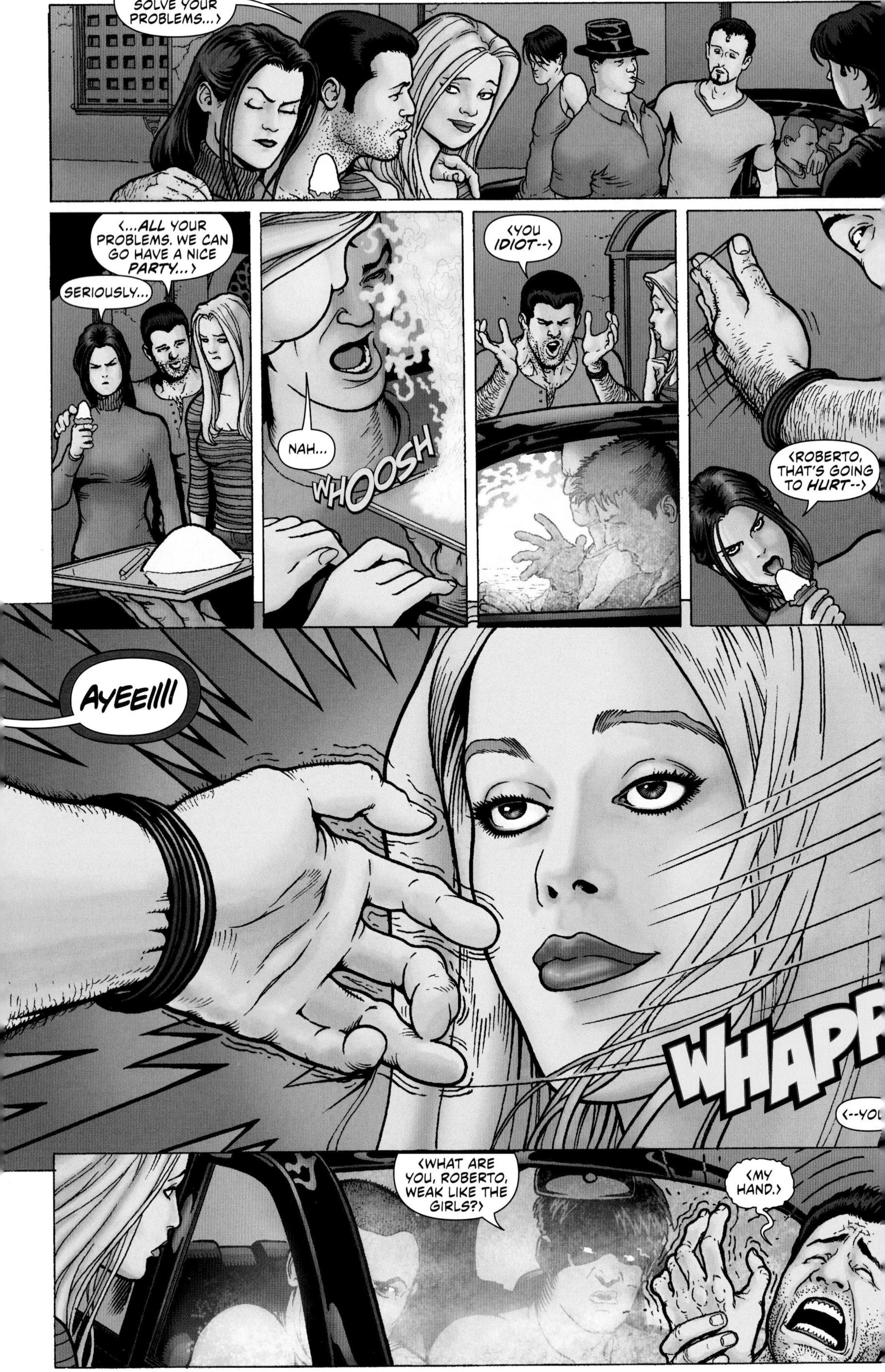

‹LET ROBERTO SOLVE YOUR PROBLEMS...›
‹...ALL YOUR PROBLEMS. WE CAN GO HAVE A NICE PARTY...›
SERIOUSLY...
NAH...
WHOOSH
‹YOU IDIOT--›
‹ROBERTO, THAT'S GOING TO HURT--›
AYEEIIII
WHAPP
‹--YOU
‹WHAT ARE YOU, ROBERTO, WEAK LIKE THE GIRLS?›
‹MY HAND.›

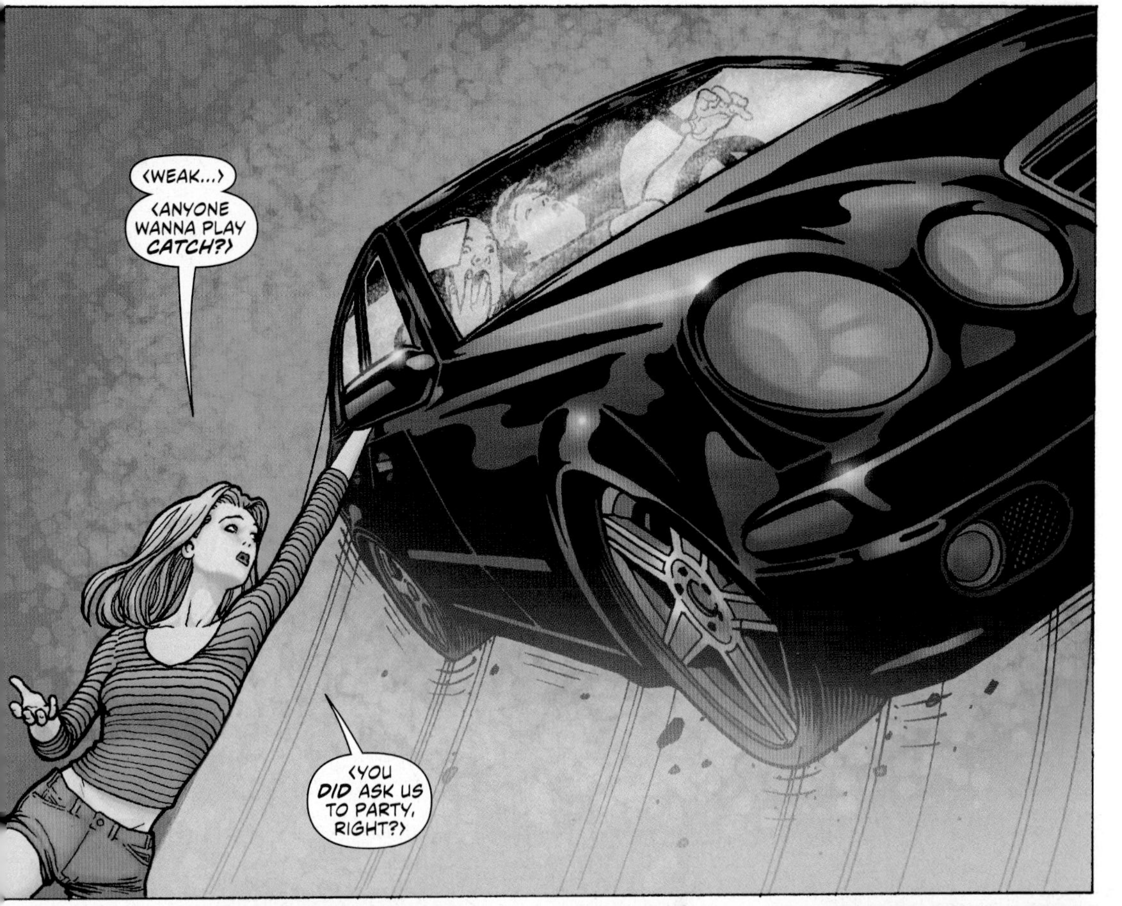

<WEAK...>
<ANYONE WANNA PLAY CATCH?>
<YOU DID ASK US TO PARTY, RIGHT?>


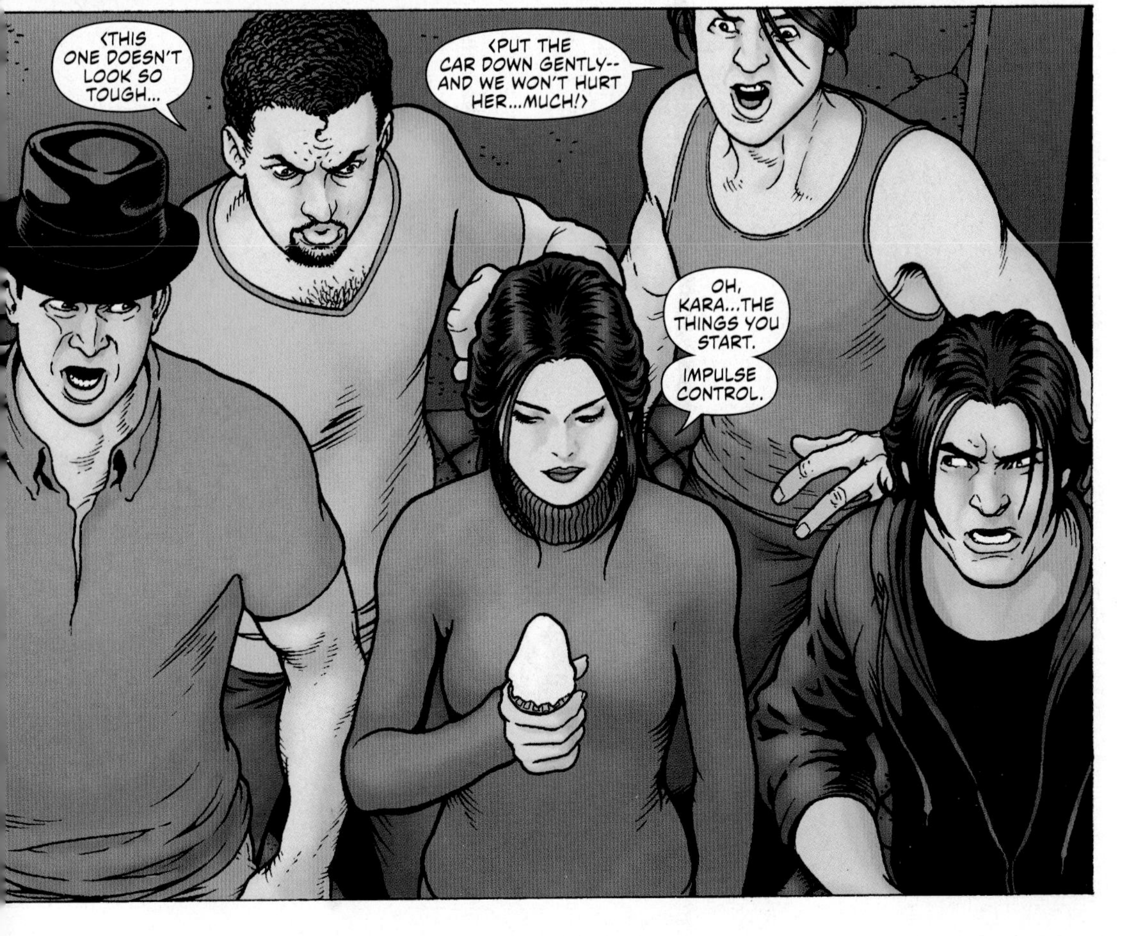

<THIS ONE DOESN'T LOOK SO TOUGH...
<PUT THE CAR DOWN GENTLY-- AND WE WON'T HURT HER...MUCH!>
OH, KARA...THE THINGS YOU START.
IMPULSE CONTROL.

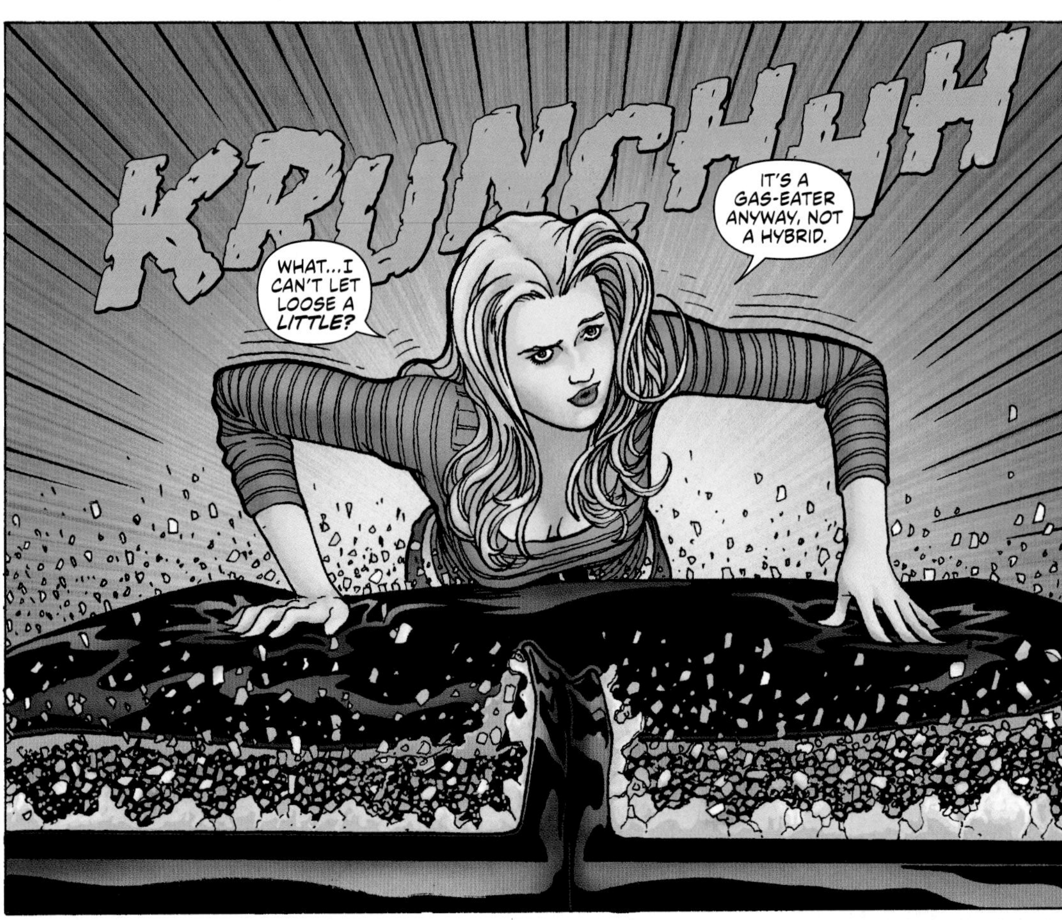
KRUNCHHH
WHAT...I CAN'T LET LOOSE A *LITTLE?*
IT'S A GAS-EATER ANYWAY, NOT A HYBRID.

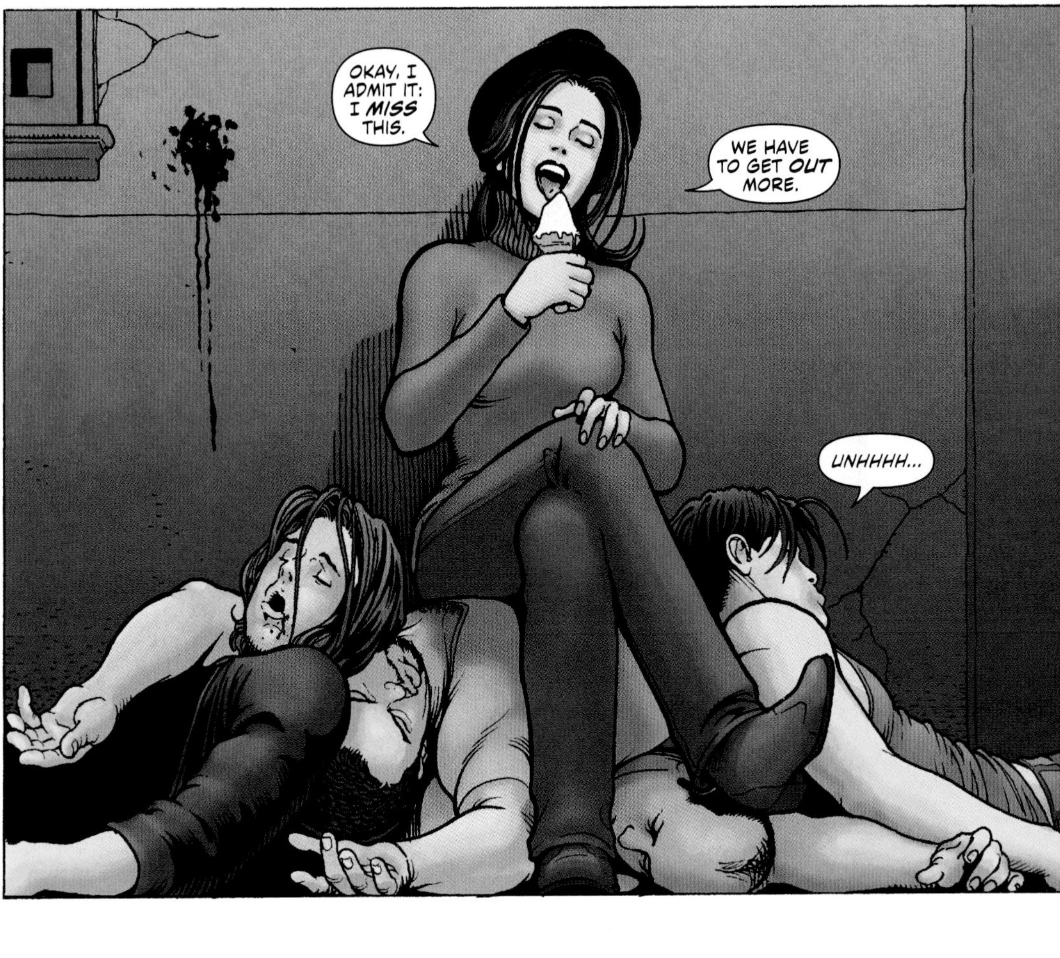
OKAY, I ADMIT IT: I *MISS* THIS.
WE HAVE TO GET *OUT* MORE.
*UNHHHH...*

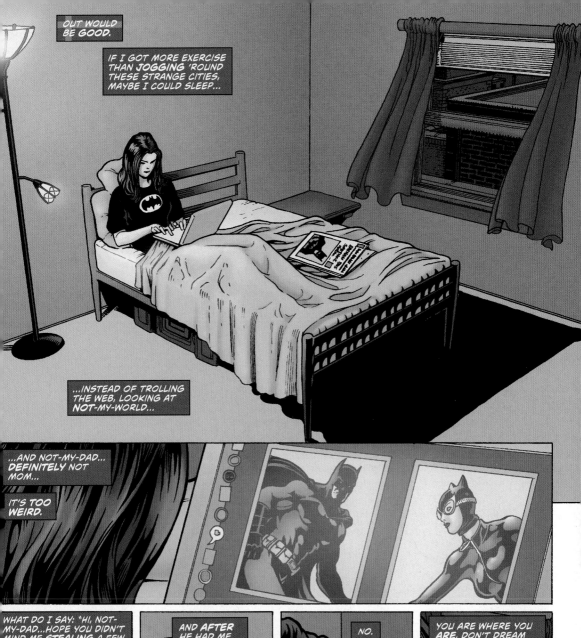

OUT WOULD BE GOOD.

IF I GOT MORE EXERCISE THAN *JOGGING* 'ROUND THESE STRANGE CITIES, MAYBE I COULD SLEEP...

...INSTEAD OF TROLLING THE WEB, LOOKING AT *NOT-MY-WORLD*...

...AND NOT-MY-DAD... DEFINITELY NOT MOM...

IT'S TOO WEIRD.

WHAT DO I SAY: "HI, NOT-MY-DAD...HOPE YOU DIDN'T MIND ME *STEALING* A FEW BUCKS...GOT ANY OPENINGS FOR A *LOST ROBIN?*"

AND *AFTER* HE HAD ME COMMITTED...

NO.

MOMLOGIC TIME:

YOU ARE WHERE YOU *ARE*, DON'T DREAM OF ELSEWHERE. MARK YOUR TERRITORY, AND LIVE IN IT.

SOUND RIGHT, TABBY?

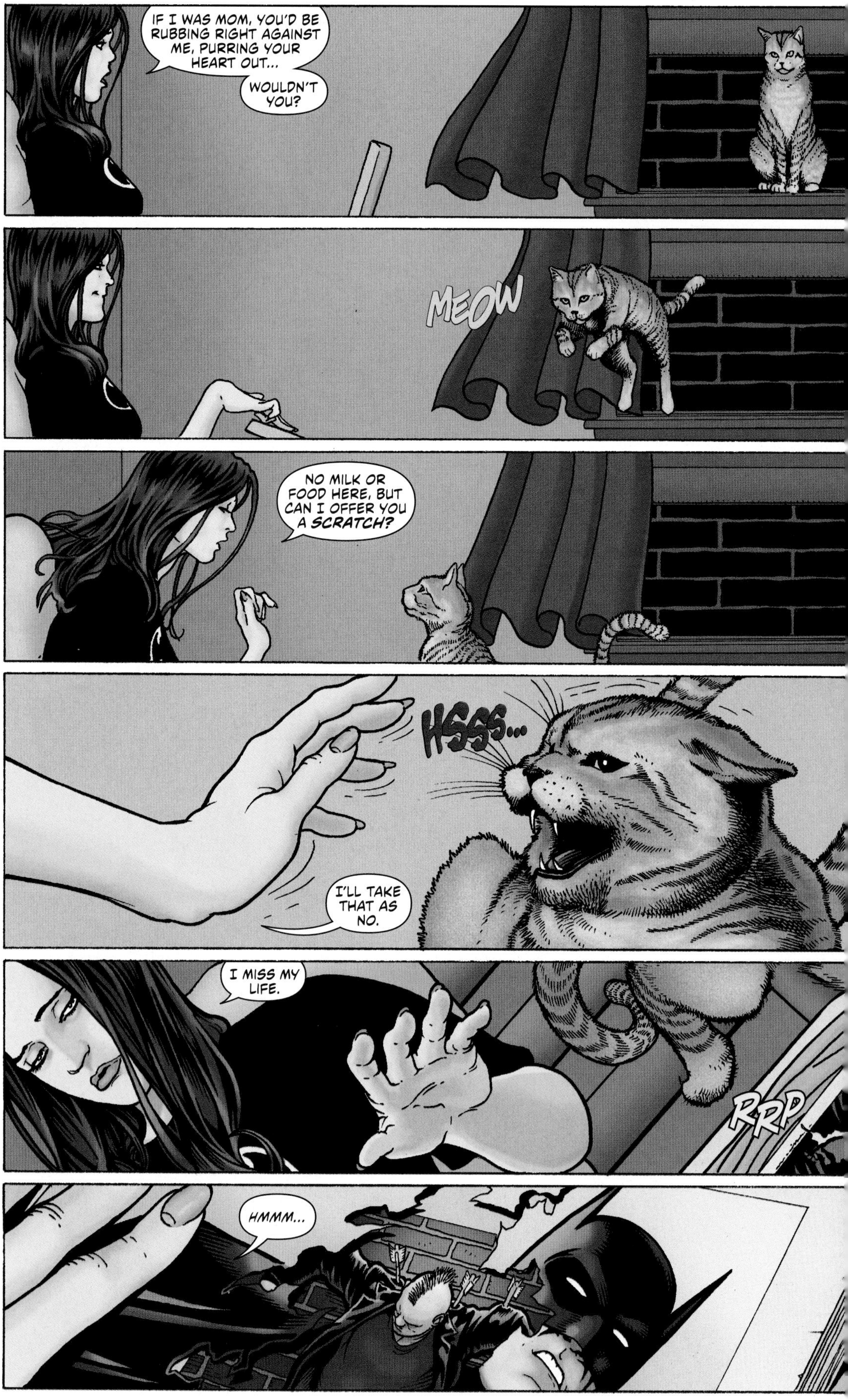

IF I WAS MOM, YOU'D BE RUBBING RIGHT AGAINST ME, PURRING YOUR HEART OUT...
WOULDN'T YOU?
MEOW
NO MILK OR FOOD HERE, BUT CAN I OFFER YOU A SCRATCH?
HSSS...
I'LL TAKE THAT AS NO.
I MISS MY LIFE.
RRP
HMMM...

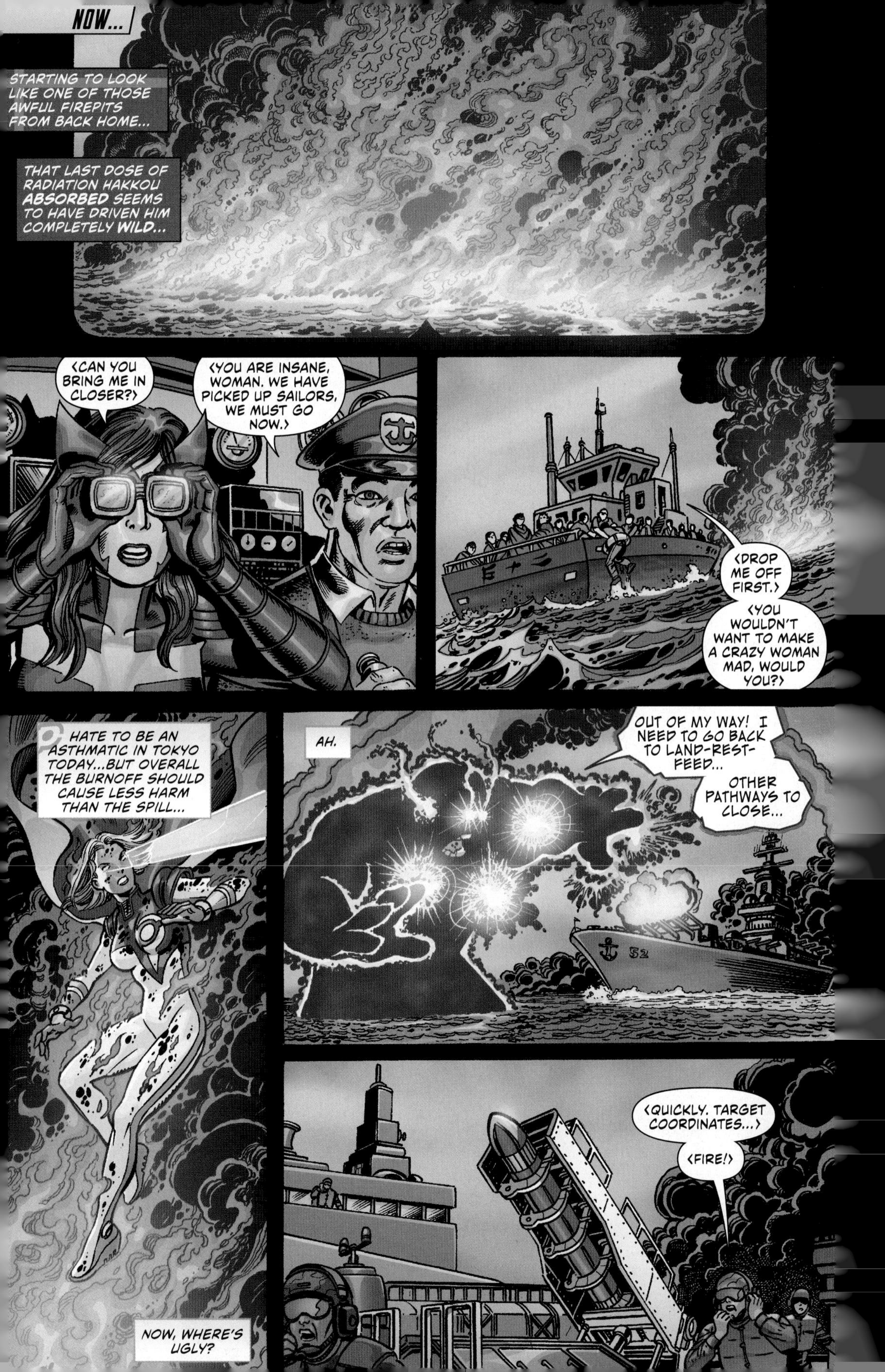
NOW...
STARTING TO LOOK LIKE ONE OF THOSE AWFUL FIREPITS FROM BACK HOME...
THAT LAST DOSE OF RADIATION HAKKOU ABSORBED SEEMS TO HAVE DRIVEN HIM COMPLETELY WILD...
‹CAN YOU BRING ME IN CLOSER?›
‹YOU ARE INSANE, WOMAN. WE HAVE PICKED UP SAILORS, WE MUST GO NOW.›
‹DROP ME OFF FIRST.›
‹YOU WOULDN'T WANT TO MAKE A CRAZY WOMAN MAD, WOULD YOU?›
HATE TO BE AN ASTHMATIC IN TOKYO TODAY...BUT OVERALL THE BURNOFF SHOULD CAUSE LESS HARM THAN THE SPILL...
NOW, WHERE'S UGLY?
AH.
OUT OF MY WAY! I NEED TO GO BACK TO LAND-REST-FEED...
OTHER PATHWAYS TO CLOSE...
‹QUICKLY. TARGET COORDINATES...›
‹FIRE!›

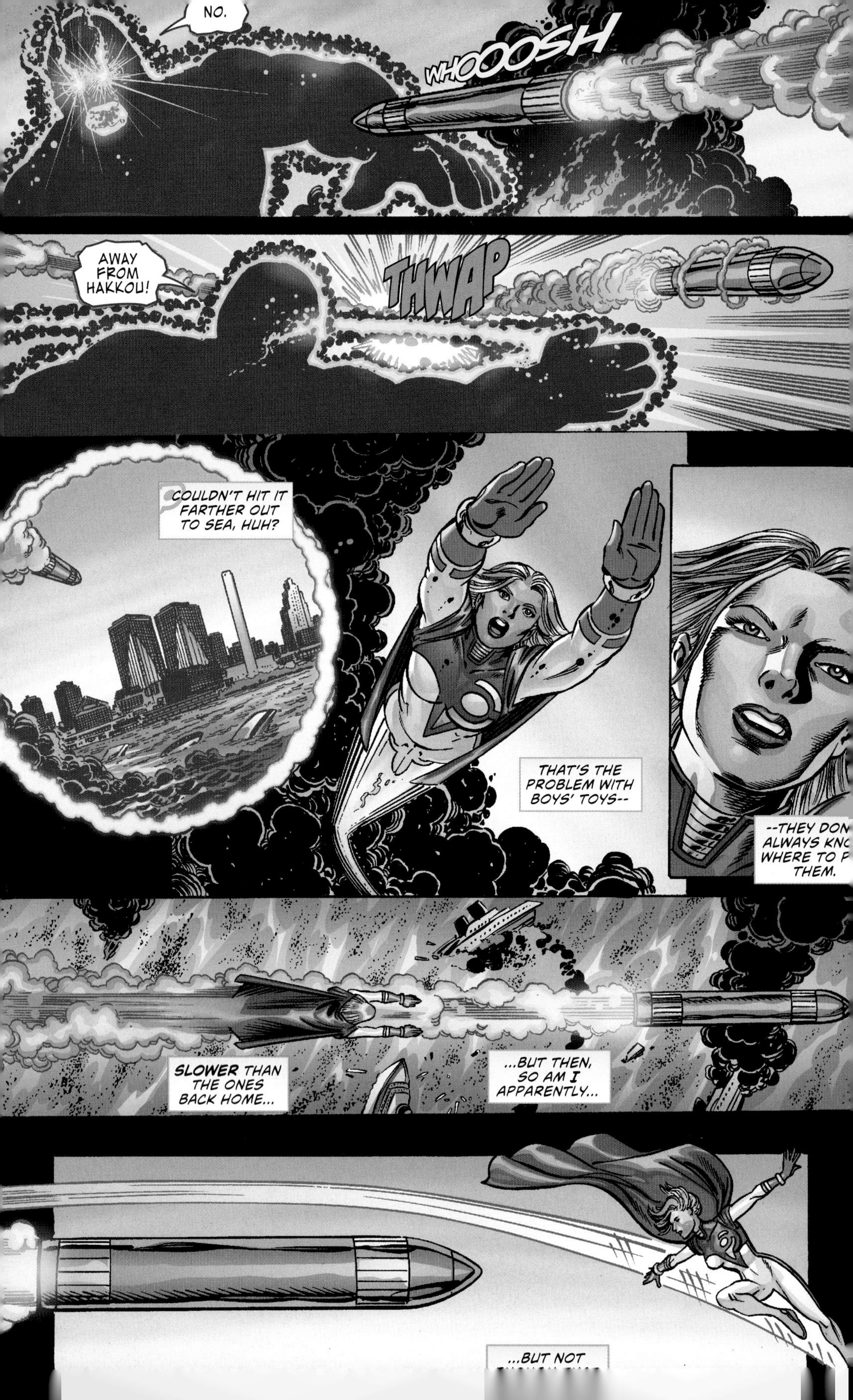
NO.
WHOOOSH
AWAY FROM HAKKOU!
THWAP
COULDN'T HIT IT FARTHER OUT TO SEA, HUH?
THAT'S THE PROBLEM WITH BOYS' TOYS--
--THEY DON ALWAYS KNO WHERE TO P THEM.
SLOWER THAN THE ONES BACK HOME...
...BUT THEN, SO AM I APPARENTLY...
...BUT NOT

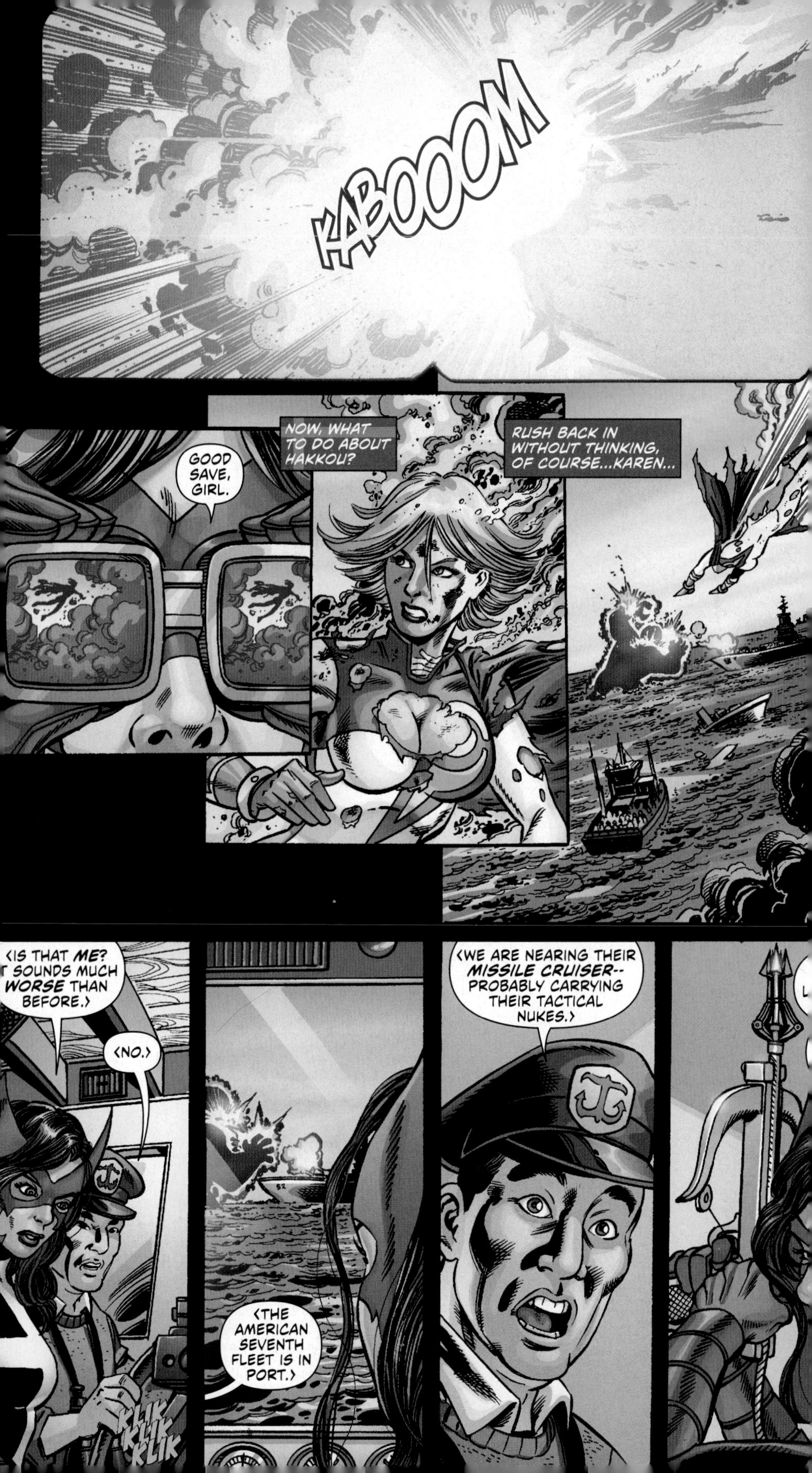
KABOOOM
GOOD SAVE, GIRL.
NOW, WHAT TO DO ABOUT HAKKOU?
RUSH BACK IN WITHOUT THINKING, OF COURSE...KAREN...
<IS THAT ME? T SOUNDS MUCH WORSE THAN BEFORE.>
<NO.>
KLIK KLIK KLIK
<THE AMERICAN SEVENTH FLEET IS IN PORT.>
<WE ARE NEARING THEIR MISSILE CRUISER-- PROBABLY CARRYING THEIR TACTICAL NUKES.>

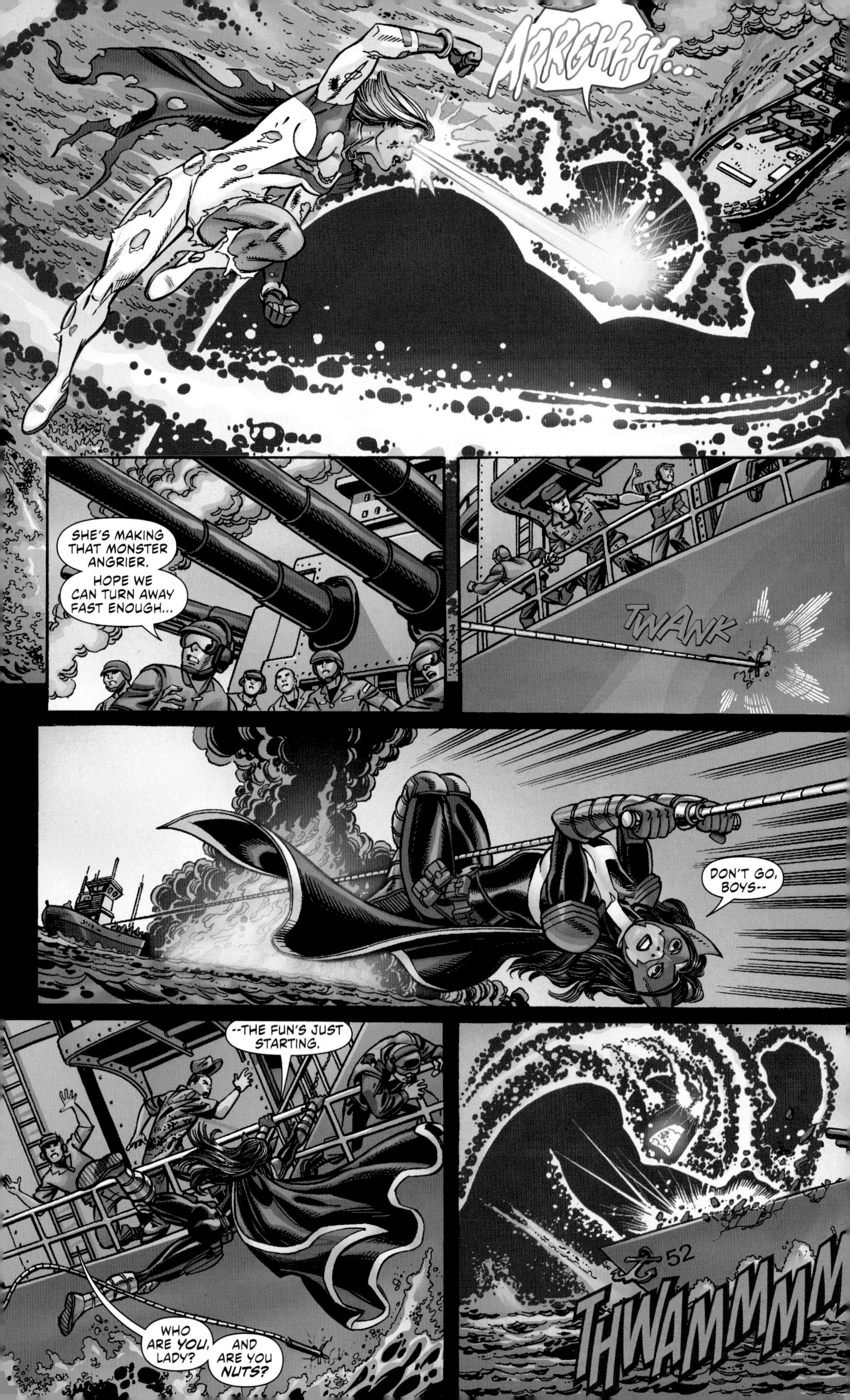
ARRGHHH...
SHE'S MAKING THAT MONSTER ANGRIER.
HOPE WE CAN TURN AWAY FAST ENOUGH...
TWANK
DON'T GO, BOYS--
--THE FUN'S JUST STARTING.
WHO ARE YOU, LADY?
AND ARE YOU NUTS?
52
THWAMMMM

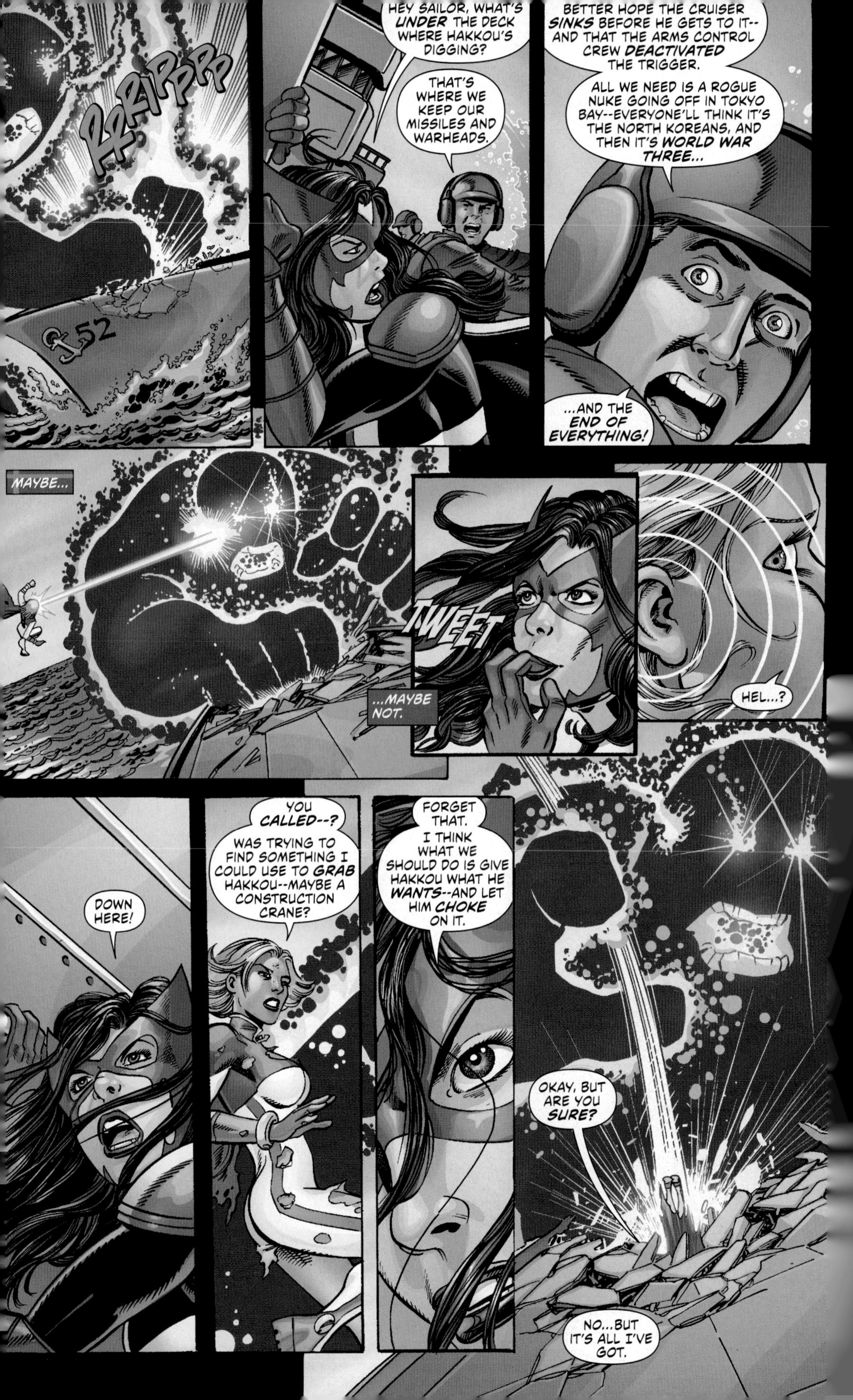
RRRIPPPP
HEY SAILOR, WHAT'S UNDER THE DECK WHERE HAKKOU'S DIGGING?
THAT'S WHERE WE KEEP OUR MISSILES AND WARHEADS.
BETTER HOPE THE CRUISER SINKS BEFORE HE GETS TO IT--AND THAT THE ARMS CONTROL CREW DEACTIVATED THE TRIGGER.
ALL WE NEED IS A ROGUE NUKE GOING OFF IN TOKYO BAY--EVERYONE'LL THINK IT'S THE NORTH KOREANS, AND THEN IT'S WORLD WAR THREE...
...AND THE END OF EVERYTHING!
MAYBE...
...MAYBE NOT.
TWEET
HEL...?
DOWN HERE!
YOU CALLED--?
WAS TRYING TO FIND SOMETHING I COULD USE TO GRAB HAKKOU--MAYBE A CONSTRUCTION CRANE?
FORGET THAT.
I THINK WHAT WE SHOULD DO IS GIVE HAKKOU WHAT HE WANTS--AND LET HIM CHOKE ON IT.
OKAY, BUT ARE YOU SURE?
NO...BUT IT'S ALL I'VE GOT.

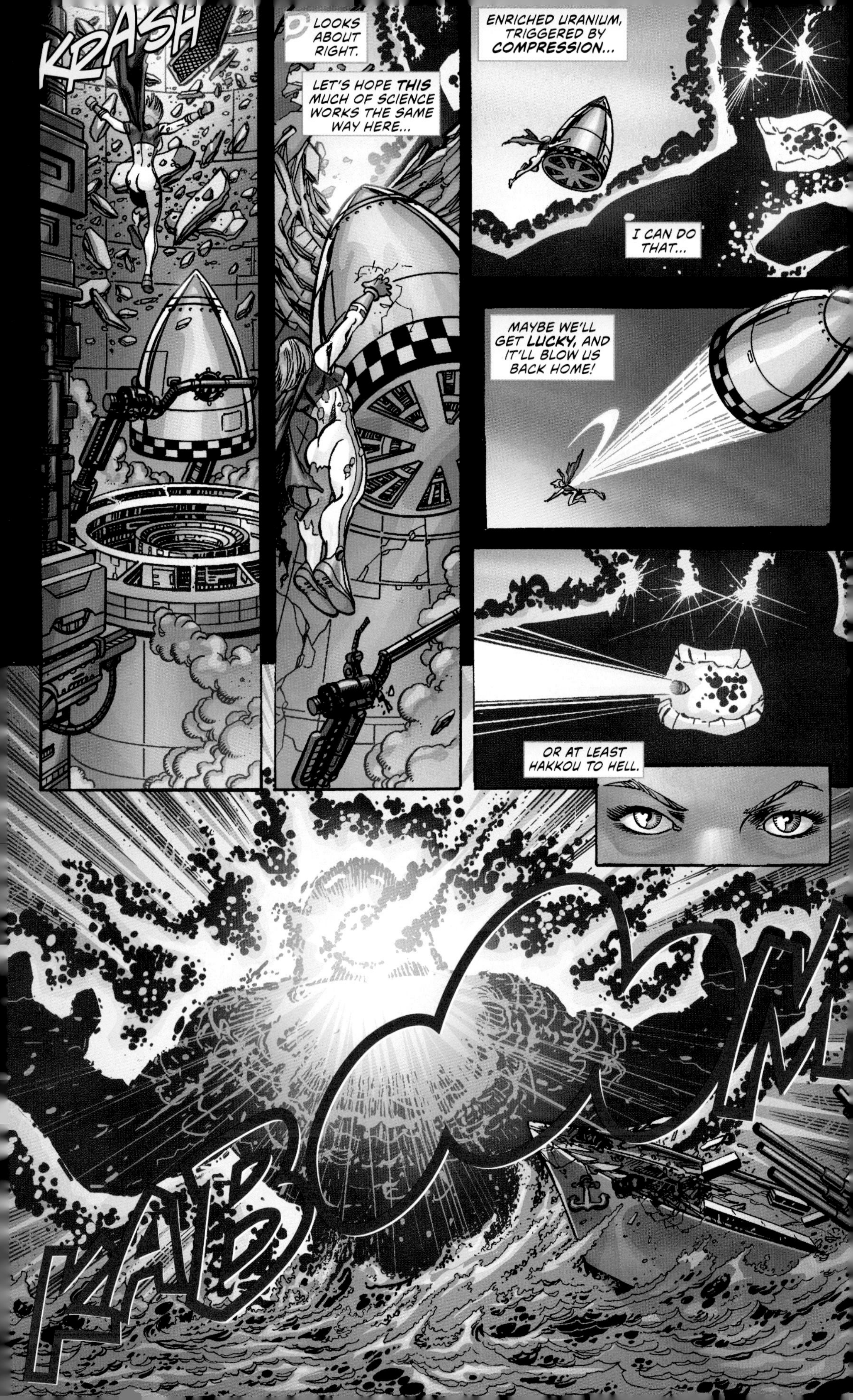
KRASH
LOOKS ABOUT RIGHT.
LET'S HOPE THIS MUCH OF SCIENCE WORKS THE SAME WAY HERE...
ENRICHED URANIUM, TRIGGERED BY COMPRESSION...
I CAN DO THAT...
MAYBE WE'LL GET LUCKY, AND IT'LL BLOW US BACK HOME!
OR AT LEAST HAKKOU TO HELL.
KABOOM

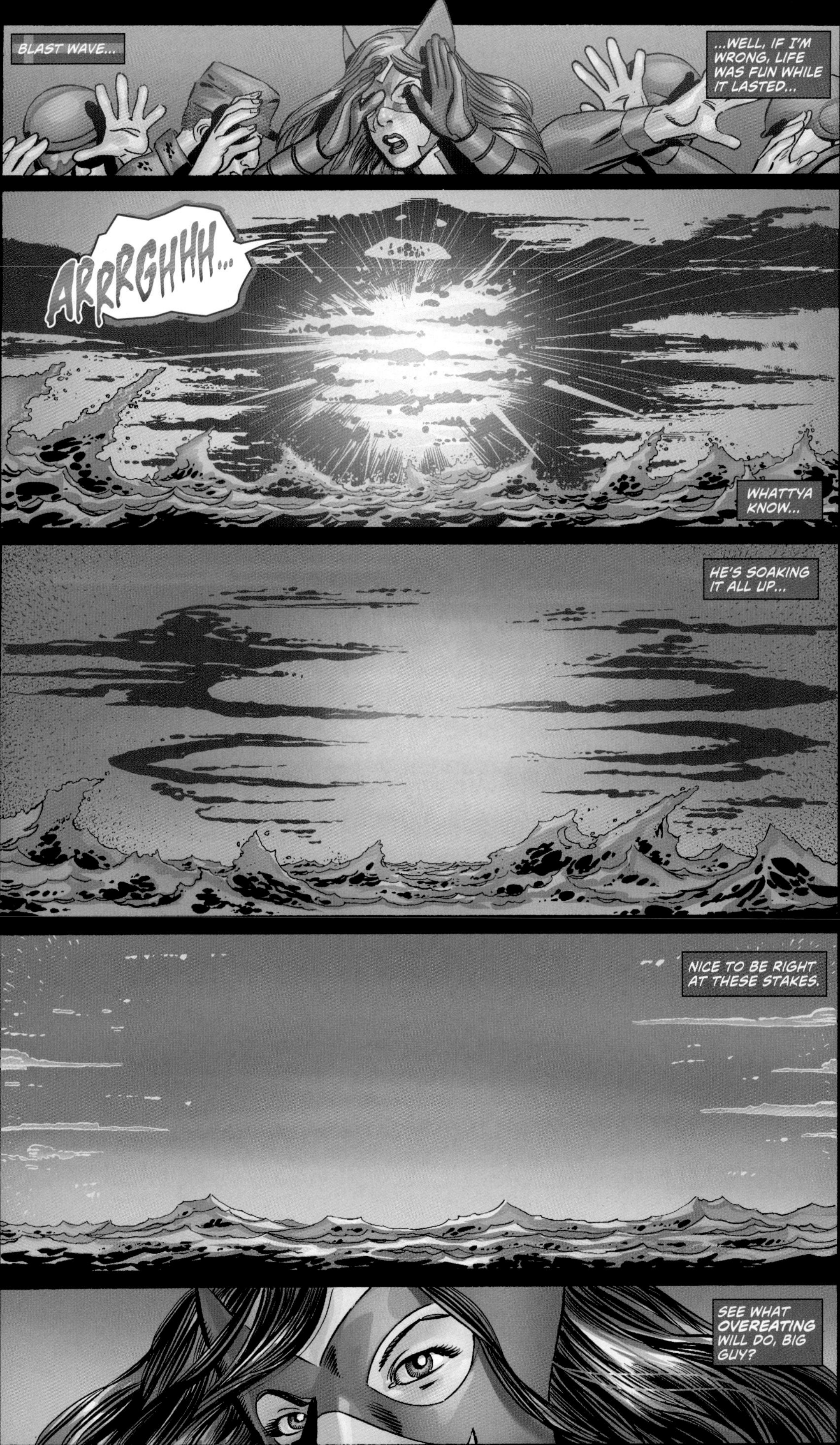
BLAST WAVE...
...WELL, IF I'M WRONG, LIFE WAS FUN WHILE IT LASTED...
ARRRGHHH...
WHATTYA KNOW...
HE'S SOAKING IT ALL UP...
NICE TO BE RIGHT AT THESE STAKES.
SEE WHAT OVEREATING WILL DO, BIG GUY?

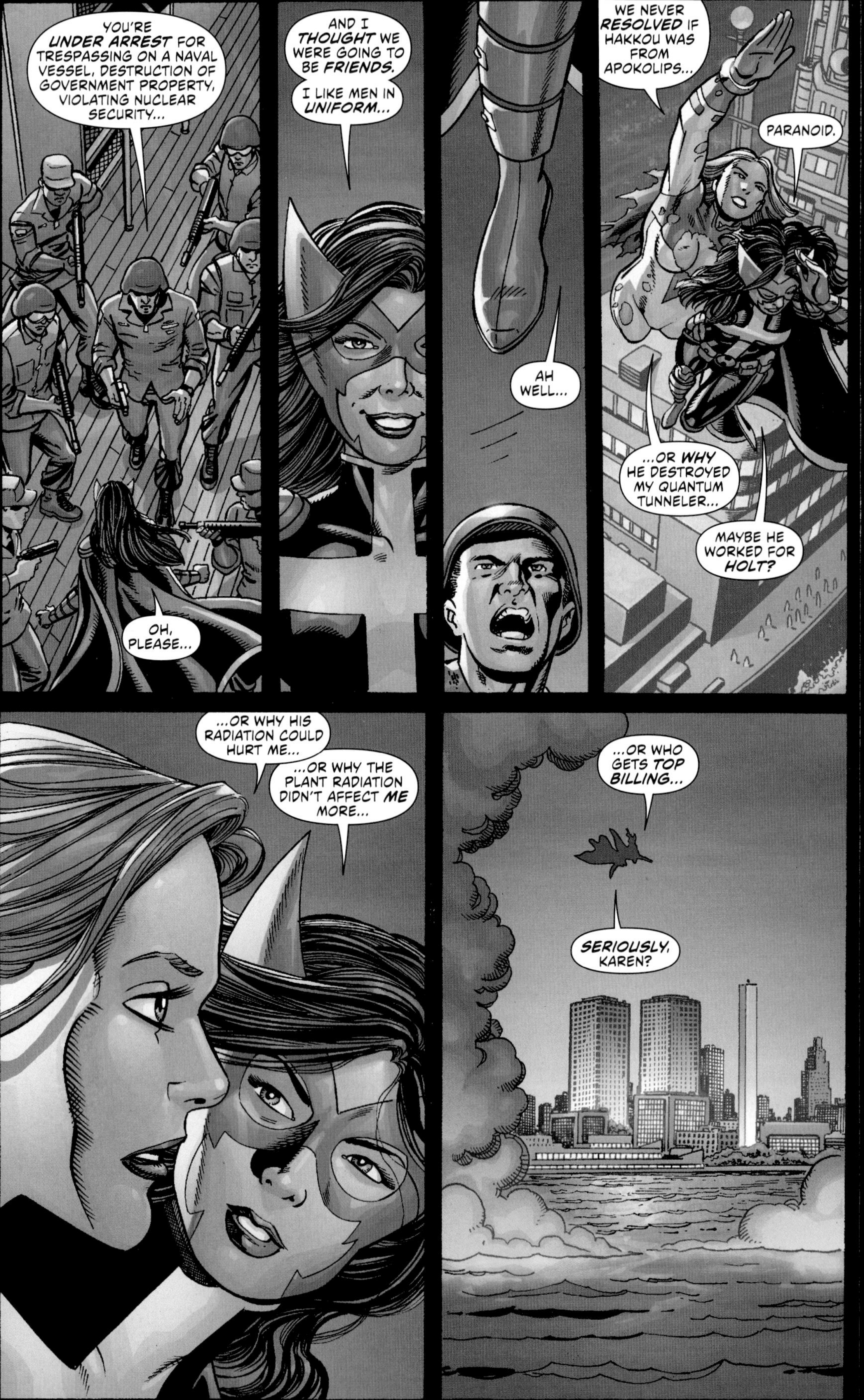
YOU'RE UNDER ARREST FOR TRESPASSING ON A NAVAL VESSEL, DESTRUCTION OF GOVERNMENT PROPERTY, VIOLATING NUCLEAR SECURITY...
OH, PLEASE...
AND I THOUGHT WE WERE GOING TO BE FRIENDS.
I LIKE MEN IN UNIFORM...
AH WELL...
WE NEVER RESOLVED IF HAKKOU WAS FROM APOKOLIPS...
PARANOID.
...OR WHY HE DESTROYED MY QUANTUM TUNNELER...
MAYBE HE WORKED FOR HOLT?
...OR WHY HIS RADIATION COULD HURT ME...
...OR WHY THE PLANT RADIATION DIDN'T AFFECT ME MORE...
...OR WHO GETS TOP BILLING...
SERIOUSLY, KAREN?

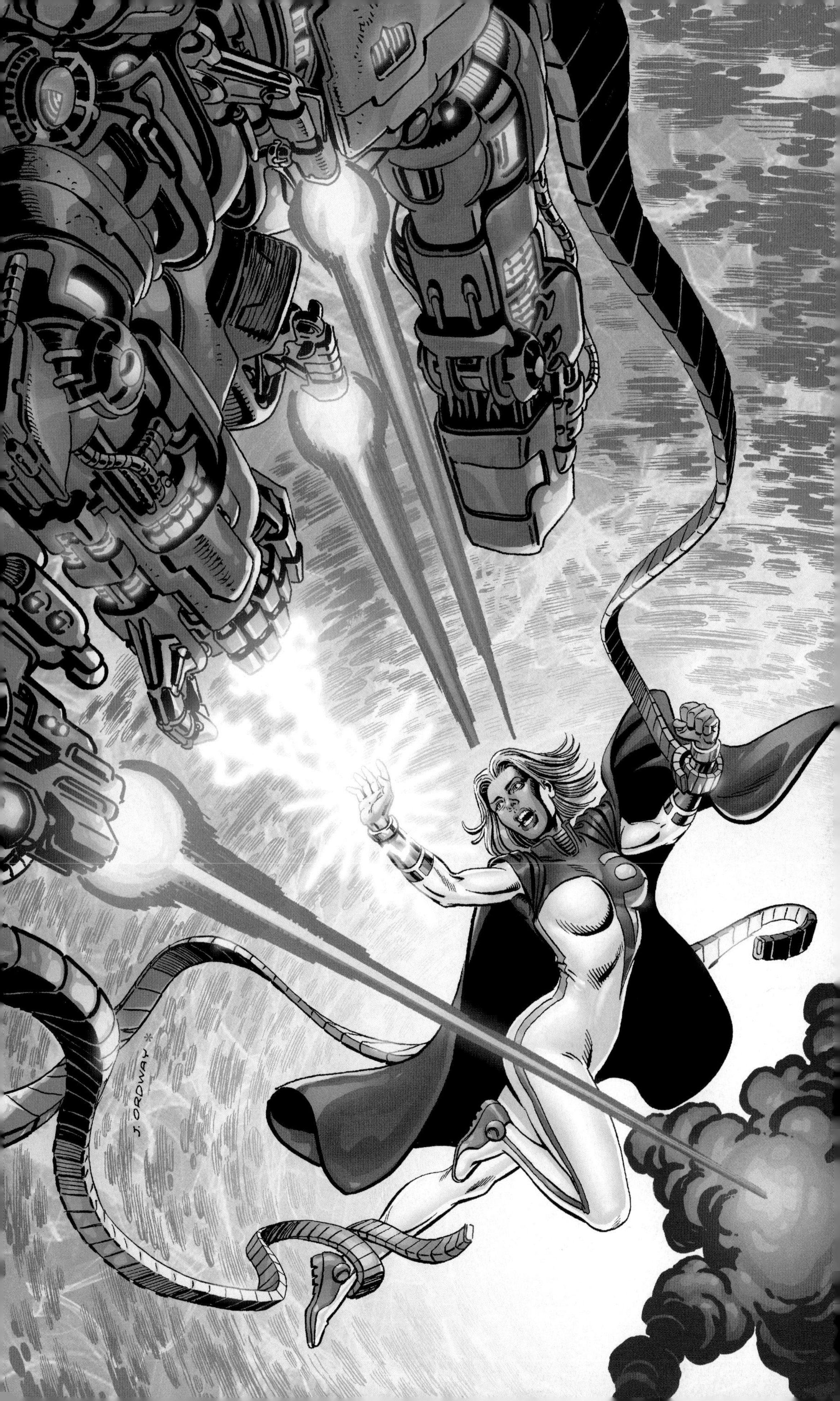
J. ORDWAY

**PAUL LEVITZ** writer **GEORGE PÉREZ** penciller (framing sequence)
**SCOTT KOBLISH** inker (framing sequence) **JERRY ORDWAY** artist (Power Girl sequence)
**WES CRAIG** penciller (Huntress sequence) **SERGE LAPOINTE** inker (Huntress sequence)

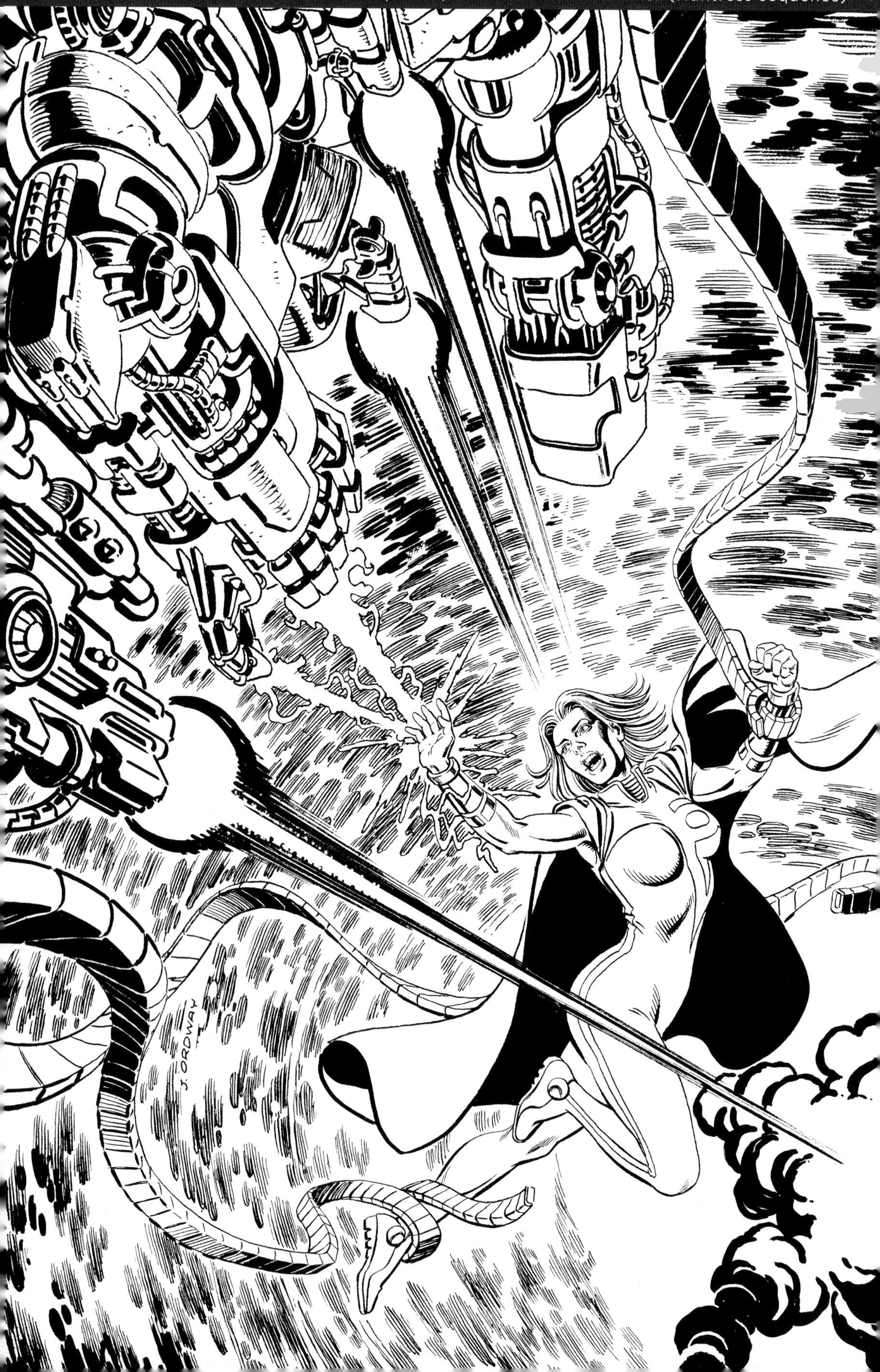
J. ORDWAY

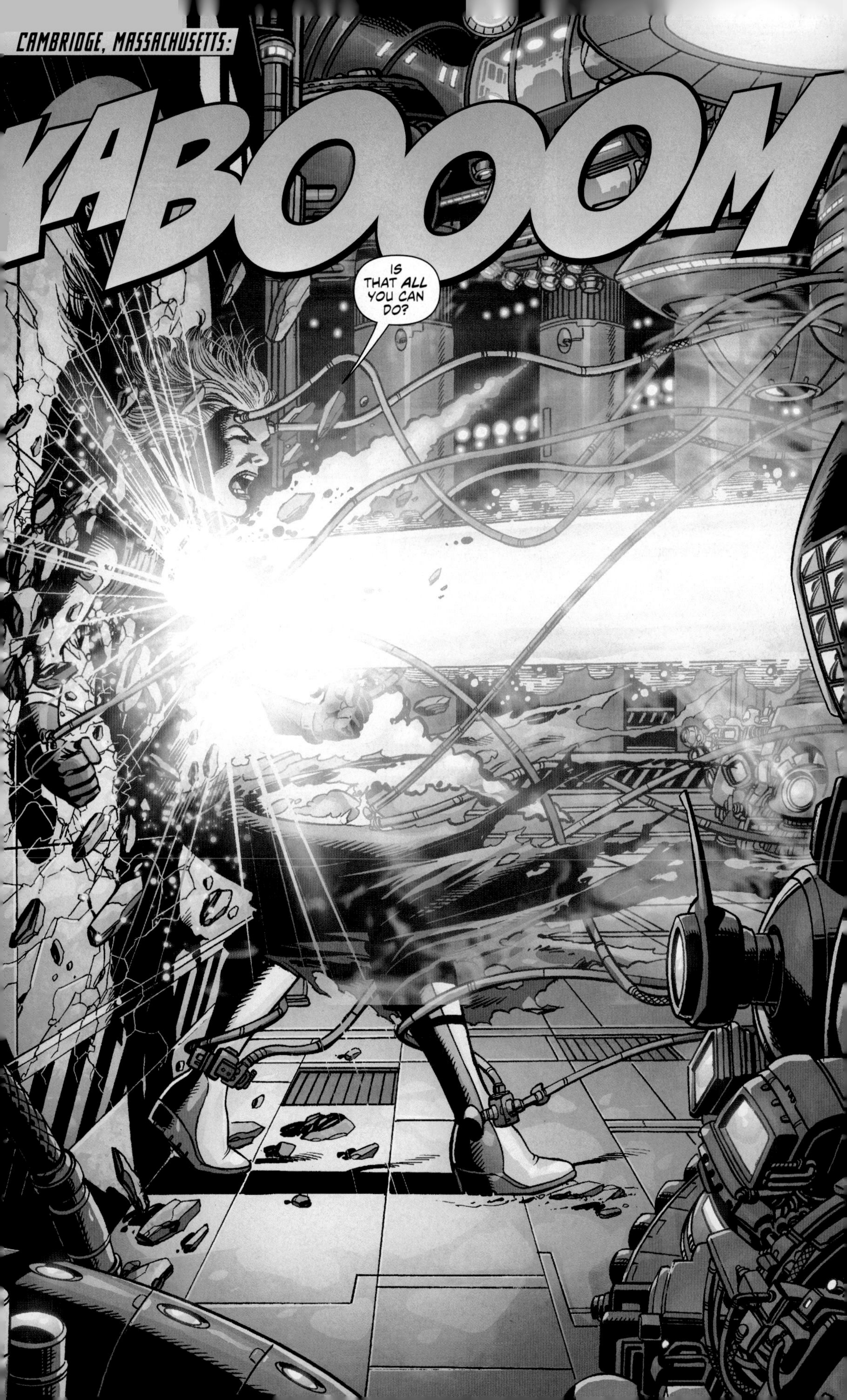

CAMBRIDGE, MASSACHUSETTS:
KABOOOM
IS THAT ALL YOU CAN DO?

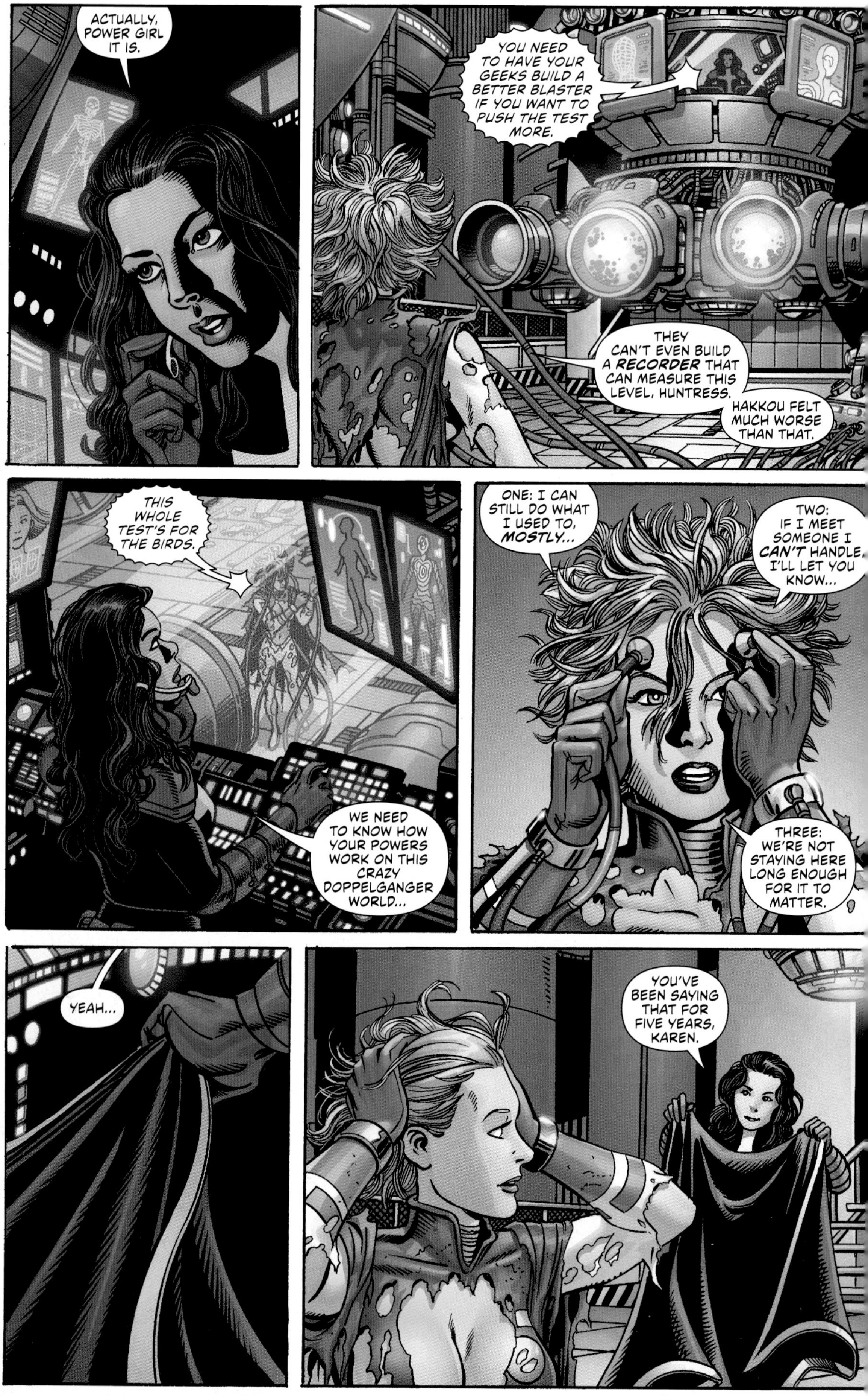

ACTUALLY, POWER GIRL IT IS.
YOU NEED TO HAVE YOUR GEEKS BUILD A BETTER BLASTER IF YOU WANT TO PUSH THE TEST MORE.
THEY CAN'T EVEN BUILD A RECORDER THAT CAN MEASURE THIS LEVEL, HUNTRESS.
HAKKOU FELT MUCH WORSE THAN THAT.
THIS WHOLE TEST'S FOR THE BIRDS.
WE NEED TO KNOW HOW YOUR POWERS WORK ON THIS CRAZY DOPPELGANGER WORLD...
ONE: I CAN STILL DO WHAT I USED TO, MOSTLY...
TWO: IF I MEET SOMEONE I CAN'T HANDLE, I'LL LET YOU KNOW...
THREE: WE'RE NOT STAYING HERE LONG ENOUGH FOR IT TO MATTER.
YEAH...
YOU'VE BEEN SAYING THAT FOR FIVE YEARS, KAREN.

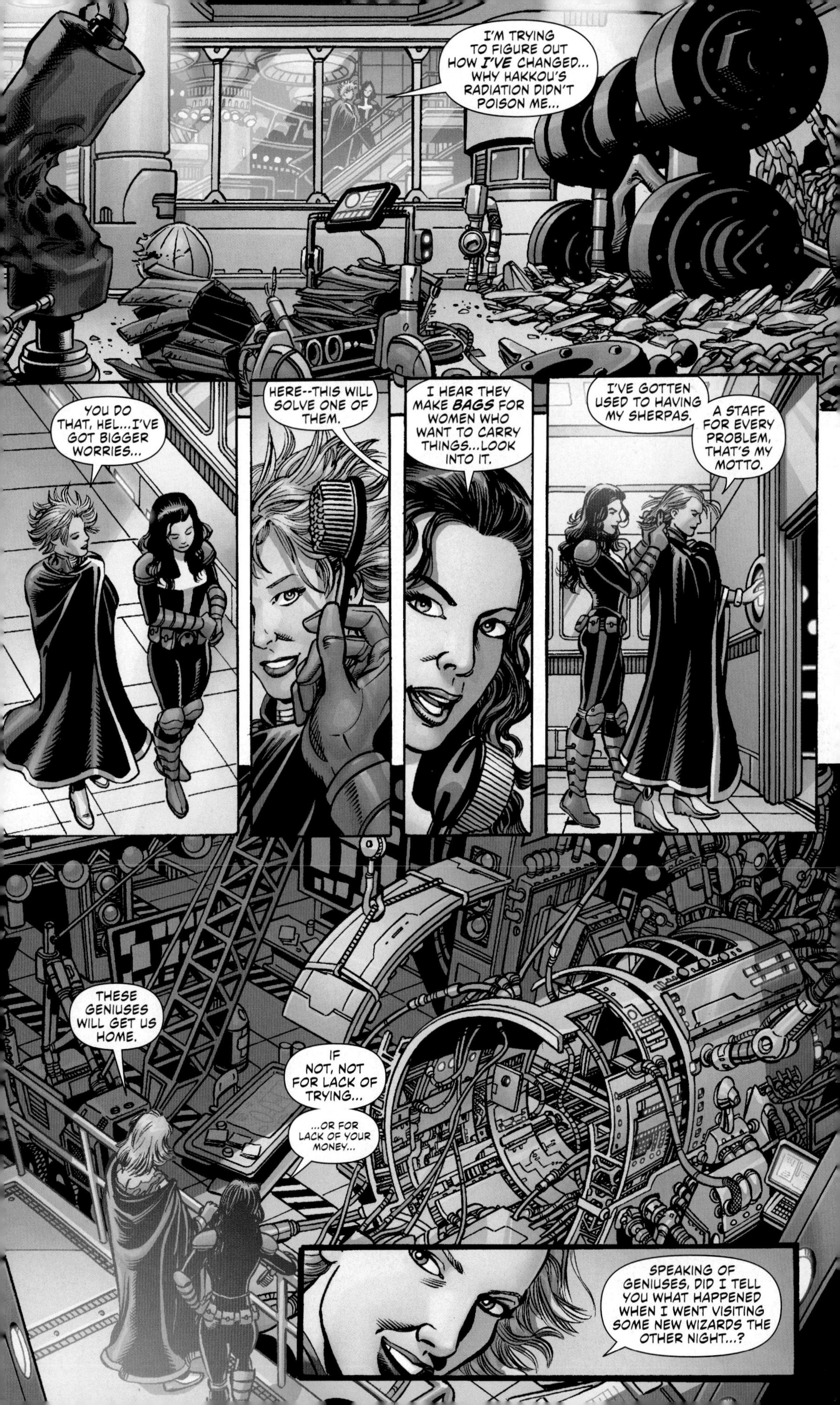
I'M TRYING TO FIGURE OUT HOW I'VE CHANGED... WHY HAKKOU'S RADIATION DIDN'T POISON ME...
YOU DO THAT, HEL...I'VE GOT BIGGER WORRIES...
HERE--THIS WILL SOLVE ONE OF THEM.
I HEAR THEY MAKE BAGS FOR WOMEN WHO WANT TO CARRY THINGS...LOOK INTO IT.
I'VE GOTTEN USED TO HAVING MY SHERPAS.
A STAFF FOR EVERY PROBLEM, THAT'S MY MOTTO.
THESE GENIUSES WILL GET US HOME.
IF NOT, NOT FOR LACK OF TRYING...
...OR FOR LACK OF YOUR MONEY...
SPEAKING OF GENIUSES, DID I TELL YOU WHAT HAPPENED WHEN I WENT VISITING SOME NEW WIZARDS THE OTHER NIGHT...?

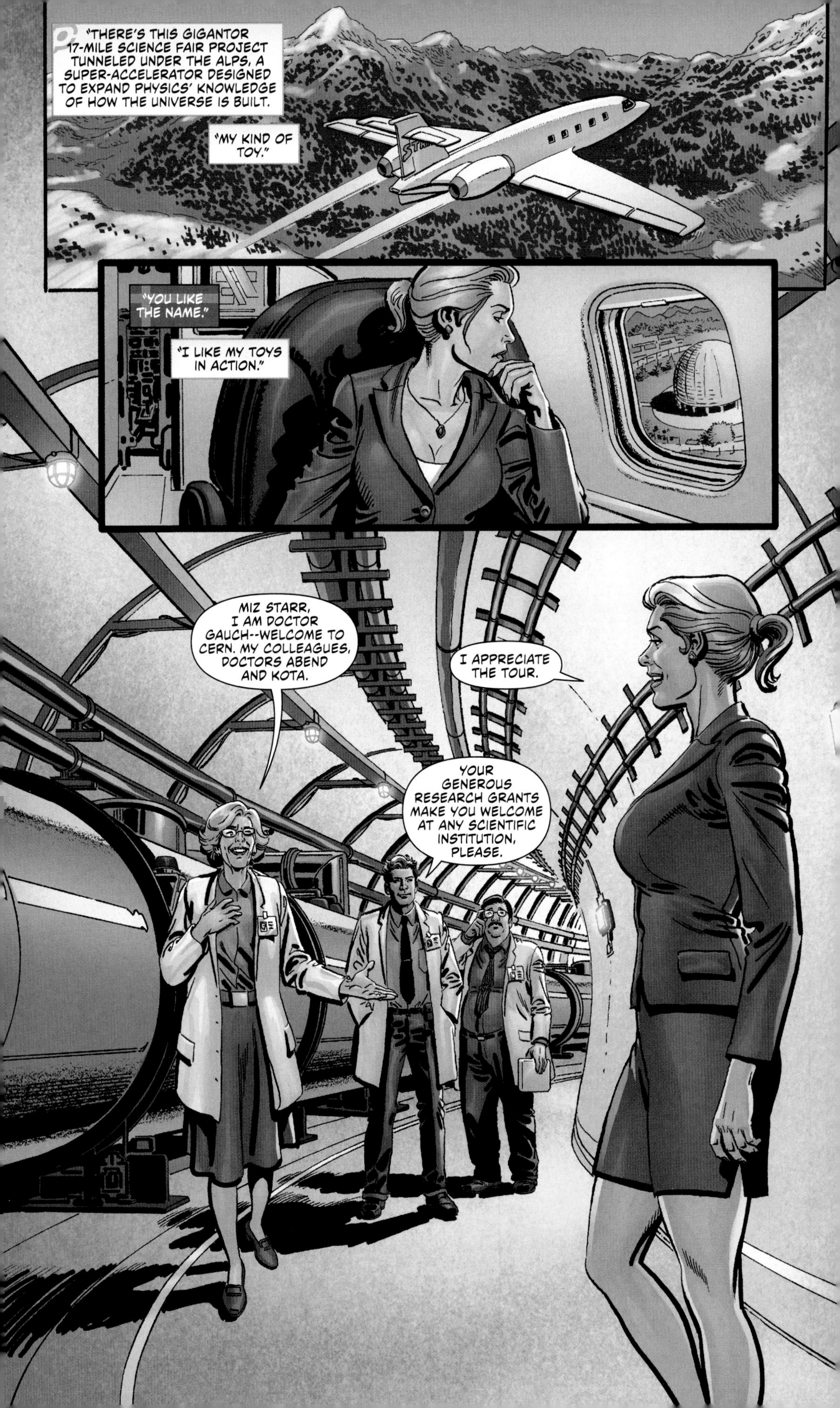

"THERE'S THIS GIGANTOR 17-MILE SCIENCE FAIR PROJECT TUNNELED UNDER THE ALPS, A SUPER-ACCELERATOR DESIGNED TO EXPAND PHYSICS' KNOWLEDGE OF HOW THE UNIVERSE IS BUILT.
"MY KIND OF TOY."
"YOU LIKE THE NAME."
"I LIKE MY TOYS IN ACTION."
MIZ STARR, I AM DOCTOR GAUCH--WELCOME TO CERN. MY COLLEAGUES, DOCTORS ABEND AND KOTA.
I APPRECIATE THE TOUR.
YOUR GENEROUS RESEARCH GRANTS MAKE YOU WELCOME AT ANY SCIENTIFIC INSTITUTION, PLEASE.

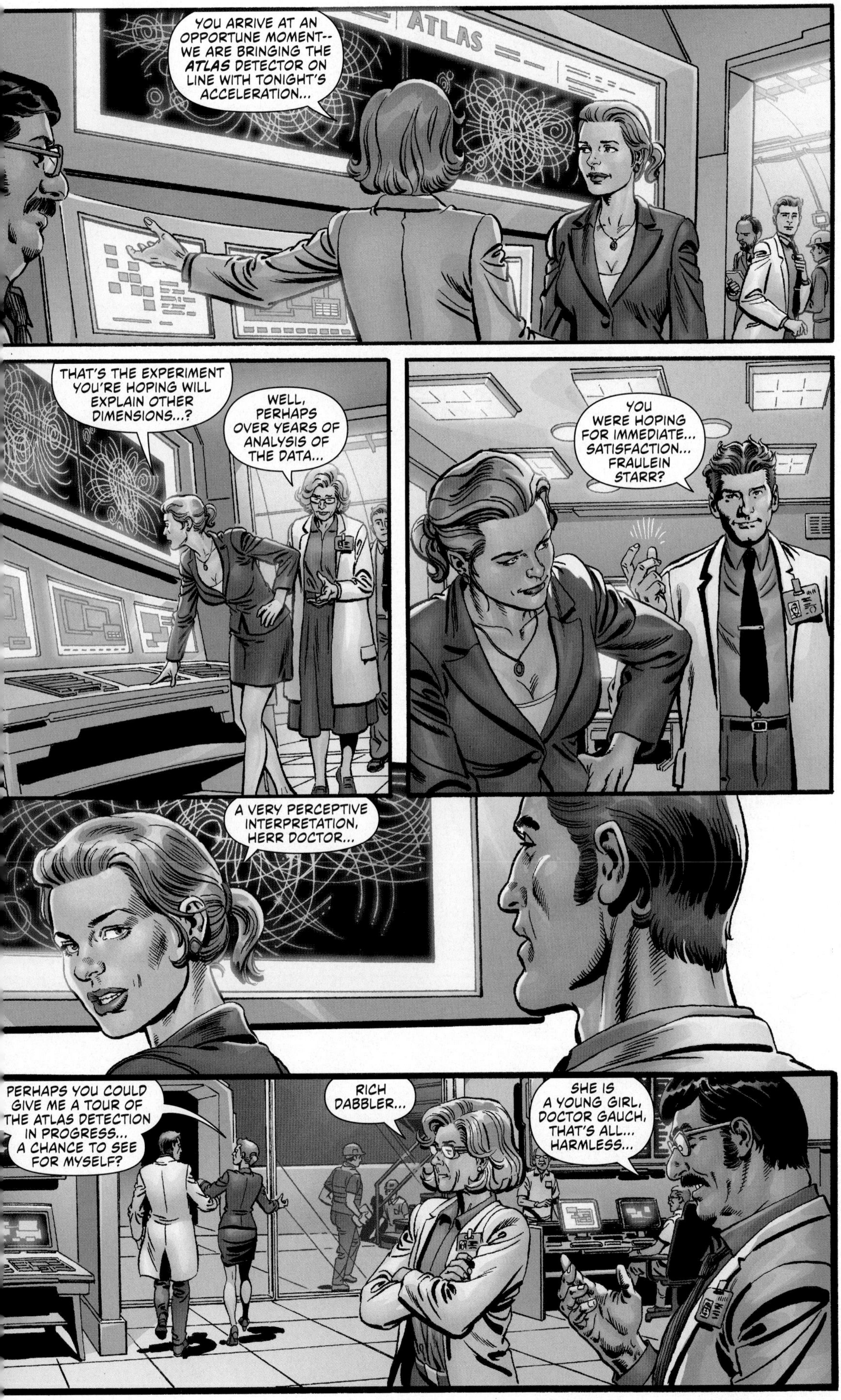
ATLAS
YOU ARRIVE AT AN OPPORTUNE MOMENT-- WE ARE BRINGING THE ATLAS DETECTOR ON LINE WITH TONIGHT'S ACCELERATION...
THAT'S THE EXPERIMENT YOU'RE HOPING WILL EXPLAIN OTHER DIMENSIONS...?
WELL, PERHAPS OVER YEARS OF ANALYSIS OF THE DATA...
YOU WERE HOPING FOR IMMEDIATE... SATISFACTION... FRAULEIN STARR?
A VERY PERCEPTIVE INTERPRETATION, HERR DOCTOR...
PERHAPS YOU COULD GIVE ME A TOUR OF THE ATLAS DETECTION IN PROGRESS... A CHANCE TO SEE FOR MYSELF?
RICH DABBLER...
SHE IS A YOUNG GIRL, DOCTOR GAUCH, THAT'S ALL... HARMLESS...

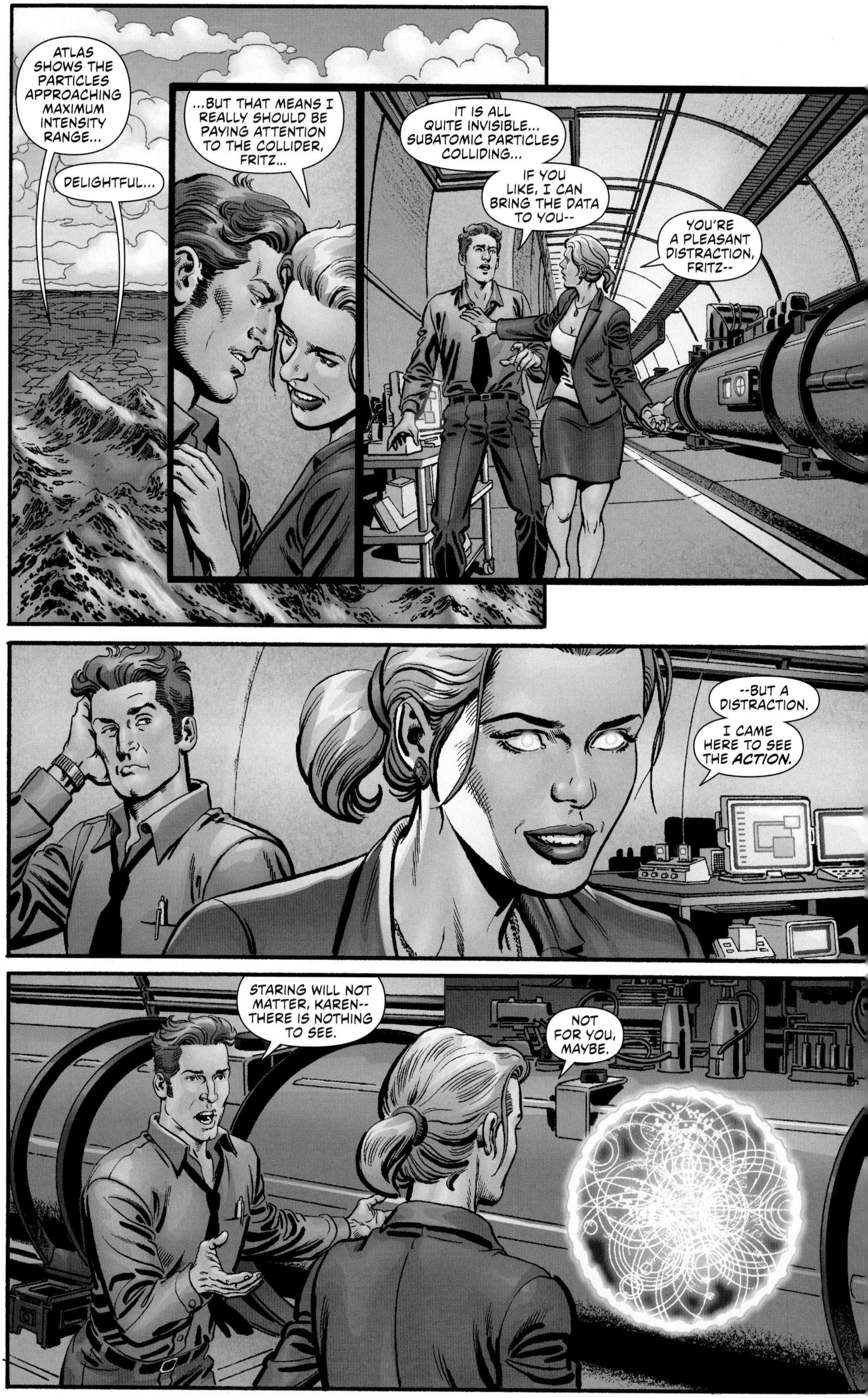
ATLAS SHOWS THE PARTICLES APPROACHING MAXIMUM INTENSITY RANGE...
DELIGHTFUL...
...BUT THAT MEANS I REALLY SHOULD BE PAYING ATTENTION TO THE COLLIDER, FRITZ...
IT IS ALL QUITE INVISIBLE... SUBATOMIC PARTICLES COLLIDING...
IF YOU LIKE, I CAN BRING THE DATA TO YOU--
YOU'RE A PLEASANT DISTRACTION, FRITZ--
--BUT A DISTRACTION.
I CAME HERE TO SEE THE *ACTION*.
STARING WILL NOT MATTER, KAREN-- THERE IS NOTHING TO SEE.
NOT FOR YOU, MAYBE.

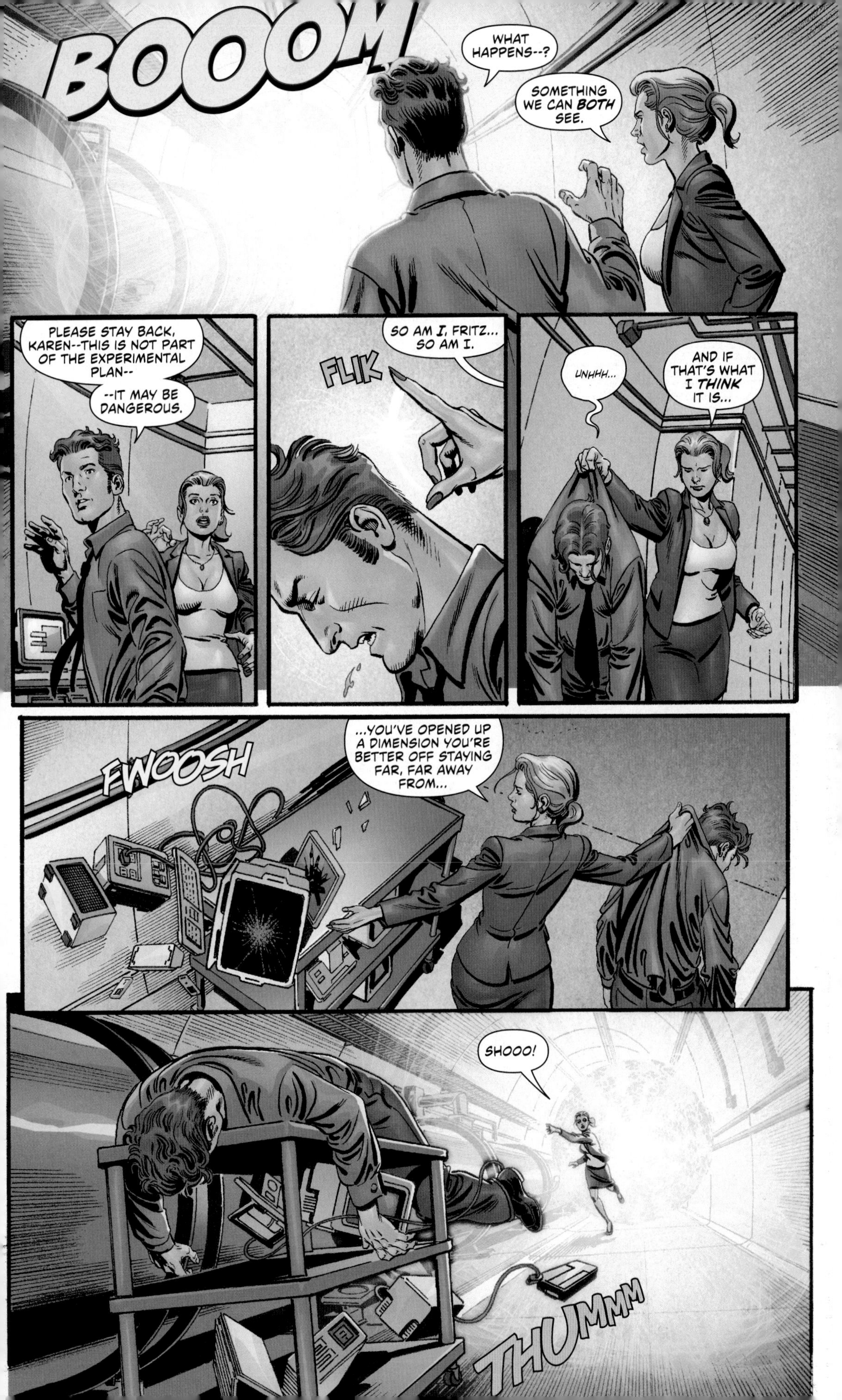
BOOOM
WHAT HAPPENS--?
SOMETHING WE CAN BOTH SEE.
PLEASE STAY BACK, KAREN--THIS IS NOT PART OF THE EXPERIMENTAL PLAN--
--IT MAY BE DANGEROUS.
SO AM I, FRITZ... SO AM I.
FLIK
UNHHH...
AND IF THAT'S WHAT I THINK IT IS...
FWOOSH
...YOU'VE OPENED UP A DIMENSION YOU'RE BETTER OFF STAYING FAR, FAR AWAY FROM...
SHOOO!
THUMMM

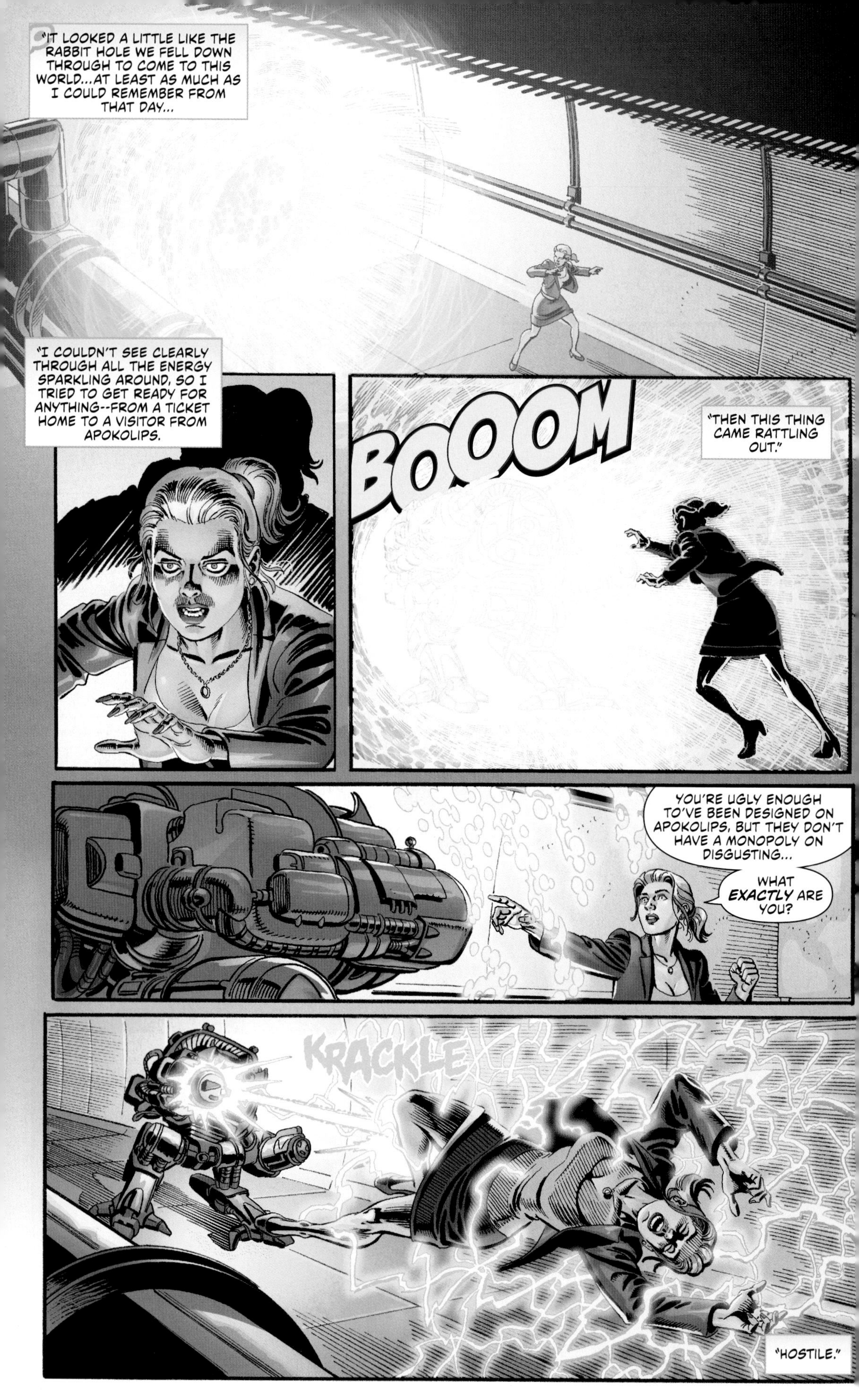
"IT LOOKED A LITTLE LIKE THE RABBIT HOLE WE FELL DOWN THROUGH TO COME TO THIS WORLD...AT LEAST AS MUCH AS I COULD REMEMBER FROM THAT DAY...
"I COULDN'T SEE CLEARLY THROUGH ALL THE ENERGY SPARKLING AROUND, SO I TRIED TO GET READY FOR ANYTHING--FROM A TICKET HOME TO A VISITOR FROM APOKOLIPS.
BOOOM
"THEN THIS THING CAME RATTLING OUT."
YOU'RE UGLY ENOUGH TO'VE BEEN DESIGNED ON APOKOLIPS, BUT THEY DON'T HAVE A MONOPOLY ON DISGUSTING...
WHAT *EXACTLY* ARE YOU?
KRACKLE
"HOSTILE."

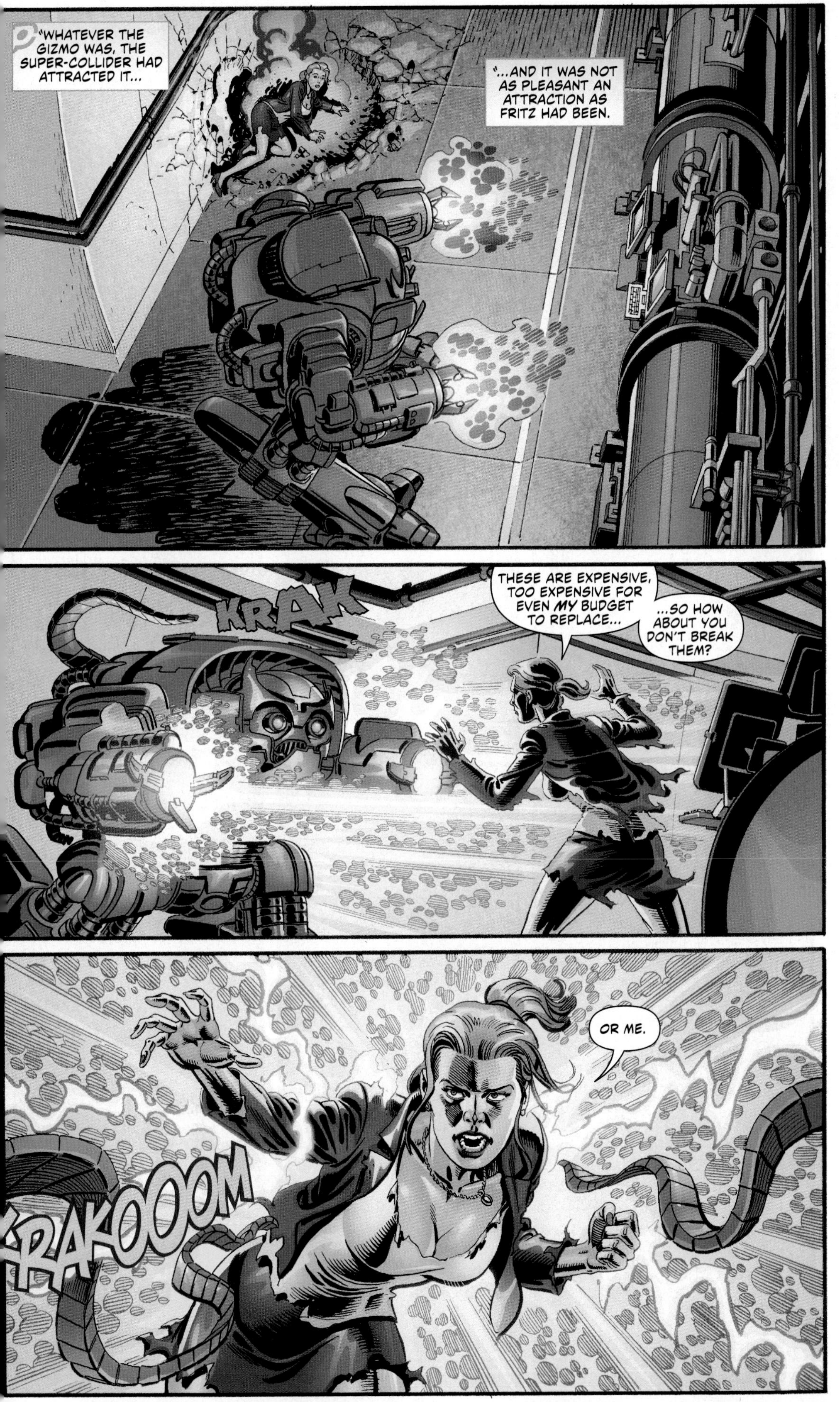
"WHATEVER THE GIZMO WAS, THE SUPER-COLLIDER HAD ATTRACTED IT...
"...AND IT WAS NOT AS PLEASANT AN ATTRACTION AS FRITZ HAD BEEN.
KRAK
THESE ARE EXPENSIVE, TOO EXPENSIVE FOR EVEN MY BUDGET TO REPLACE...
...SO HOW ABOUT YOU DON'T BREAK THEM?
OR ME.
KRAKOOOM

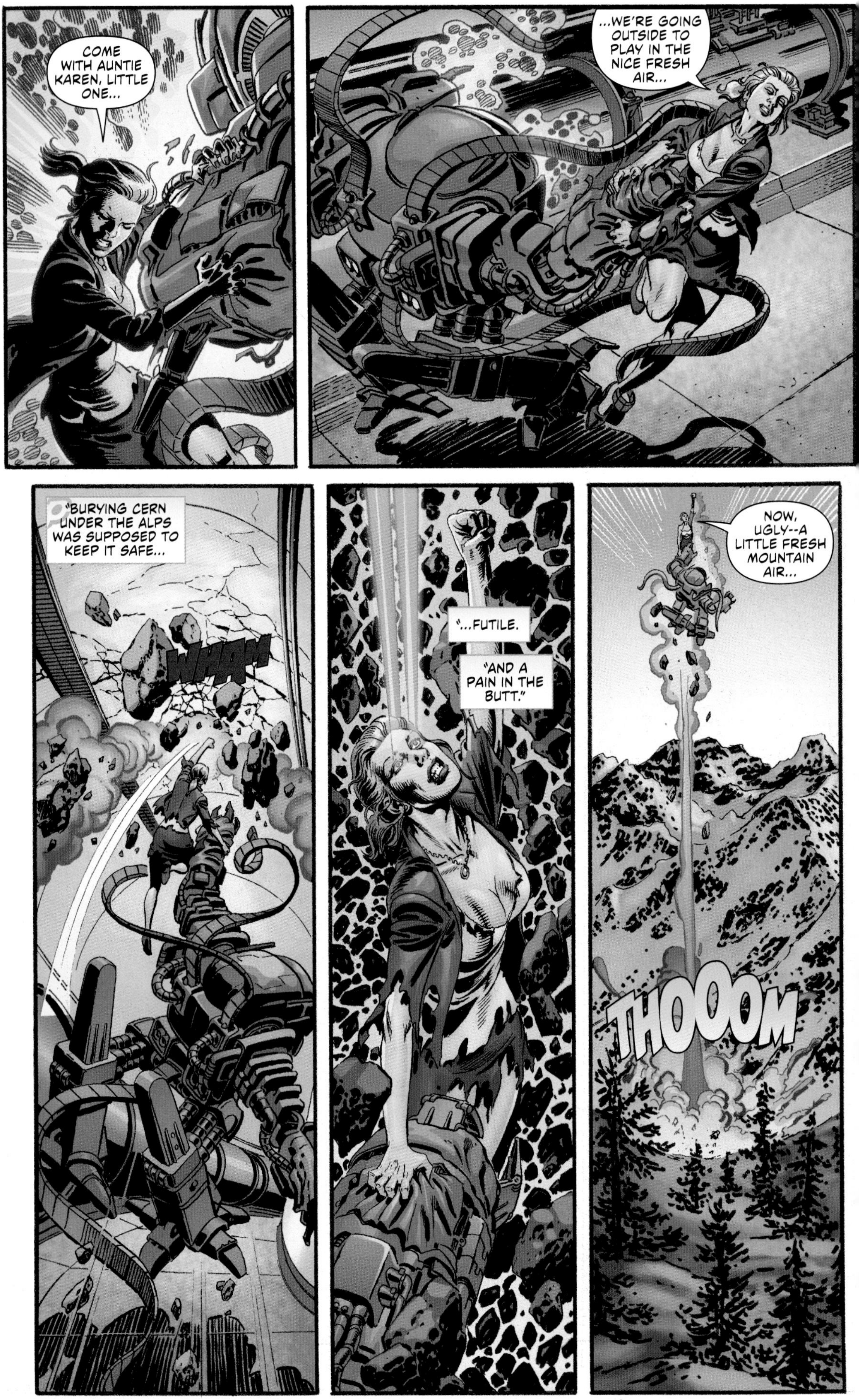
COME WITH AUNTIE KAREN, LITTLE ONE...
...WE'RE GOING OUTSIDE TO PLAY IN THE NICE FRESH AIR...
"BURYING CERN UNDER THE ALPS WAS SUPPOSED TO KEEP IT SAFE...
WHAM
"...FUTILE.
"AND A PAIN IN THE BUTT."
NOW, UGLY--A LITTLE FRESH MOUNTAIN AIR...
THOOOM

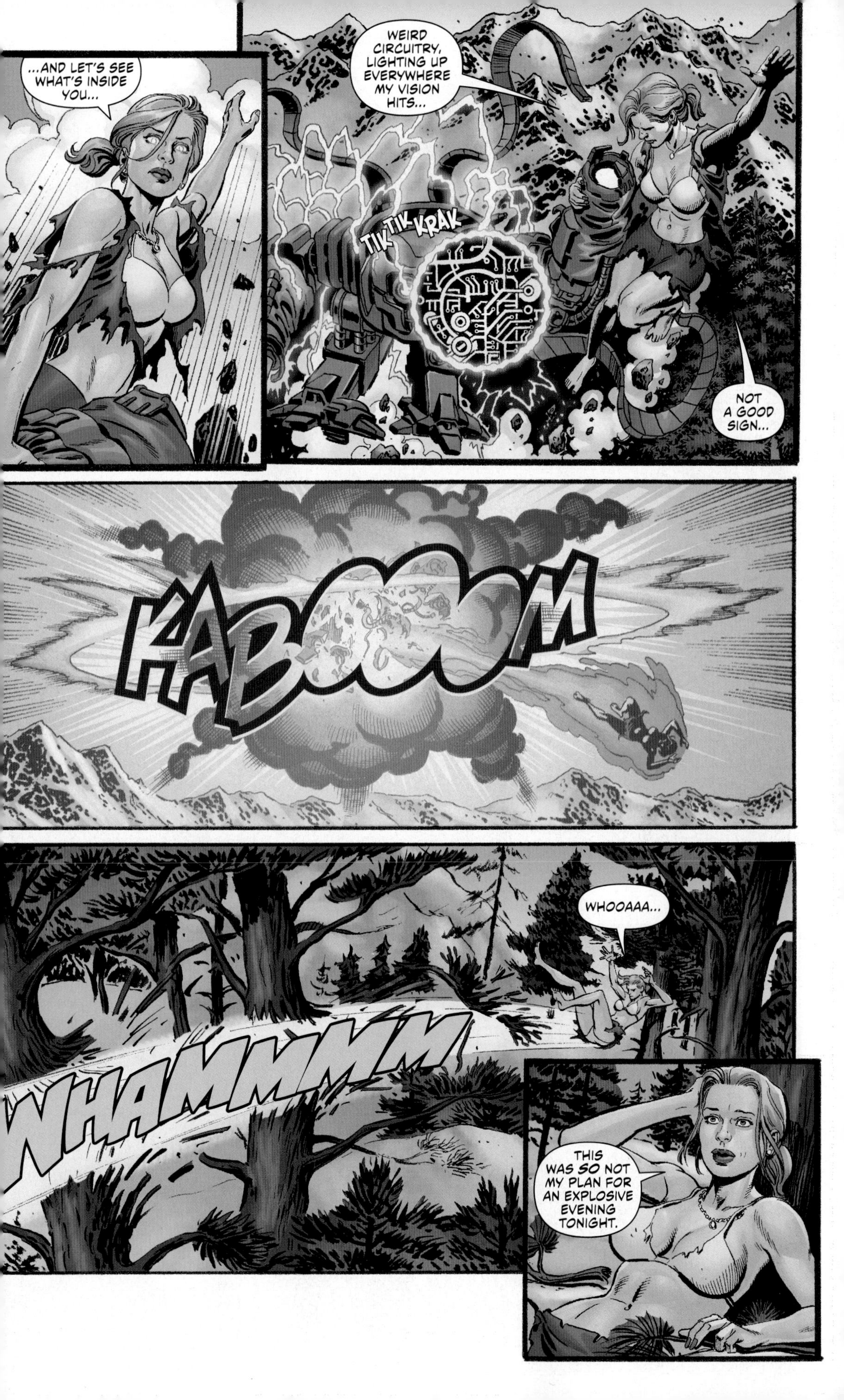
...AND LET'S SEE WHAT'S INSIDE YOU...
WEIRD CIRCUITRY, LIGHTING UP EVERYWHERE MY VISION HITS...
TIK TIK KRAK
NOT A GOOD SIGN...
KABOOOM
WHOOAAA...
WHAMMMMM
THIS WAS SO NOT MY PLAN FOR AN EXPLOSIVE EVENING TONIGHT.

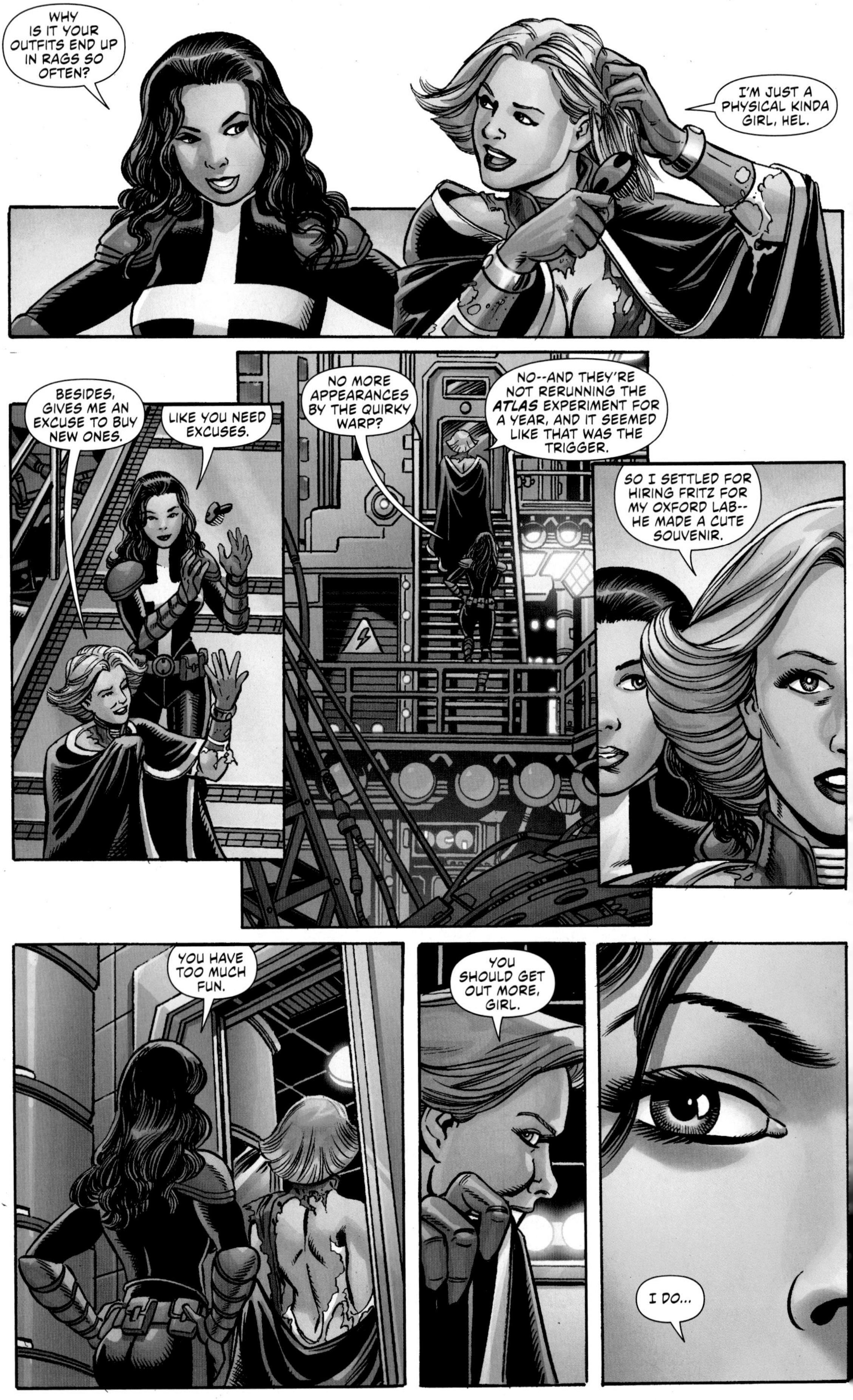
WHY IS IT YOUR OUTFITS END UP IN RAGS SO OFTEN?
I'M JUST A PHYSICAL KINDA GIRL, HEL.
BESIDES, GIVES ME AN EXCUSE TO BUY NEW ONES.
LIKE YOU NEED EXCUSES.
NO MORE APPEARANCES BY THE QUIRKY WARP?
NO--AND THEY'RE NOT RERUNNING THE *ATLAS* EXPERIMENT FOR A YEAR, AND IT SEEMED LIKE THAT WAS THE TRIGGER.
SO I SETTLED FOR HIRING FRITZ FOR MY OXFORD LAB--HE MADE A CUTE SOUVENIR.
YOU HAVE TOO MUCH FUN.
YOU SHOULD GET OUT MORE, GIRL.
I DO...

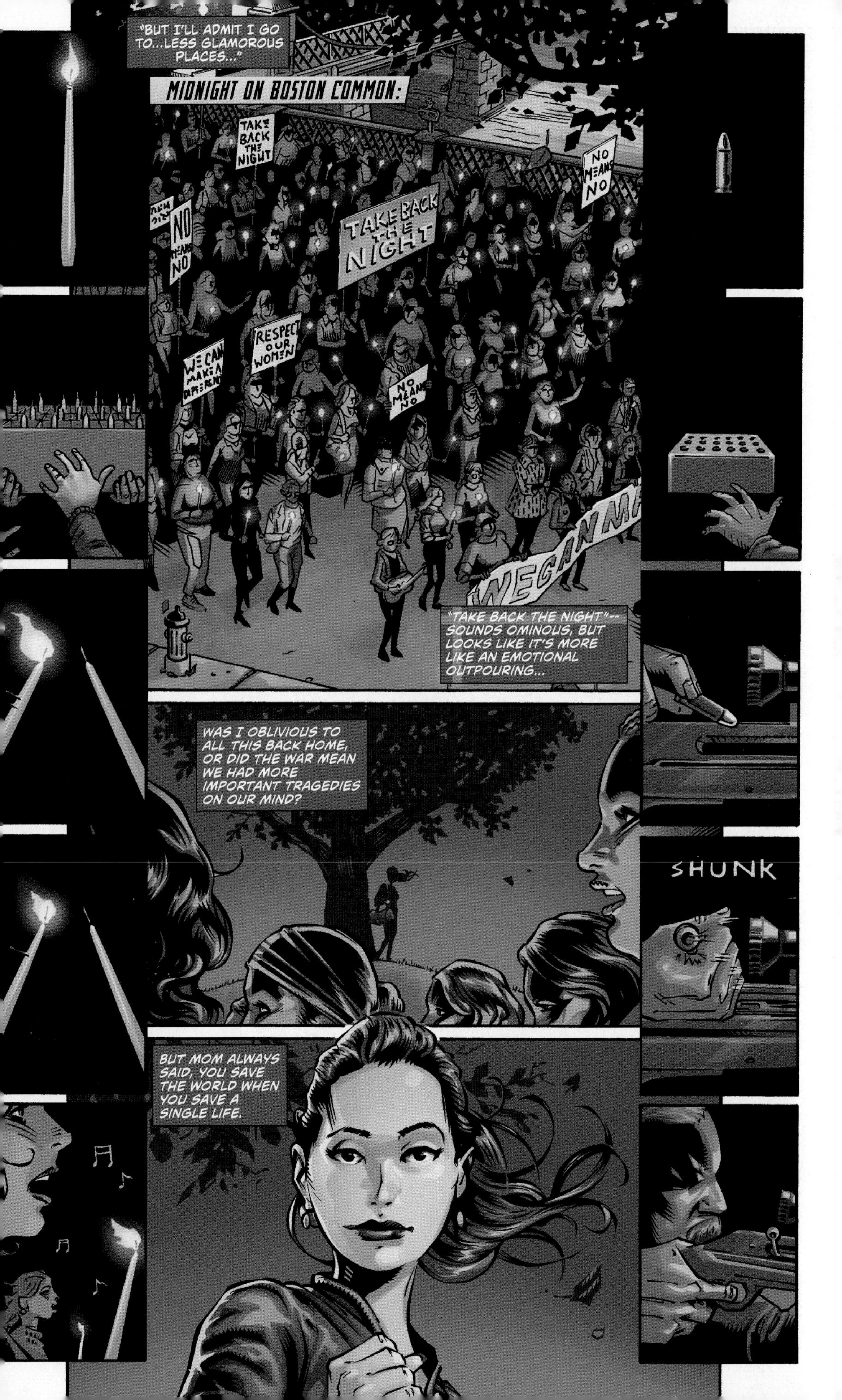
"BUT I'LL ADMIT I GO TO...LESS GLAMOROUS PLACES..."
MIDNIGHT ON BOSTON COMMON:
TAKE BACK THE NIGHT
NO MEANS NO
TAKE BACK THE NIGHT
NO MEANS NO
RESPECT OUR WOMEN
WE CAN MAKE A DIFFERENCE
NO MEANS NO
WE CAN MA
"TAKE BACK THE NIGHT"--SOUNDS OMINOUS, BUT LOOKS LIKE IT'S MORE LIKE AN EMOTIONAL OUTPOURING...
WAS I OBLIVIOUS TO ALL THIS BACK HOME, OR DID THE WAR MEAN WE HAD MORE IMPORTANT TRAGEDIES ON OUR MIND?
SHUNK
BUT MOM ALWAYS SAID, YOU SAVE THE WORLD WHEN YOU SAVE A SINGLE LIFE.

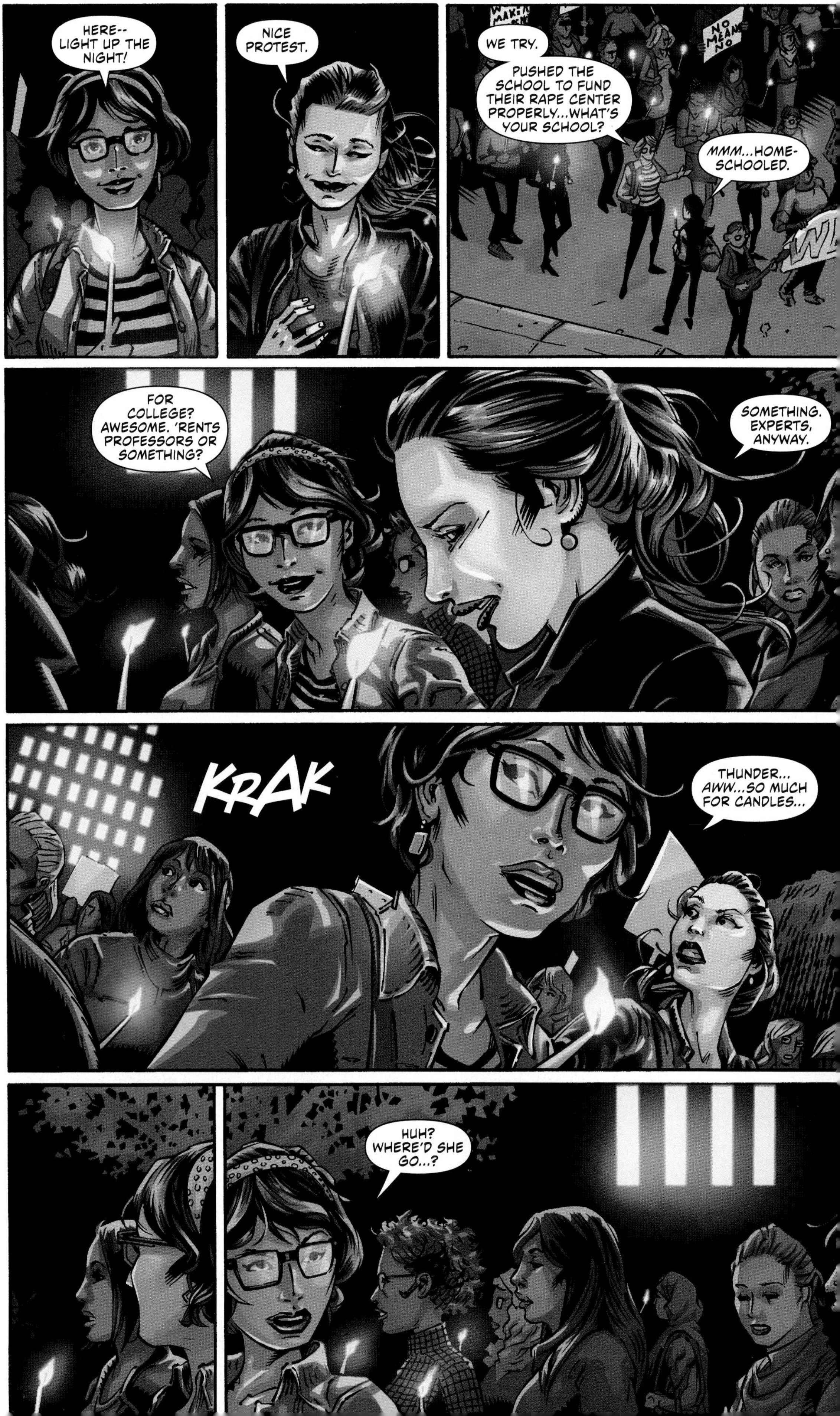
HERE--
LIGHT UP THE NIGHT!
NICE PROTEST.
NO MEANS NO
WE TRY.
PUSHED THE SCHOOL TO FUND THEIR RAPE CENTER PROPERLY...WHAT'S YOUR SCHOOL?
MMM...HOME-SCHOOLED.
FOR COLLEGE? AWESOME. 'RENTS PROFESSORS OR SOMETHING?
SOMETHING. EXPERTS, ANYWAY.
KRAK
THUNDER... AWW...SO MUCH FOR CANDLES...
HUH? WHERE'D SHE GO...?

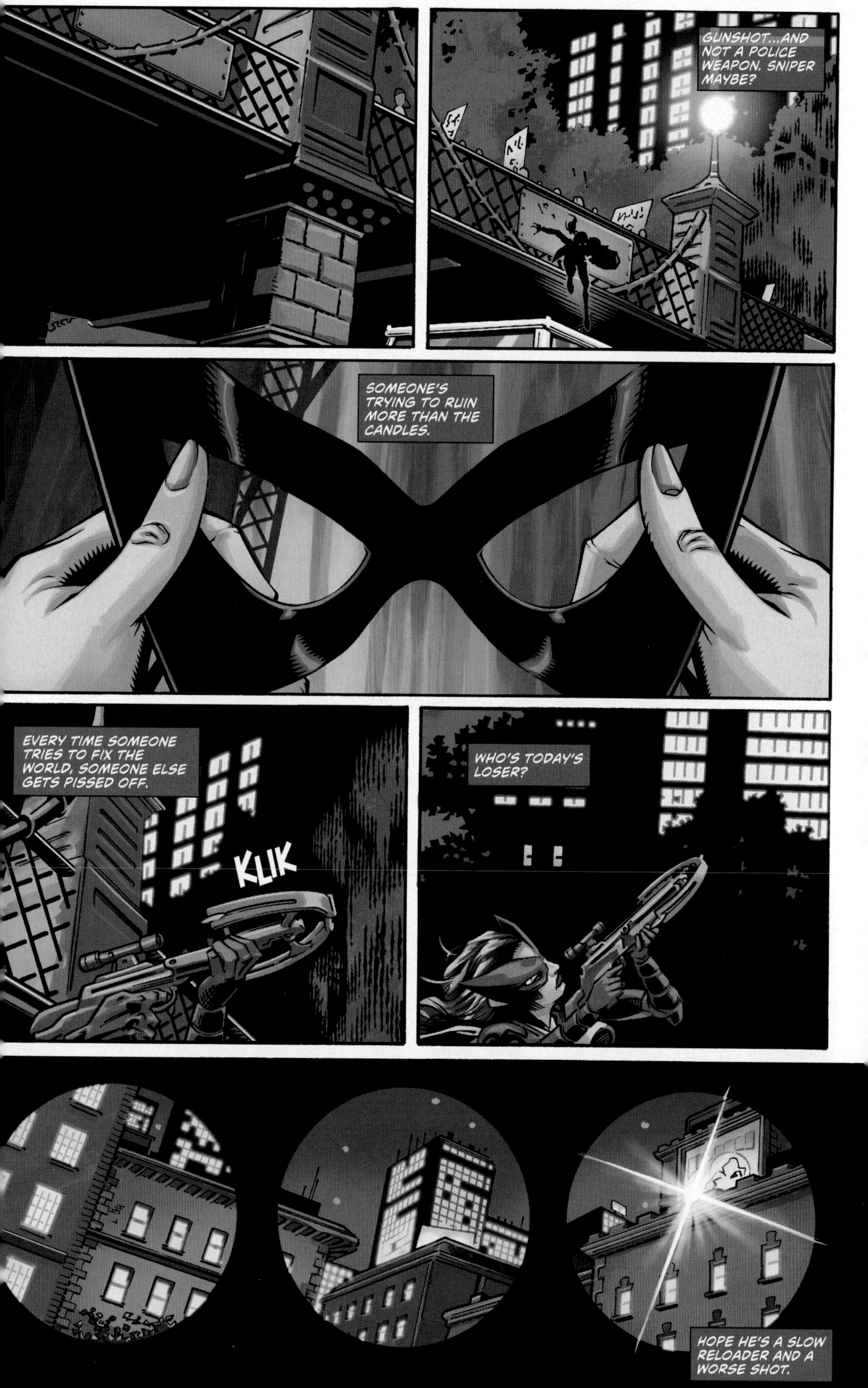
GUNSHOT...AND NOT A POLICE WEAPON. SNIPER MAYBE?
SOMEONE'S TRYING TO RUIN MORE THAN THE CANDLES.
EVERY TIME SOMEONE TRIES TO FIX THE WORLD, SOMEONE ELSE GETS PISSED OFF.
KLIK
WHO'S TODAY'S LOSER?
HOPE HE'S A SLOW RELOADER AND A WORSE SHOT.

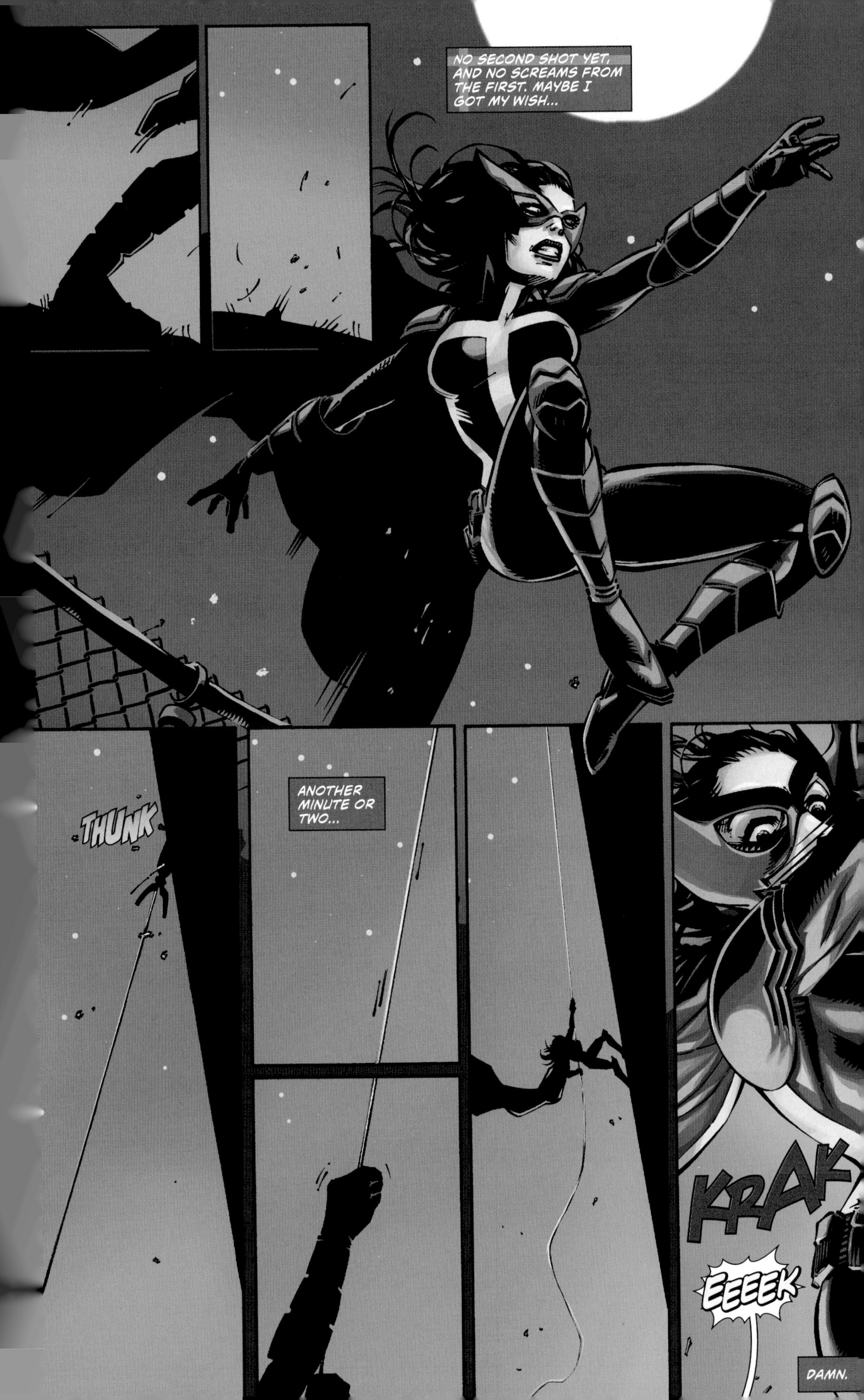
NO SECOND SHOT YET, AND NO SCREAMS FROM THE FIRST. MAYBE I GOT MY WISH...
THUNK
ANOTHER MINUTE OR TWO...
KRAK
EEEEK
DAMN.

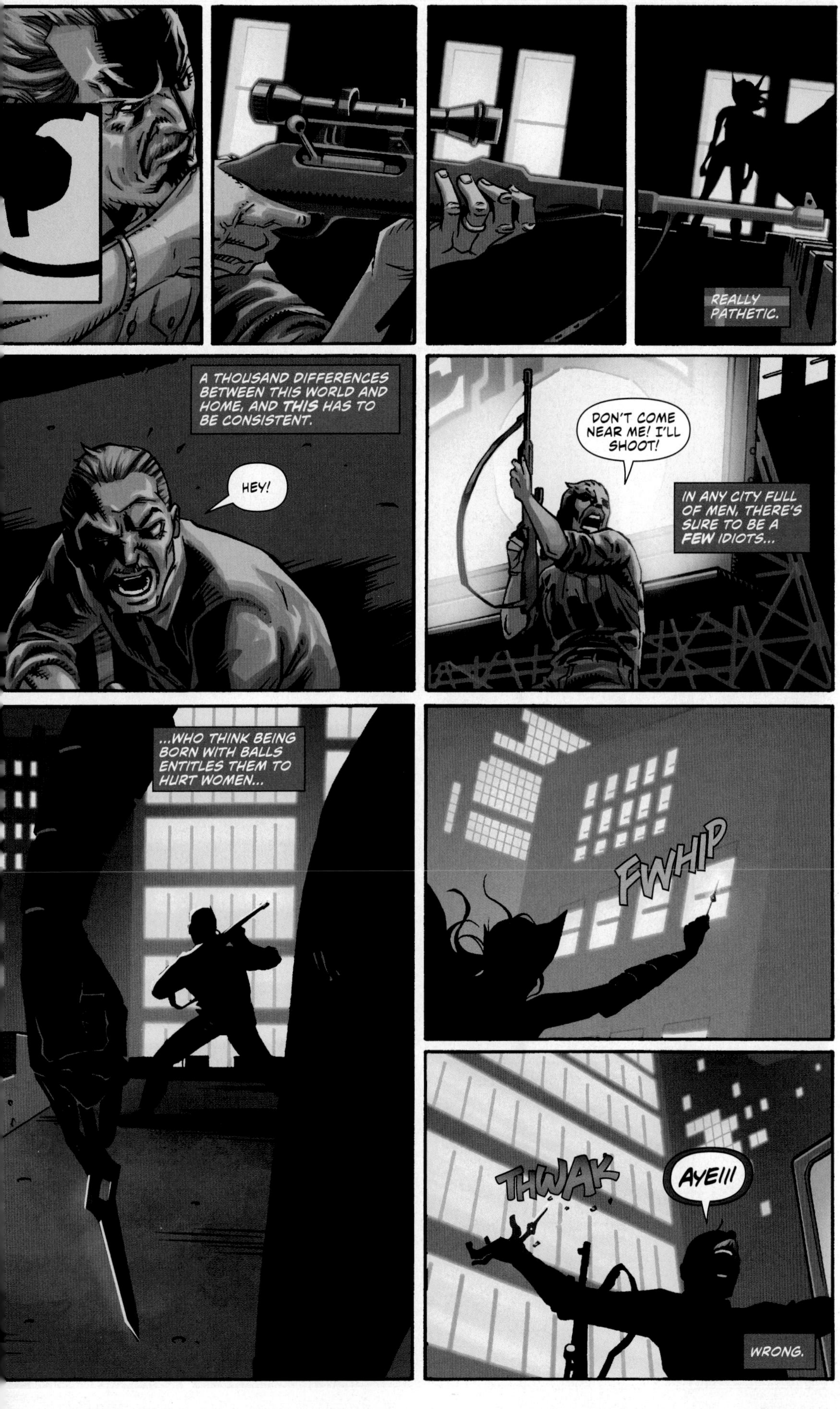
REALLY PATHETIC.
A THOUSAND DIFFERENCES BETWEEN THIS WORLD AND HOME, AND THIS HAS TO BE CONSISTENT.
HEY!
DON'T COME NEAR ME! I'LL SHOOT!
IN ANY CITY FULL OF MEN, THERE'S SURE TO BE A FEW IDIOTS...
...WHO THINK BEING BORN WITH BALLS ENTITLES THEM TO HURT WOMEN...
FWHIP
THWAK
AYEIII
WRONG.

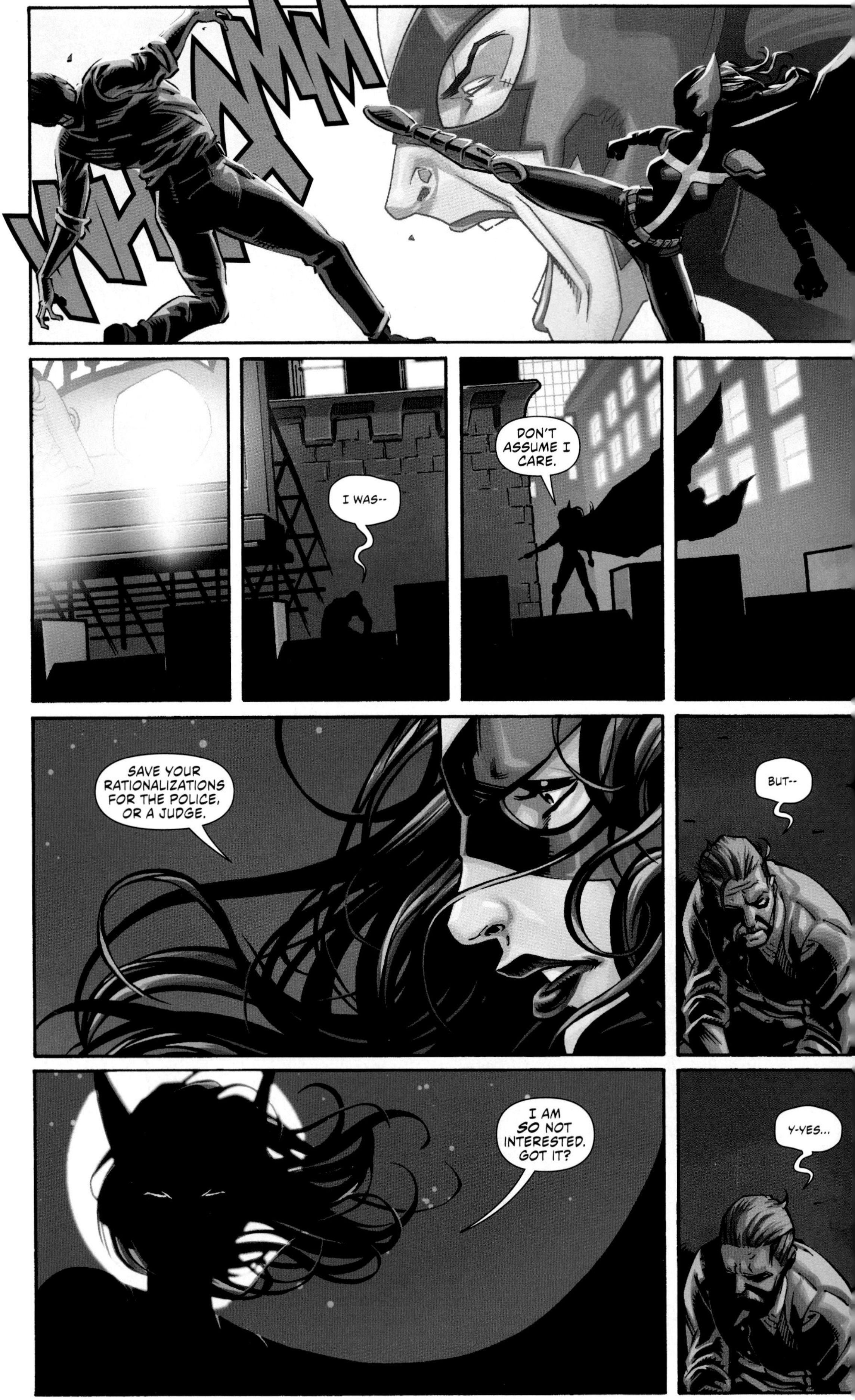
WHAMM
I WAS--
DON'T ASSUME I CARE.
SAVE YOUR RATIONALIZATIONS FOR THE POLICE, OR A JUDGE.
BUT--
I AM SO NOT INTERESTED. GOT IT?
Y-YES...

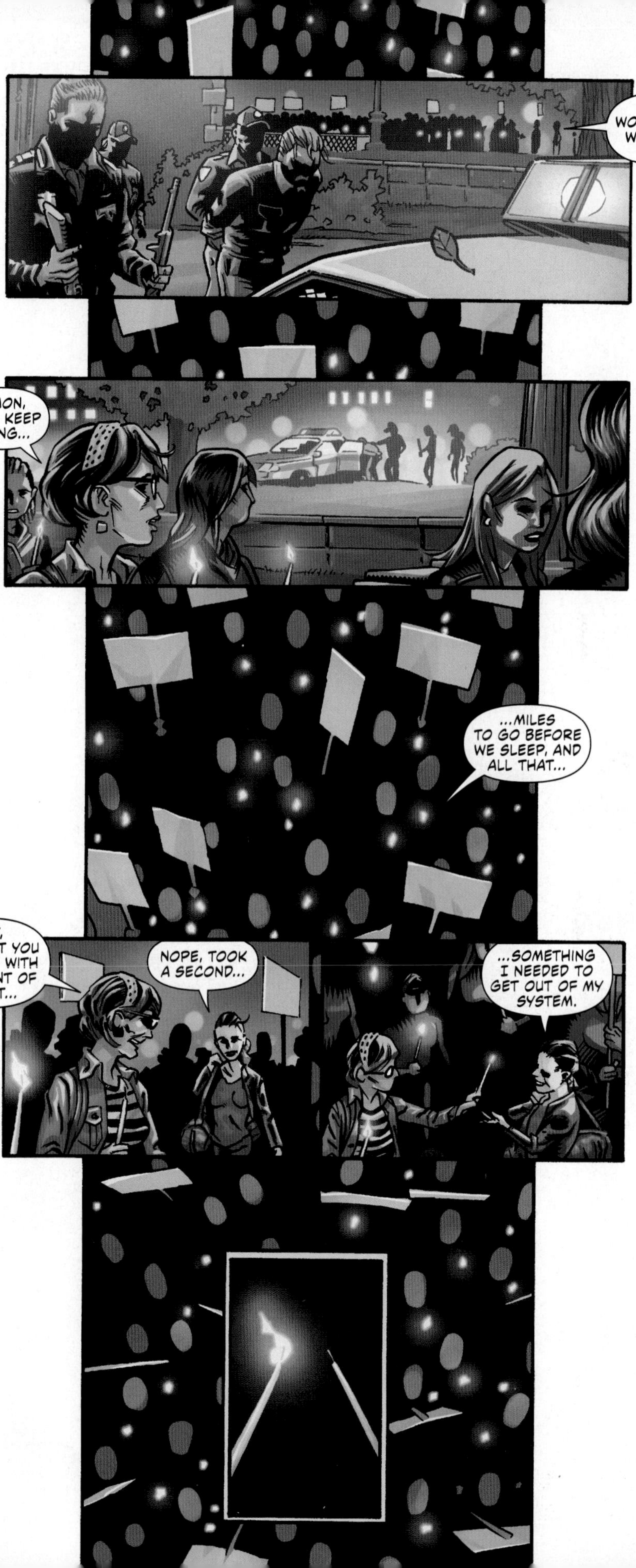
WOW... WONDER WHAT WENT DOWN THERE?
C'MON, LET'S KEEP GOING...
...MILES TO GO BEFORE WE SLEEP, AND ALL THAT...
HEY, THOUGHT YOU RAN OFF WITH THE FAINT OF HEART...
NOPE, TOOK A SECOND...
...SOMETHING I NEEDED TO GET OUT OF MY SYSTEM.

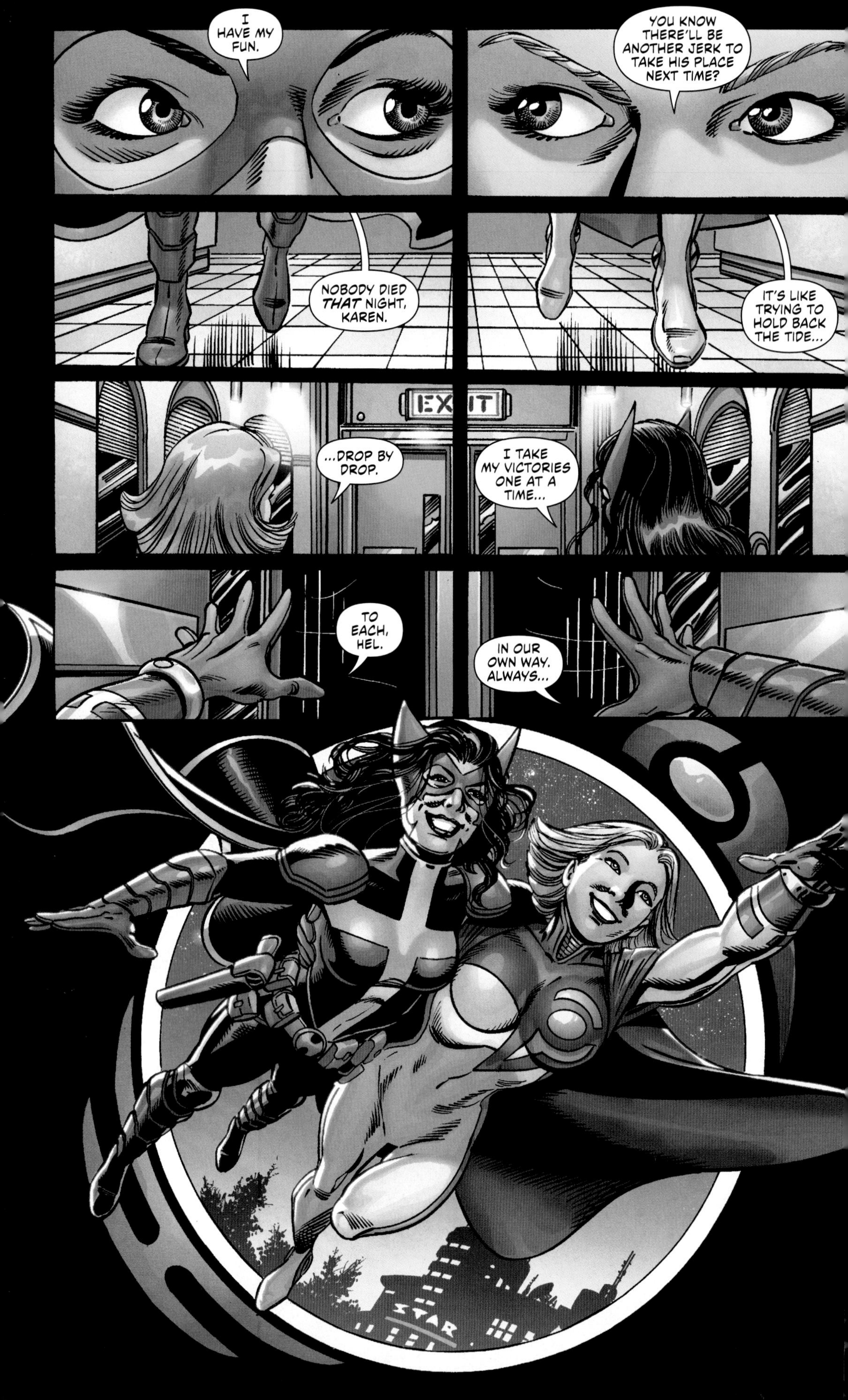
I HAVE MY FUN.
YOU KNOW THERE'LL BE ANOTHER JERK TO TAKE HIS PLACE NEXT TIME?
NOBODY DIED *THAT* NIGHT, KAREN.
IT'S LIKE TRYING TO HOLD BACK THE TIDE...
...DROP BY DROP.
EXIT
I TAKE MY VICTORIES ONE AT A TIME...
TO EACH, HEL.
IN OUR OWN WAY. ALWAYS...
STAR

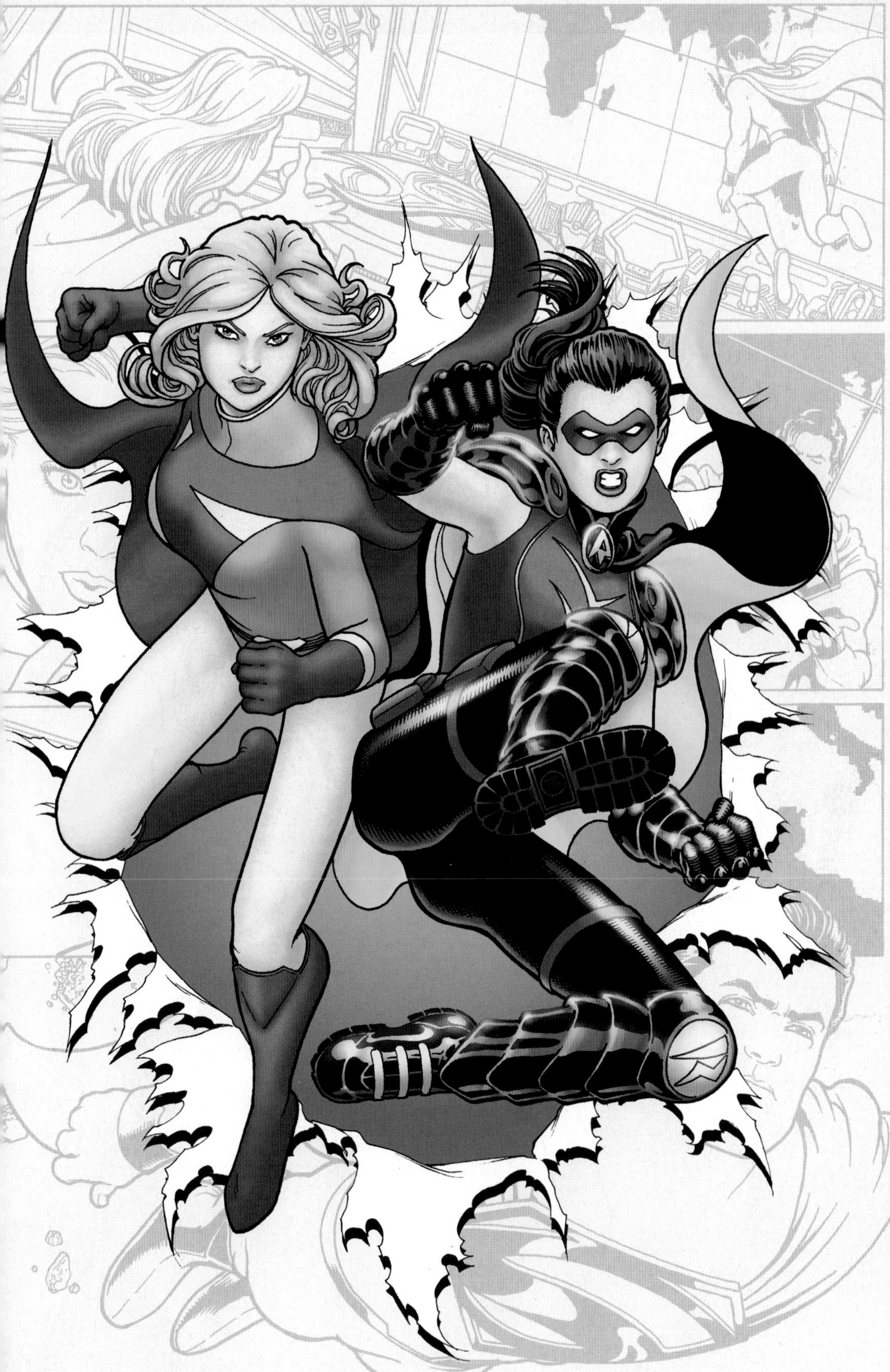

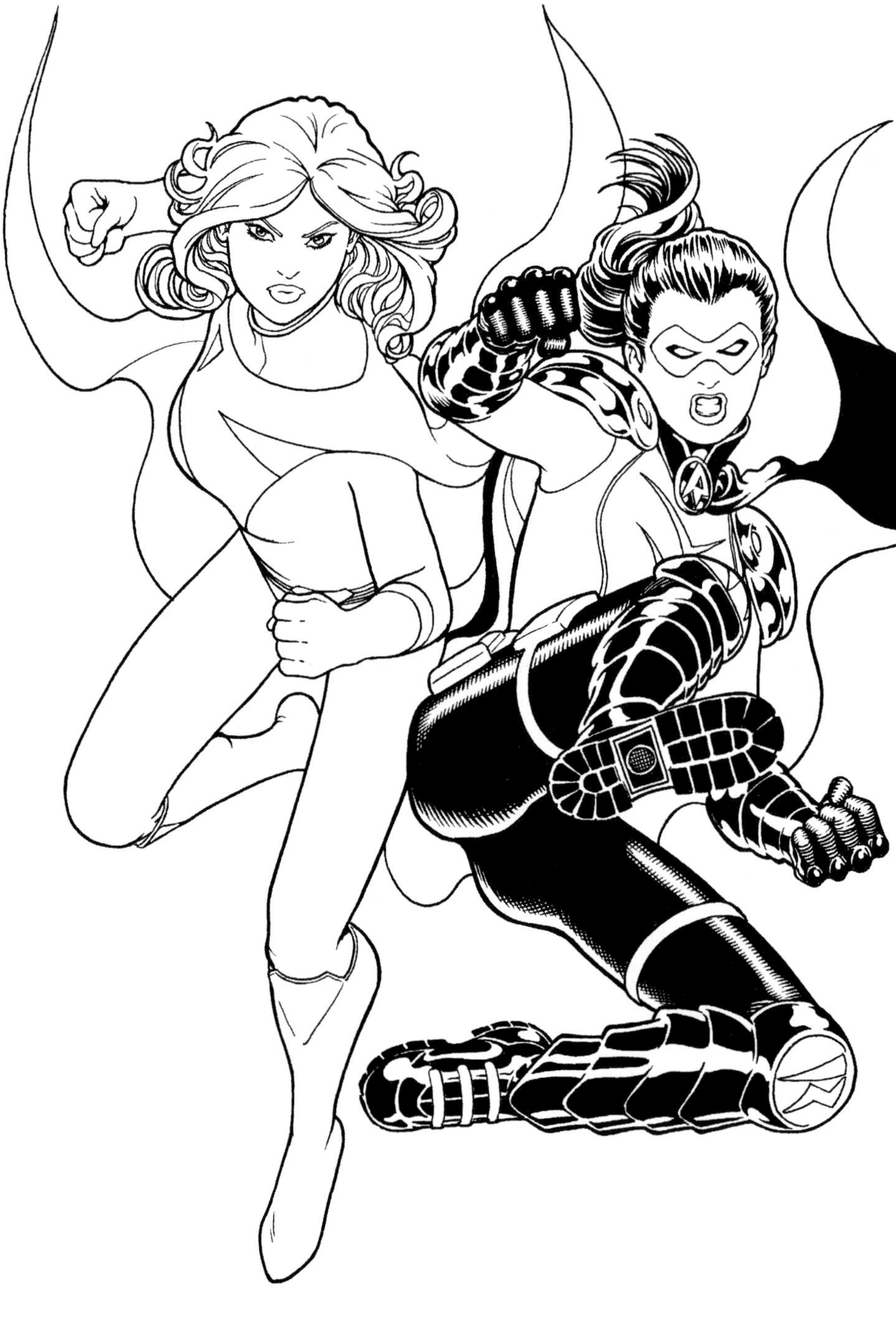

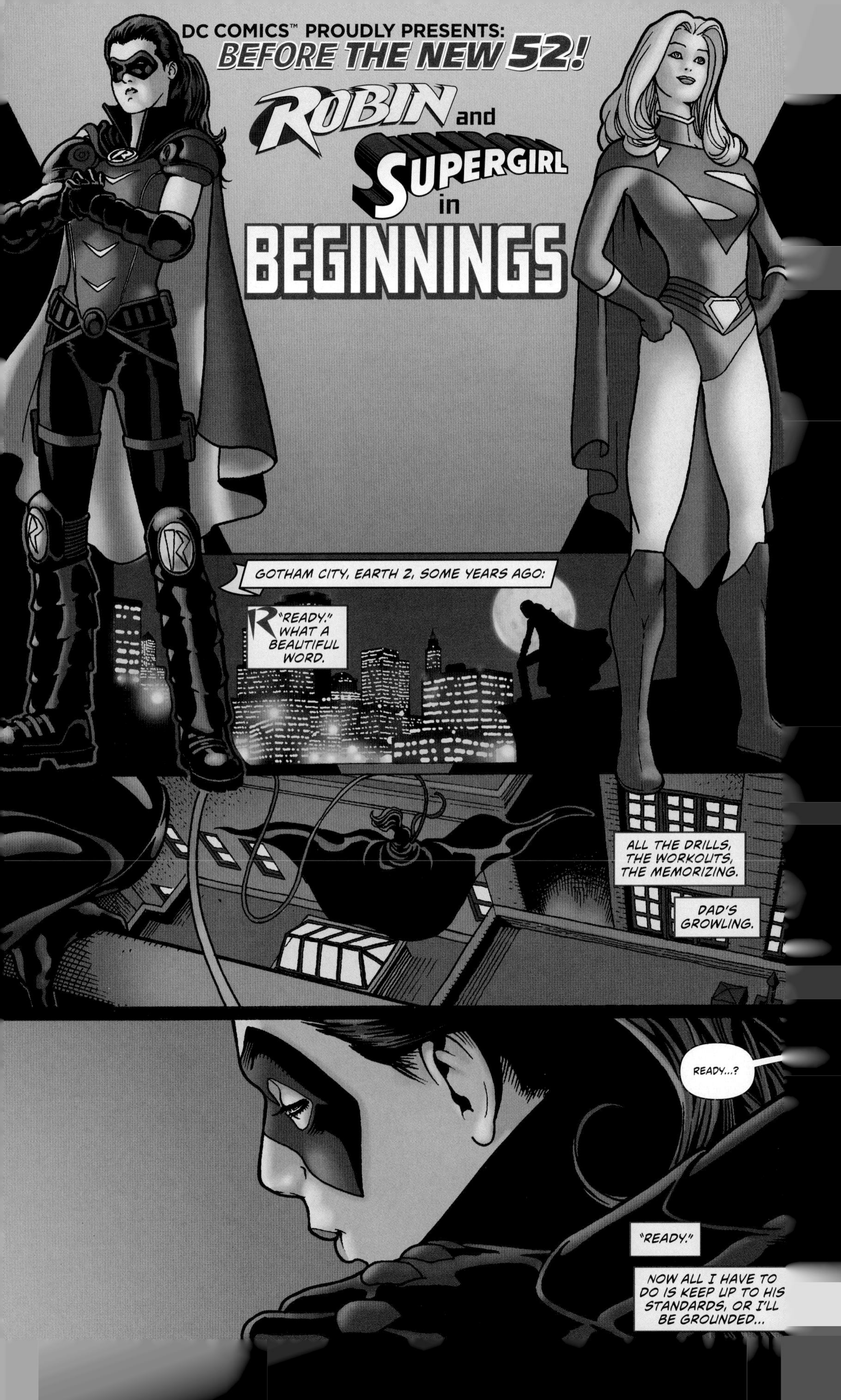

DC COMICS™ PROUDLY PRESENTS:
BEFORE THE NEW 52!
ROBIN and SUPERGIRL in
BEGINNINGS
GOTHAM CITY, EARTH 2, SOME YEARS AGO:
"READY." WHAT A BEAUTIFUL WORD.
ALL THE DRILLS, THE WORKOUTS, THE MEMORIZING.
DAD'S GROWLING.
READY...?
"READY."
NOW ALL I HAVE TO DO IS KEEP UP TO HIS STANDARDS, OR I'LL BE GROUNDED...

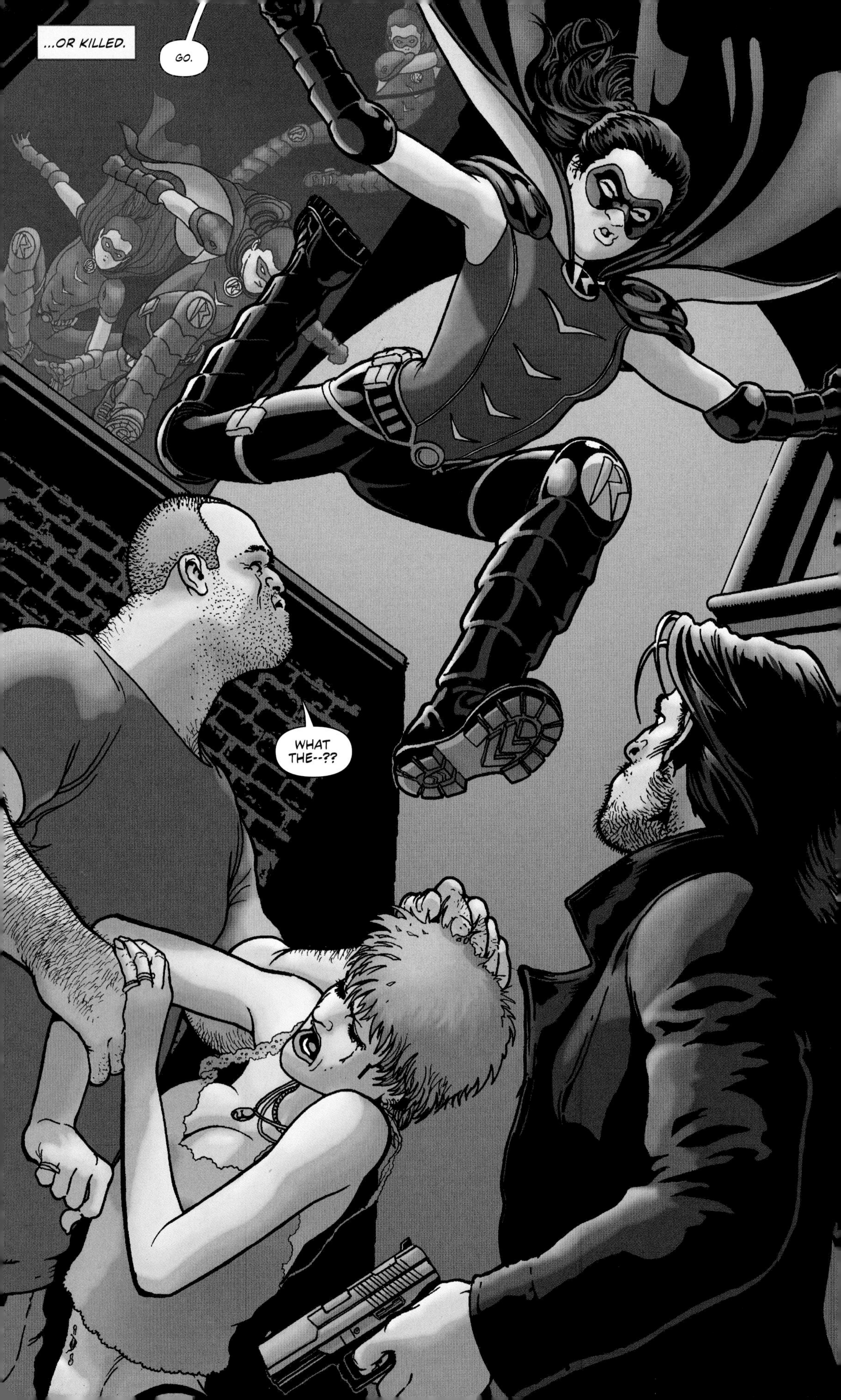
...OR KILLED.
GO.
WHAT THE--??

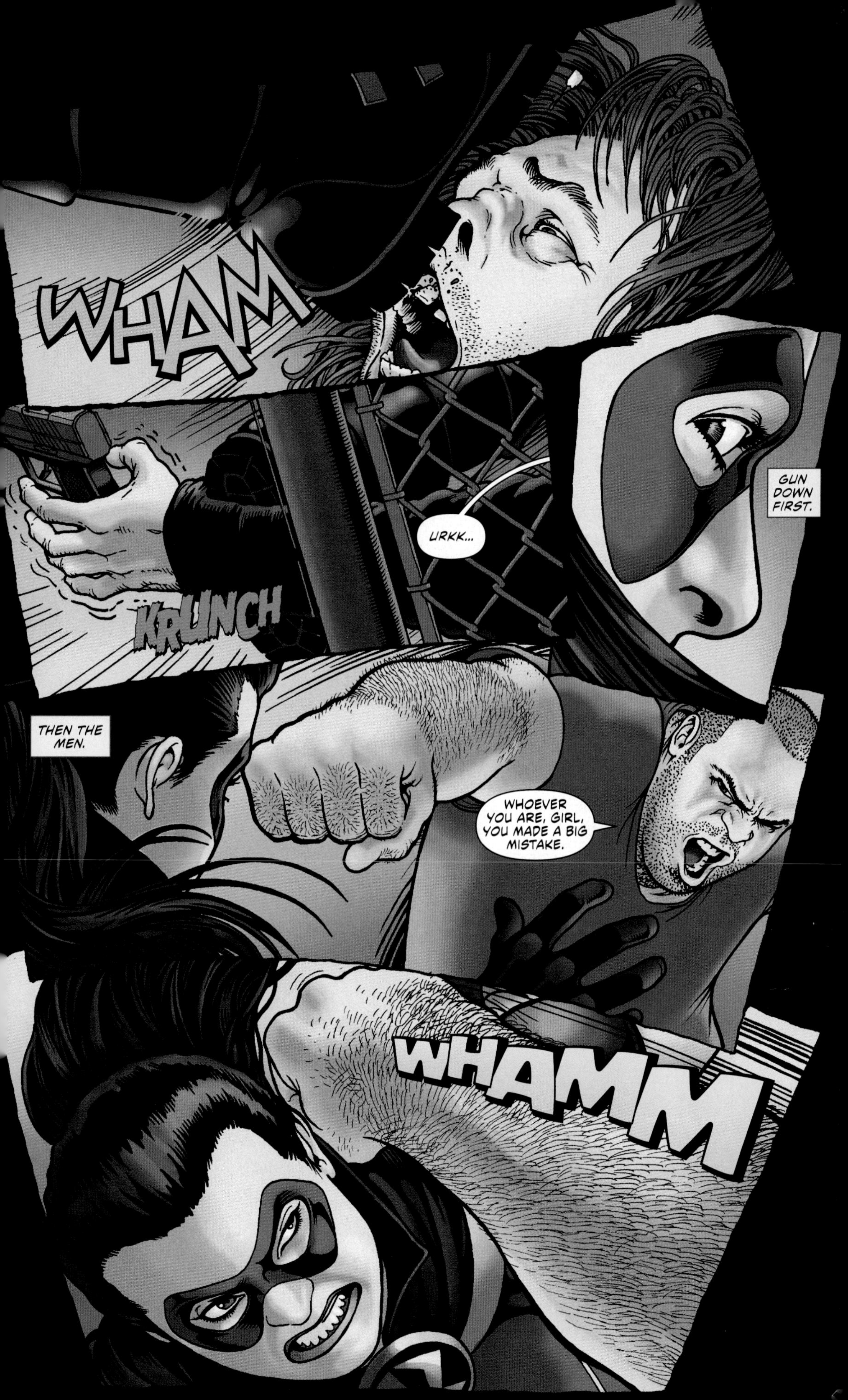
WHAM
GUN DOWN FIRST.
URKK...
KRUNCH
THEN THE MEN.
WHOEVER YOU ARE, GIRL, YOU MADE A BIG MISTAKE.
WHAMM

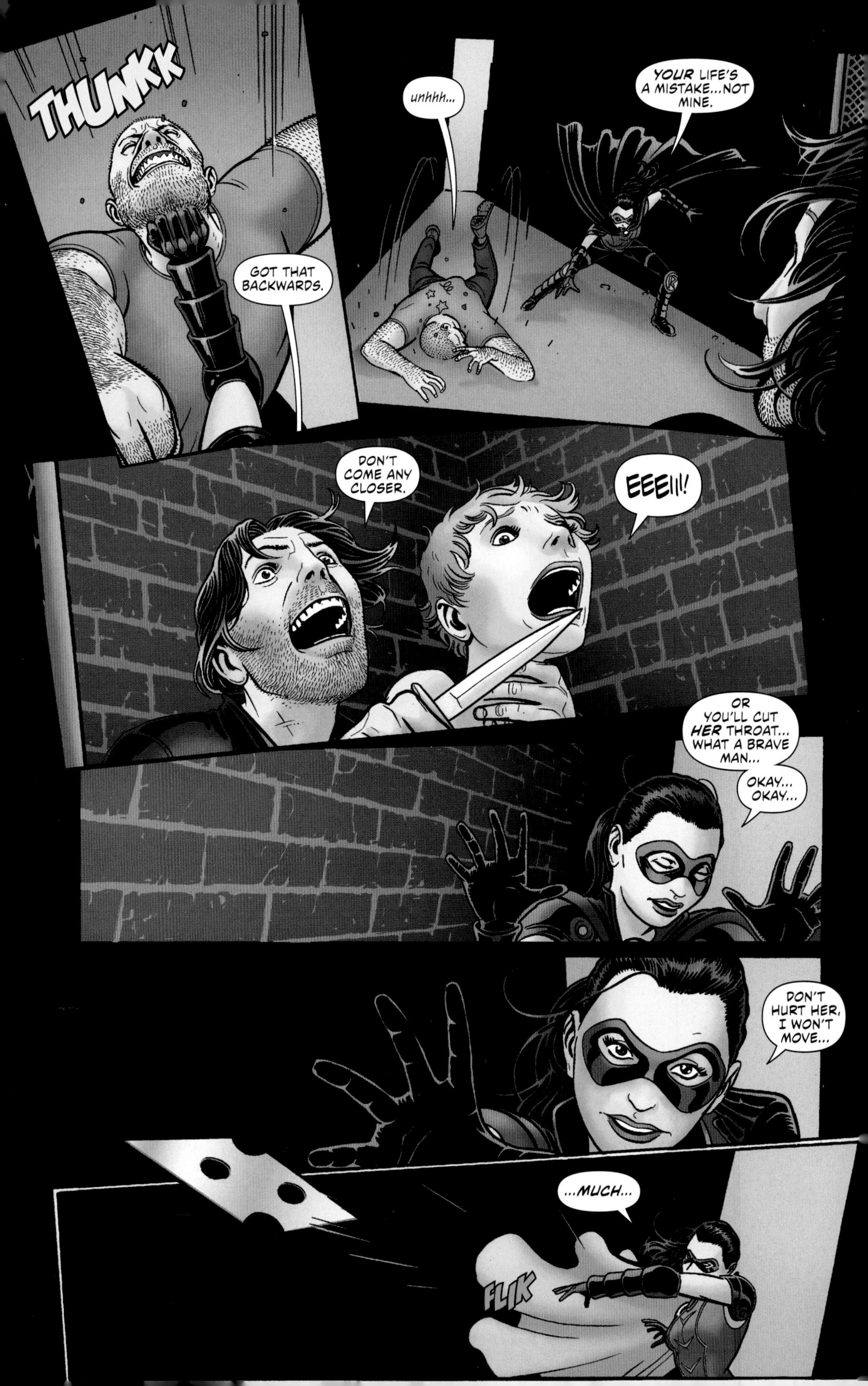
THUNKK
GOT THAT BACKWARDS.
unhhh...
YOUR LIFE'S A MISTAKE...NOT MINE.
DON'T COME ANY CLOSER.
EEEIII!
OR YOU'LL CUT HER THROAT... WHAT A BRAVE MAN...
OKAY... OKAY...
DON'T HURT HER, I WON'T MOVE...
...MUCH...
FLIK

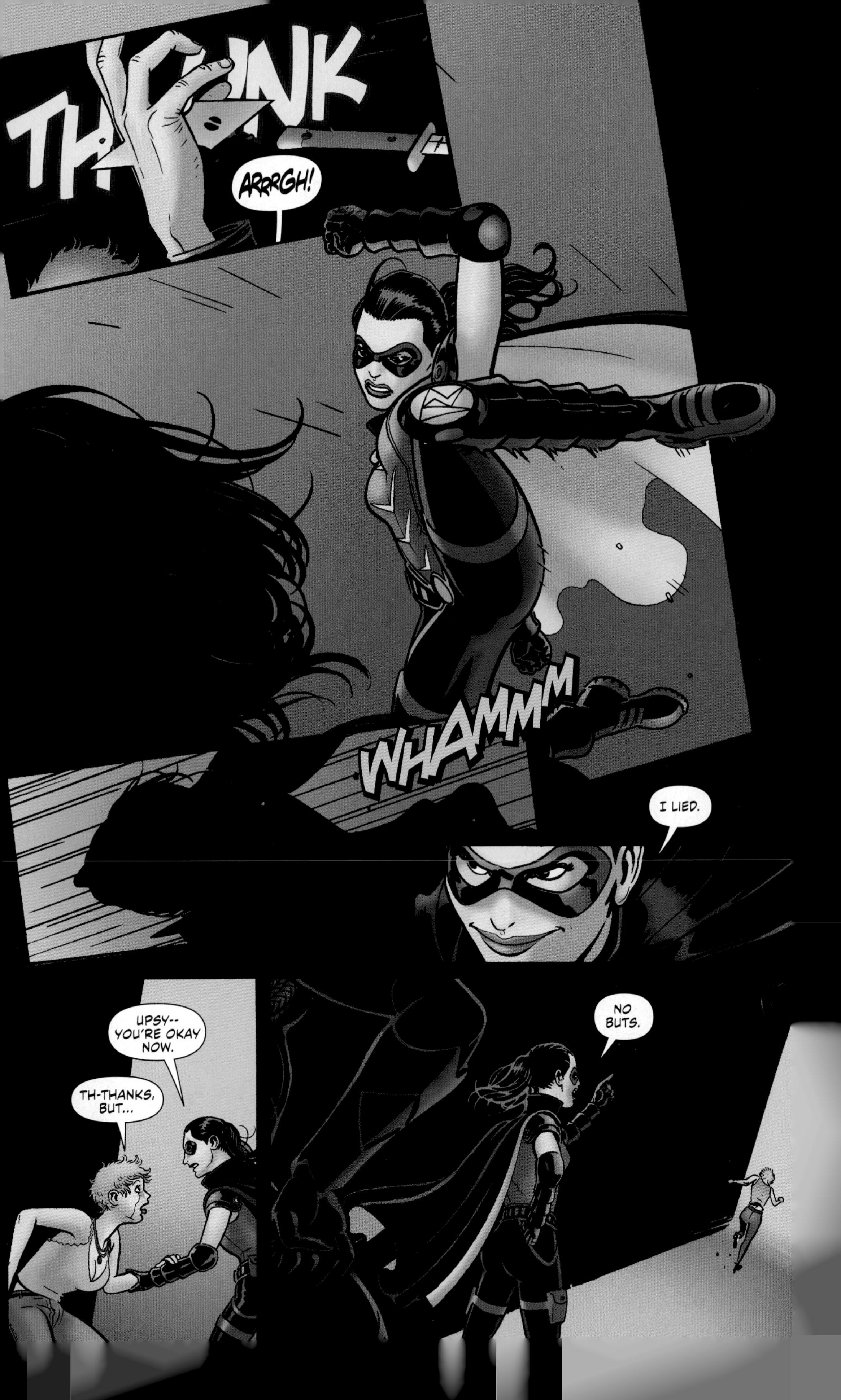

THUNK
ARRRGH!
WHAMMM
I LIED.
UPSY--
YOU'RE OKAY
NOW.
TH-THANKS,
BUT...
NO
BUTS.

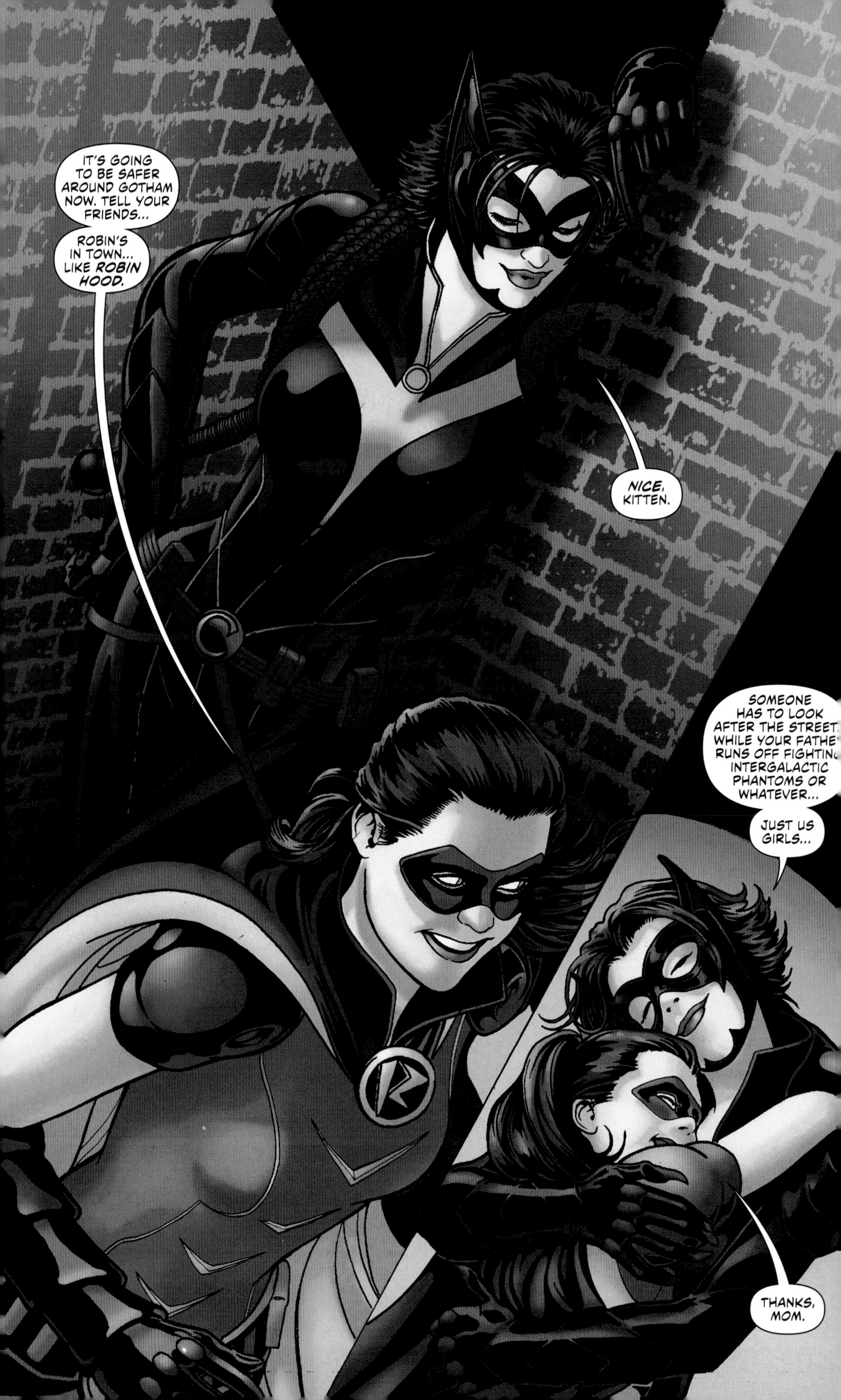
IT'S GOING TO BE SAFER AROUND GOTHAM NOW. TELL YOUR FRIENDS...
ROBIN'S IN TOWN... LIKE *ROBIN HOOD.*
*NICE,* KITTEN.
SOMEONE HAS TO LOOK AFTER THE STREET WHILE YOUR FATHE RUNS OFF FIGHTIN INTERGALACTIC PHANTOMS OR WHATEVER...
JUST US GIRLS...
THANKS, MOM.

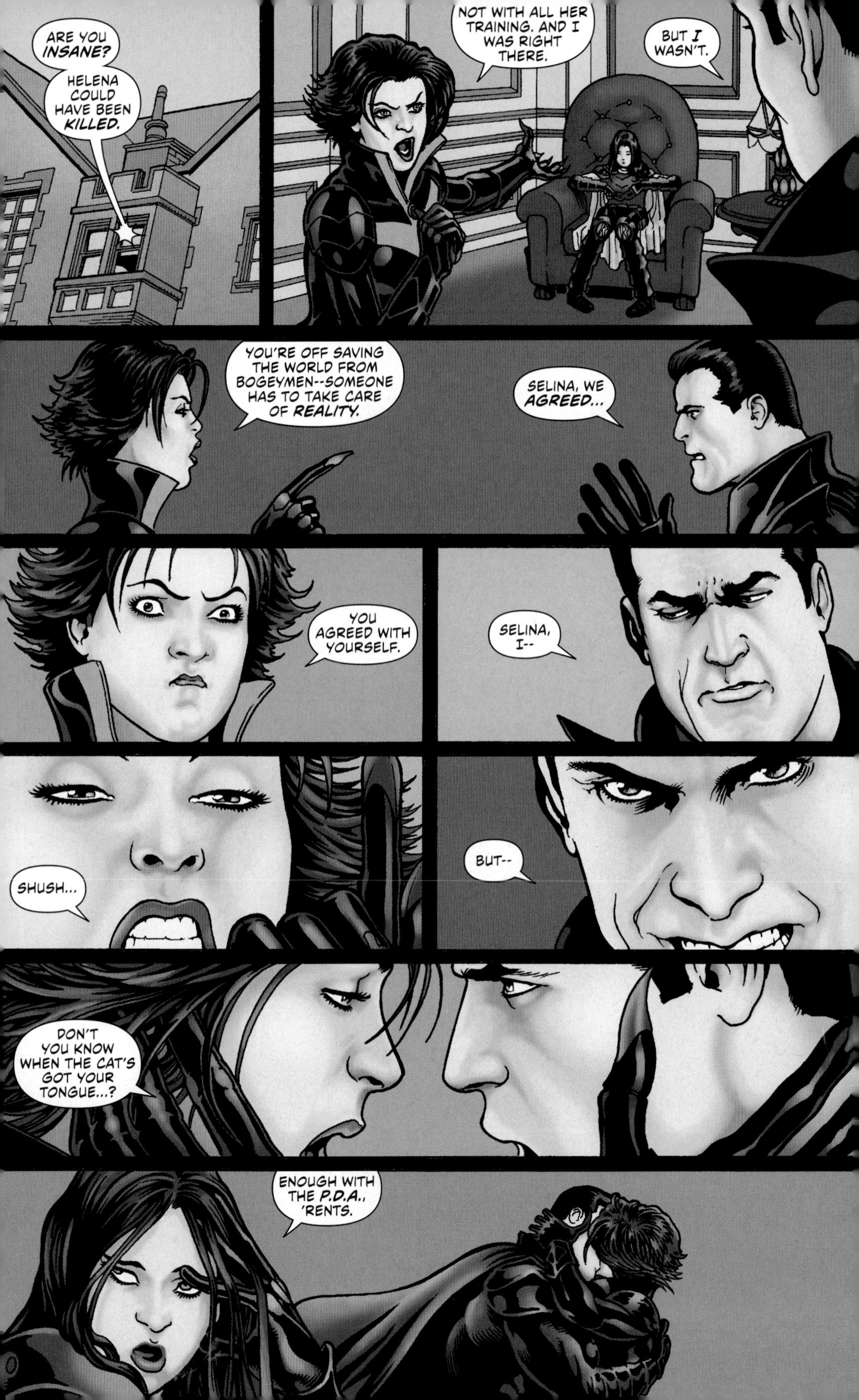

ARE YOU INSANE?
HELENA COULD HAVE BEEN KILLED.
NOT WITH ALL HER TRAINING. AND I WAS RIGHT THERE.
BUT I WASN'T.
YOU'RE OFF SAVING THE WORLD FROM BOGEYMEN--SOMEONE HAS TO TAKE CARE OF REALITY.
SELINA, WE AGREED...
YOU AGREED WITH YOURSELF.
SELINA, I--
SHUSH...
BUT--
DON'T YOU KNOW WHEN THE CAT'S GOT YOUR TONGUE...?
ENOUGH WITH THE P.D.A., 'RENTS.

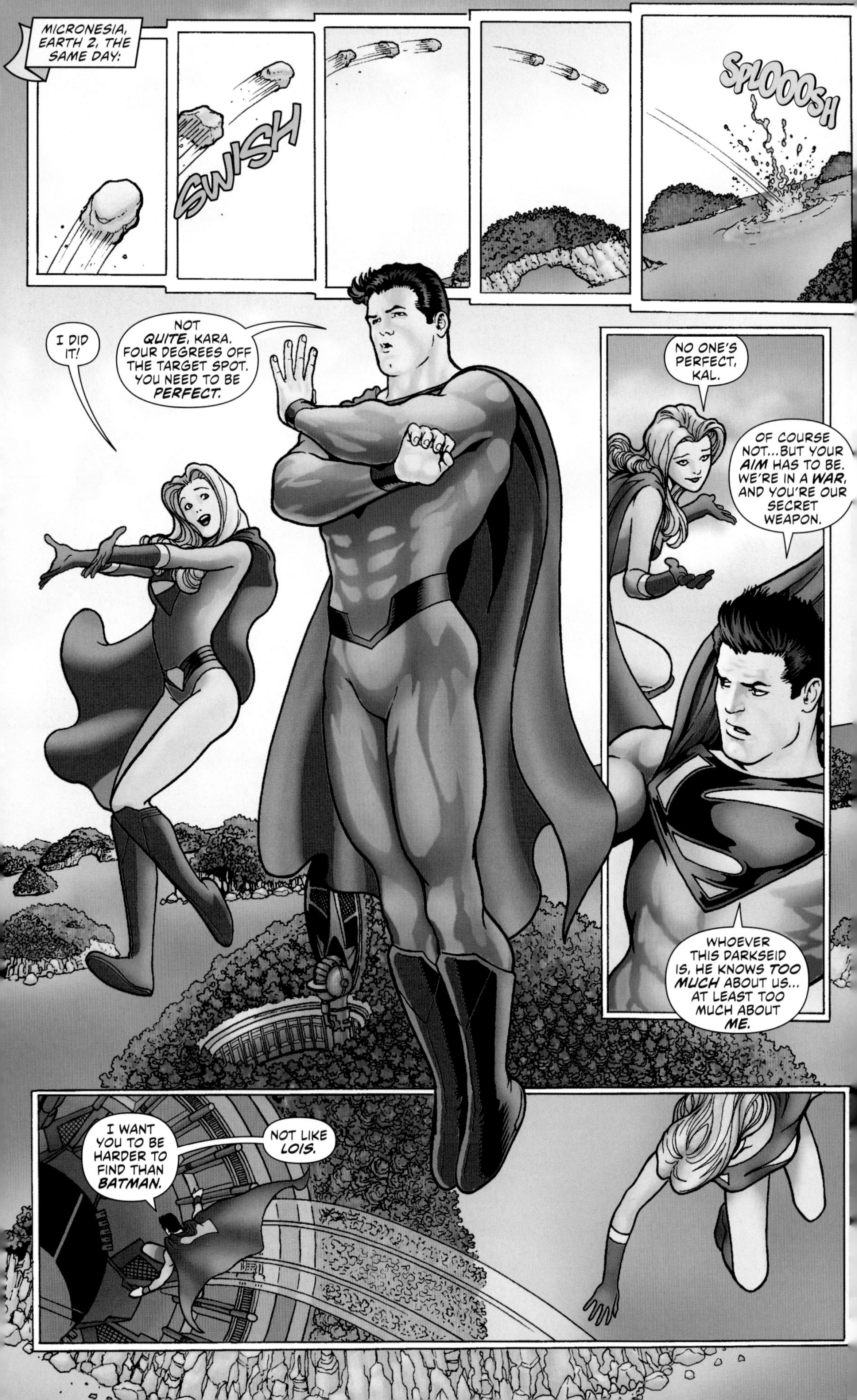
MICRONESIA, EARTH 2, THE SAME DAY:
SWISH
SPLOOOSH
I DID IT!
NOT QUITE, KARA. FOUR DEGREES OFF THE TARGET SPOT. YOU NEED TO BE PERFECT.
NO ONE'S PERFECT, KAL.
OF COURSE NOT...BUT YOUR AIM HAS TO BE. WE'RE IN A WAR, AND YOU'RE OUR SECRET WEAPON.
WHOEVER THIS DARKSEID IS, HE KNOWS TOO MUCH ABOUT US... AT LEAST TOO MUCH ABOUT ME.
I WANT YOU TO BE HARDER TO FIND THAN BATMAN.
NOT LIKE LOIS.

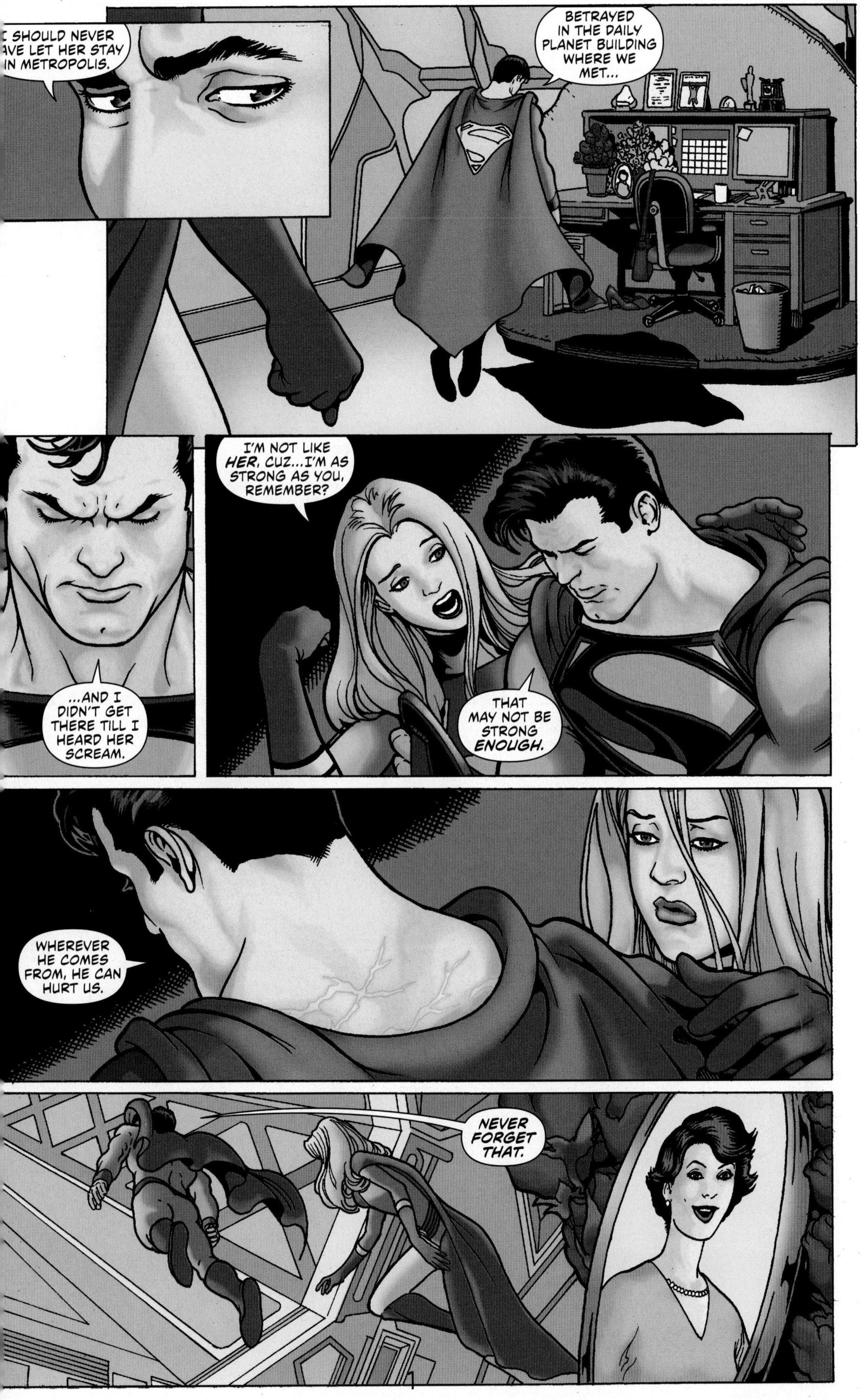
I SHOULD NEVER HAVE LET HER STAY IN METROPOLIS.
BETRAYED IN THE DAILY PLANET BUILDING WHERE WE MET...
...AND I DIDN'T GET THERE TILL I HEARD HER SCREAM.
I'M NOT LIKE HER, CUZ...I'M AS STRONG AS YOU, REMEMBER?
THAT MAY NOT BE STRONG ENOUGH.
WHEREVER HE COMES FROM, HE CAN HURT US.
NEVER FORGET THAT.

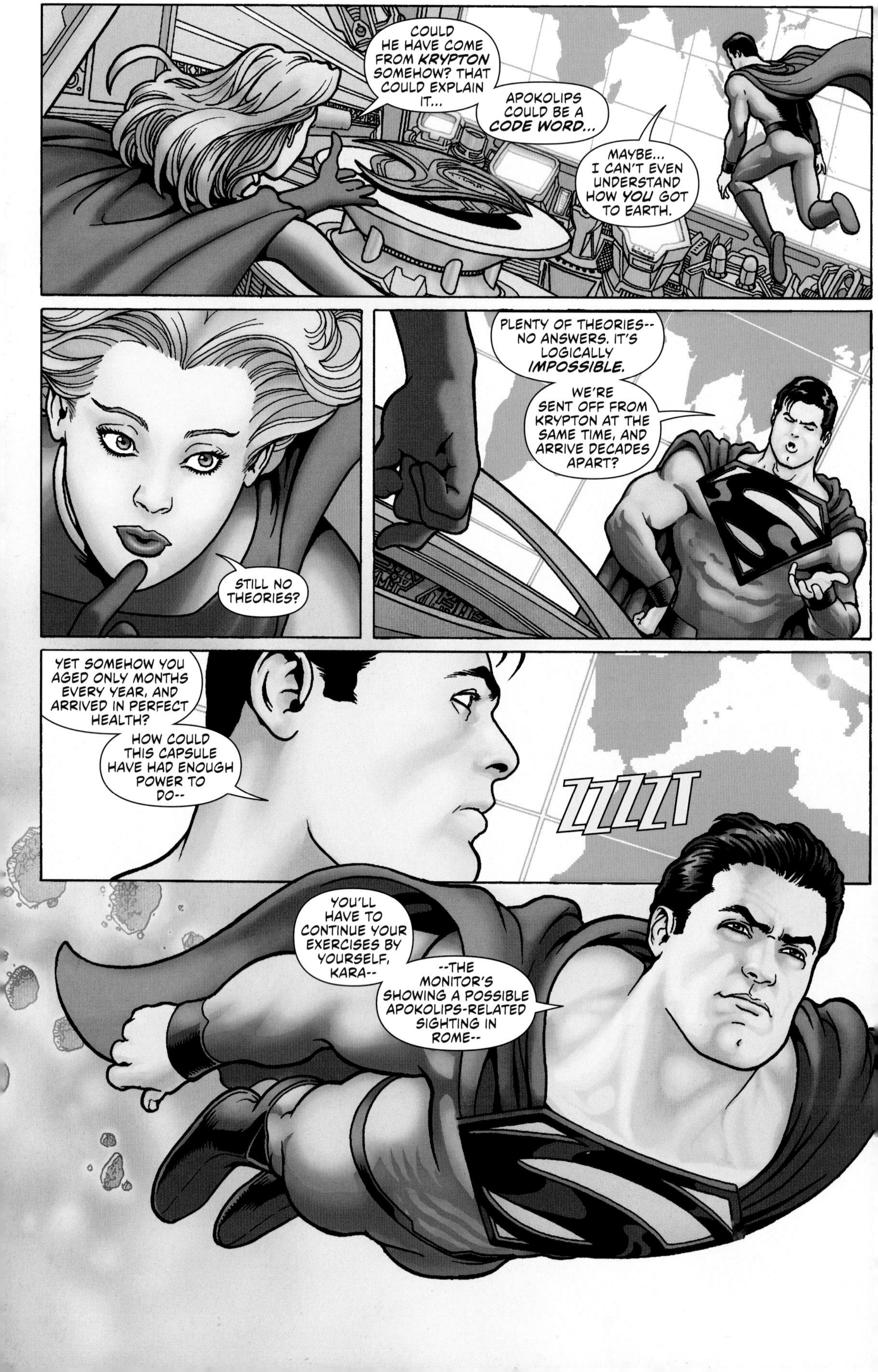

COULD HE HAVE COME FROM KRYPTON SOMEHOW? THAT COULD EXPLAIN IT...
APOKOLIPS COULD BE A CODE WORD...
MAYBE... I CAN'T EVEN UNDERSTAND HOW YOU GOT TO EARTH.
STILL NO THEORIES?
PLENTY OF THEORIES-- NO ANSWERS. IT'S LOGICALLY IMPOSSIBLE.
WE'RE SENT OFF FROM KRYPTON AT THE SAME TIME, AND ARRIVE DECADES APART?
YET SOMEHOW YOU AGED ONLY MONTHS EVERY YEAR, AND ARRIVED IN PERFECT HEALTH?
HOW COULD THIS CAPSULE HAVE HAD ENOUGH POWER TO DO--
ZZZZT
YOU'LL HAVE TO CONTINUE YOUR EXERCISES BY YOURSELF, KARA--
--THE MONITOR'S SHOWING A POSSIBLE APOKOLIPS-RELATED SIGHTING IN ROME--

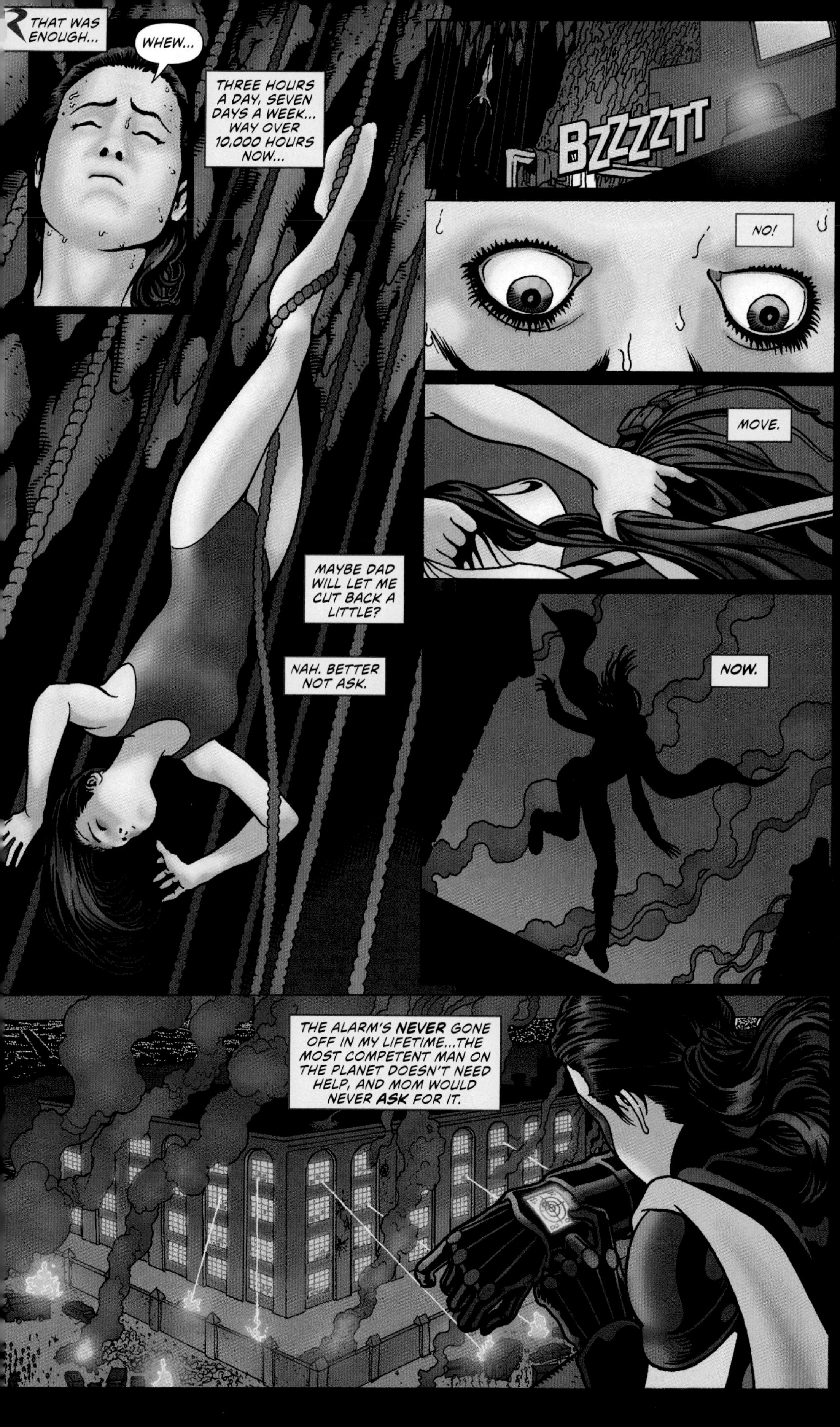
THAT WAS ENOUGH...
WHEW...
THREE HOURS A DAY, SEVEN DAYS A WEEK... WAY OVER 10,000 HOURS NOW...
MAYBE DAD WILL LET ME CUT BACK A LITTLE?
NAH. BETTER NOT ASK.
BZZZZTT
NO!
MOVE.
NOW.
THE ALARM'S NEVER GONE OFF IN MY LIFETIME...THE MOST COMPETENT MAN ON THE PLANET DOESN'T NEED HELP, AND MOM WOULD NEVER ASK FOR IT.

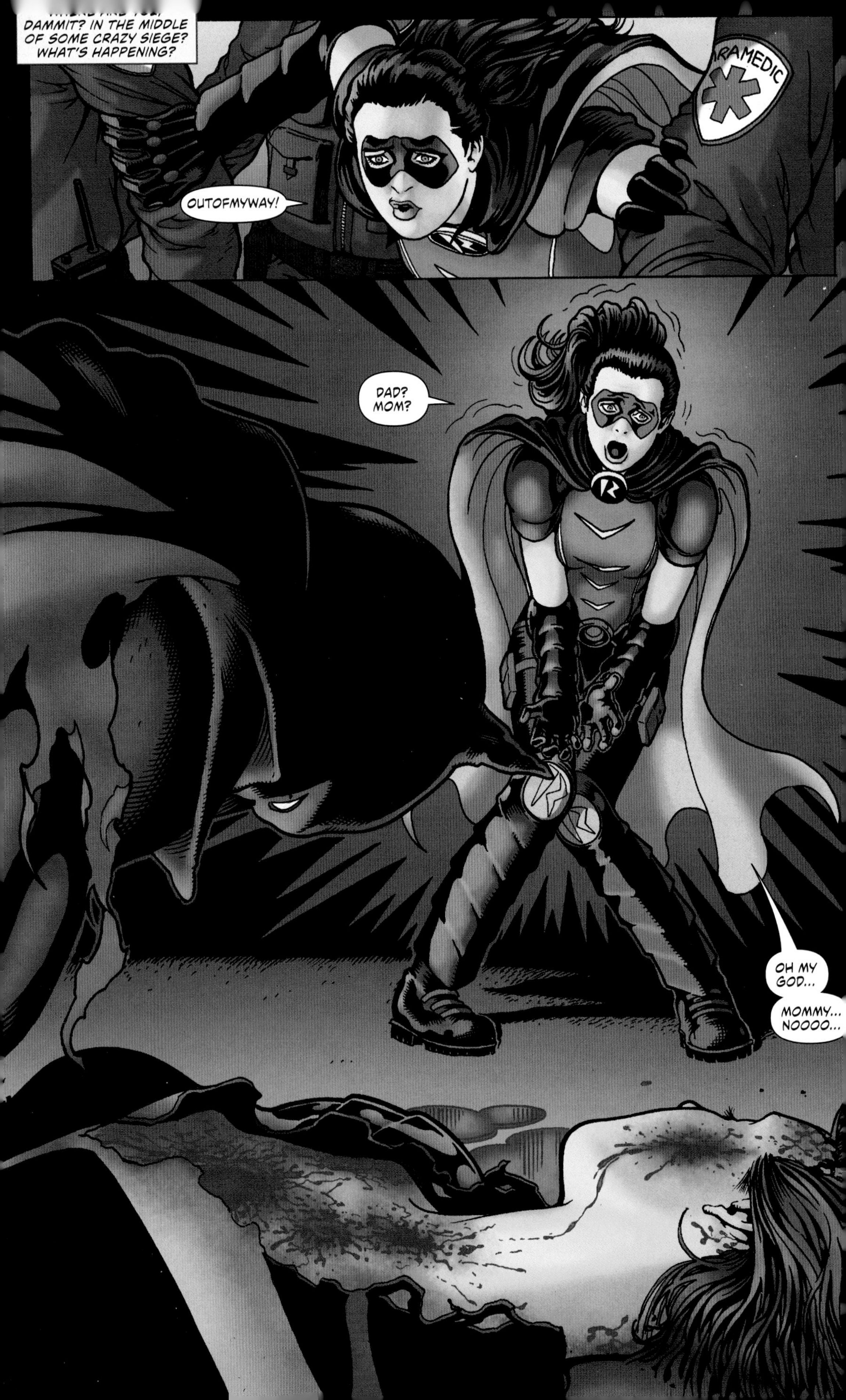
DAMMIT? IN THE MIDDLE OF SOME CRAZY SIEGE? WHAT'S HAPPENING?
PARAMEDIC
OUTOFMYWAY!
DAD? MOM?
OH MY GOD...
MOMMY... NOOOO...

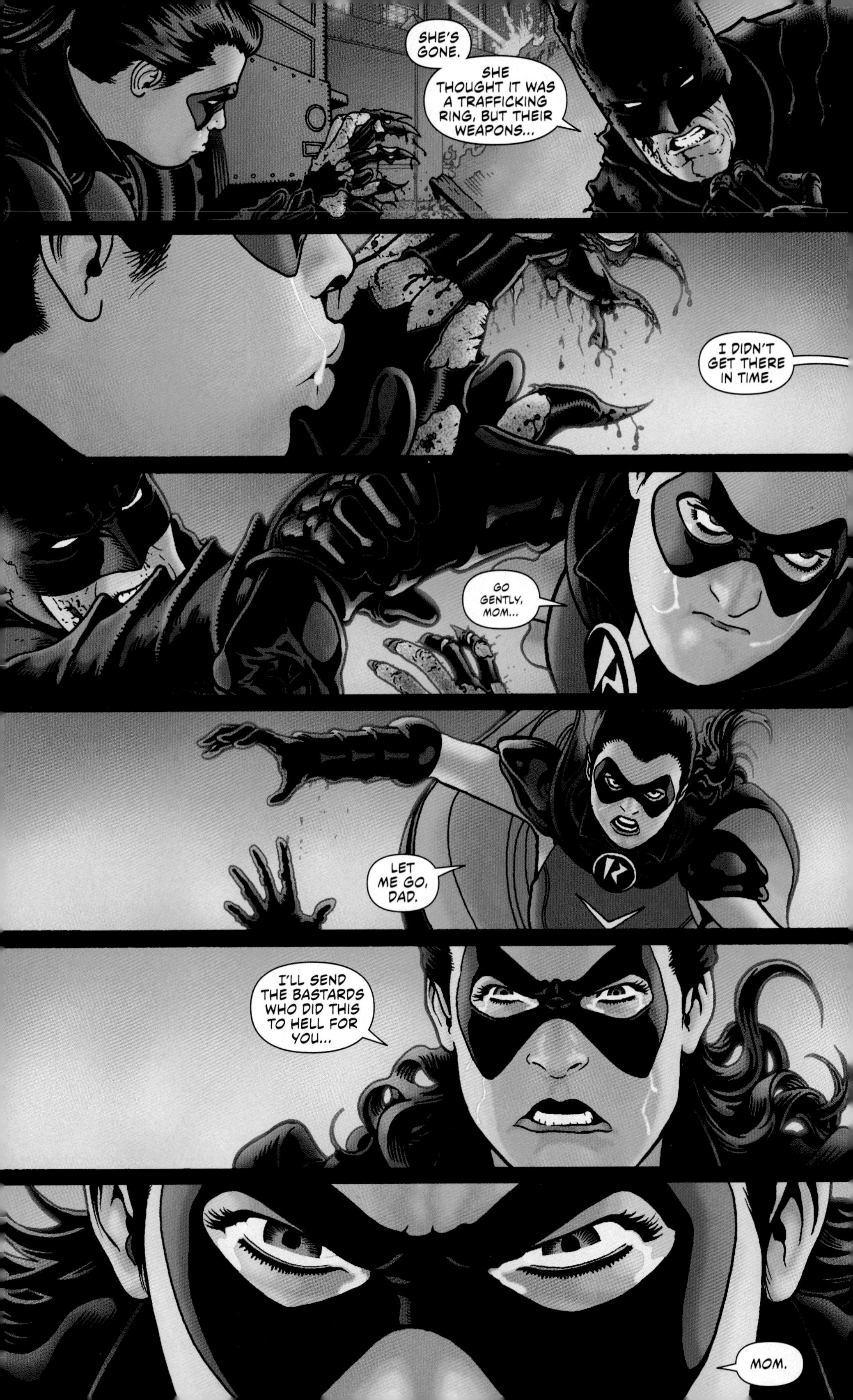
SHE'S GONE.
SHE THOUGHT IT WAS A TRAFFICKING RING, BUT THEIR WEAPONS...
I DIDN'T GET THERE IN TIME.
GO GENTLY, MOM...
LET ME GO, DAD.
I'LL SEND THE BASTARDS WHO DID THIS TO HELL FOR YOU...
MOM.

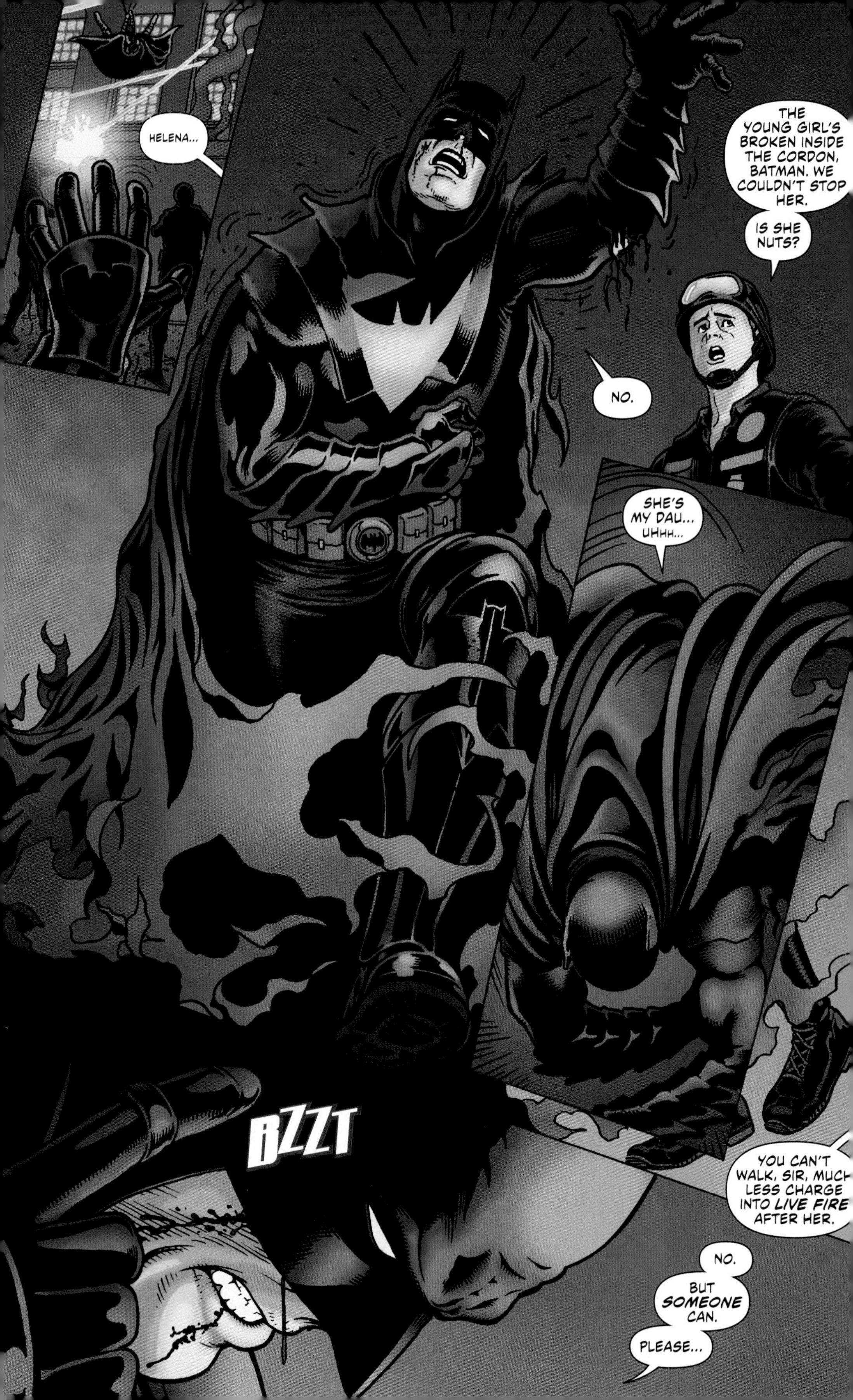
HELENA...
THE YOUNG GIRL'S BROKEN INSIDE THE CORDON, BATMAN. WE COULDN'T STOP HER.
IS SHE NUTS?
NO.
SHE'S MY DAU... UHHH...
BZZT
YOU CAN'T WALK, SIR, MUCH LESS CHARGE INTO LIVE FIRE AFTER HER.
NO.
BUT SOMEONE CAN.
PLEASE...

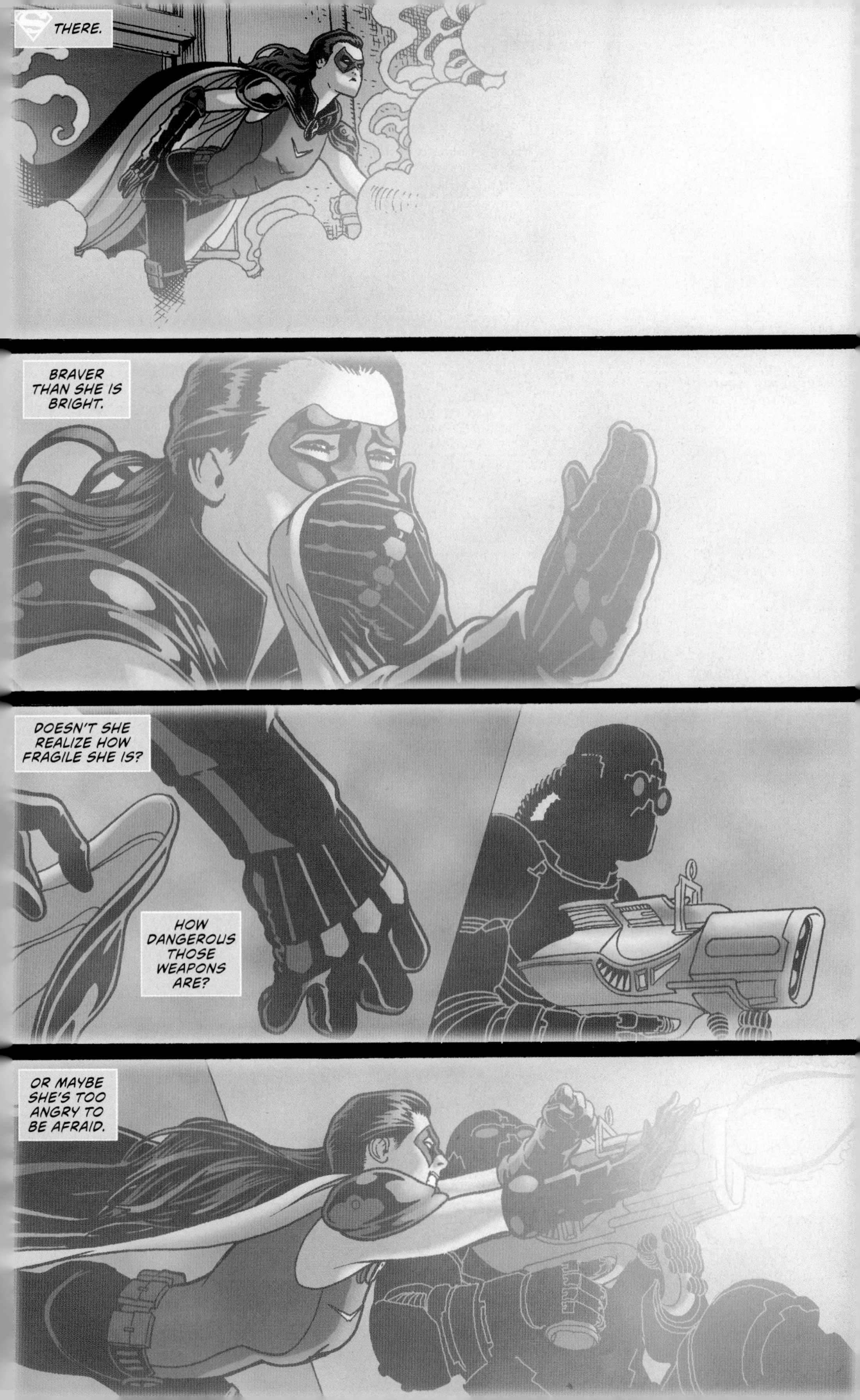
THERE.
BRAVER THAN SHE IS BRIGHT.
DOESN'T SHE REALIZE HOW FRAGILE SHE IS?
HOW DANGEROUS THOSE WEAPONS ARE?
OR MAYBE SHE'S TOO ANGRY TO BE AFRAID.

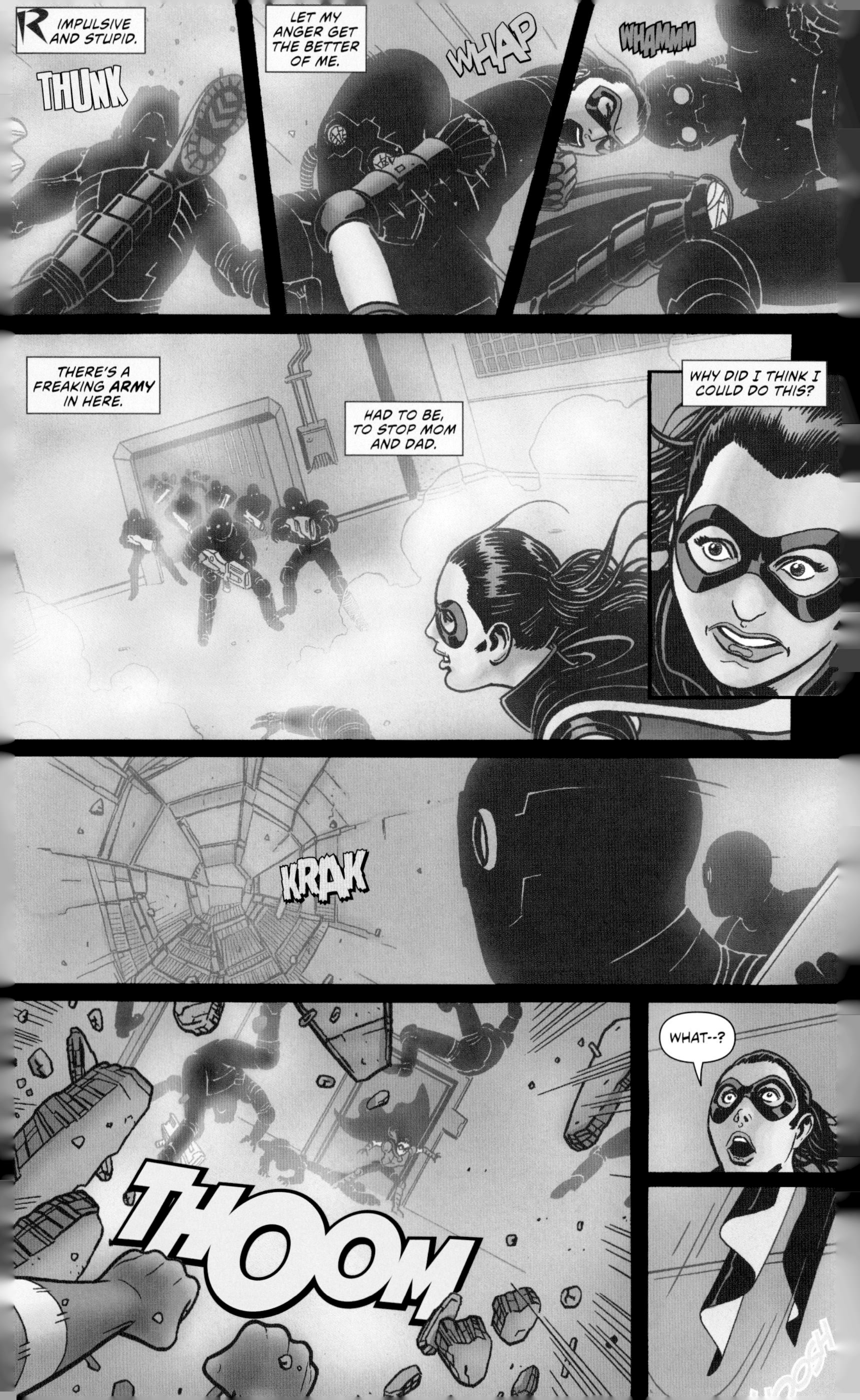
IMPULSIVE AND STUPID.
THUNK
LET MY ANGER GET THE BETTER OF ME.
WHAP
WHAMMM
THERE'S A FREAKING ARMY IN HERE.
HAD TO BE, TO STOP MOM AND DAD.
WHY DID I THINK I COULD DO THIS?
KRAK
WHAT--?
THOOM

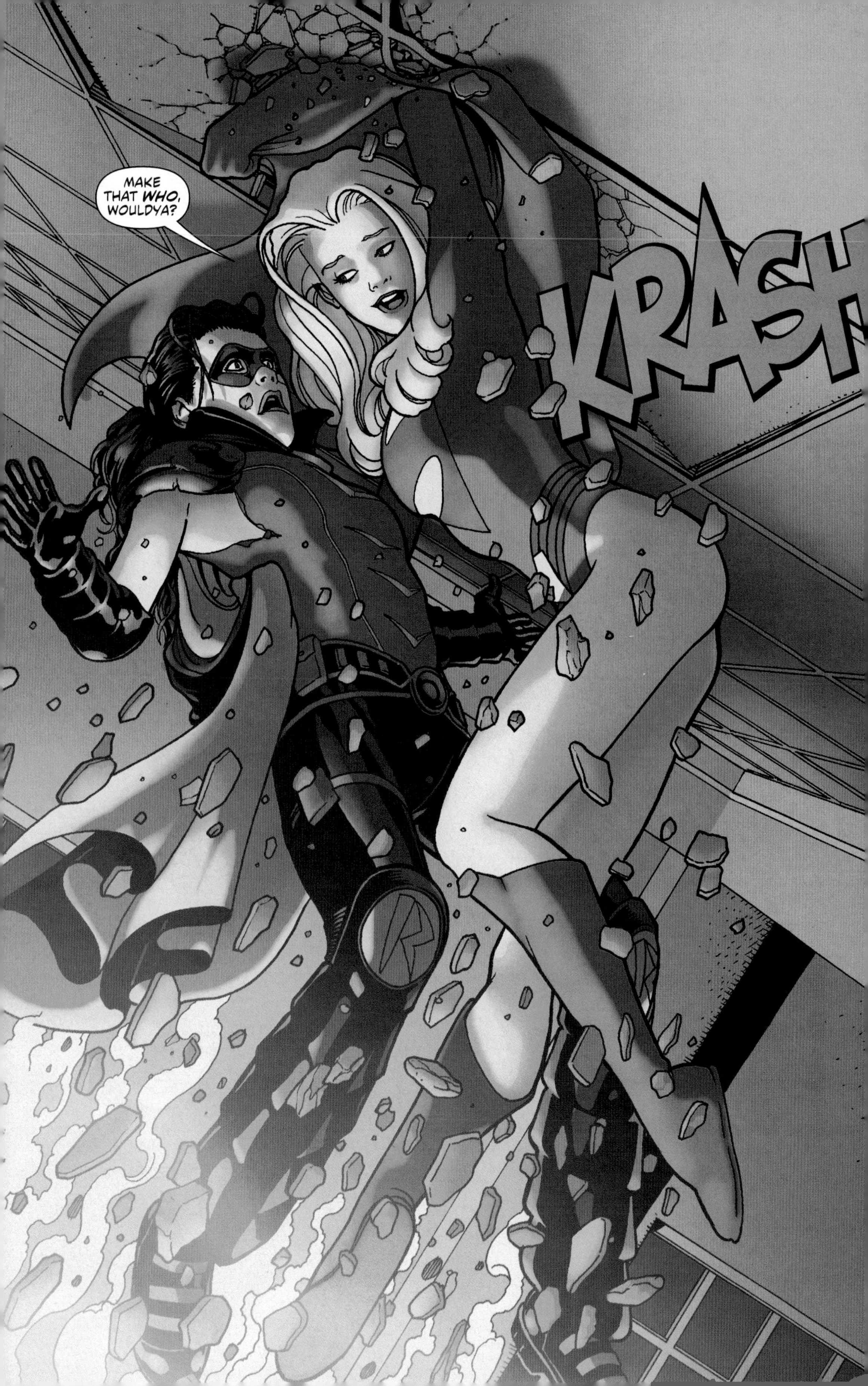
MAKE THAT WHO, WOULDYA?
KRASH

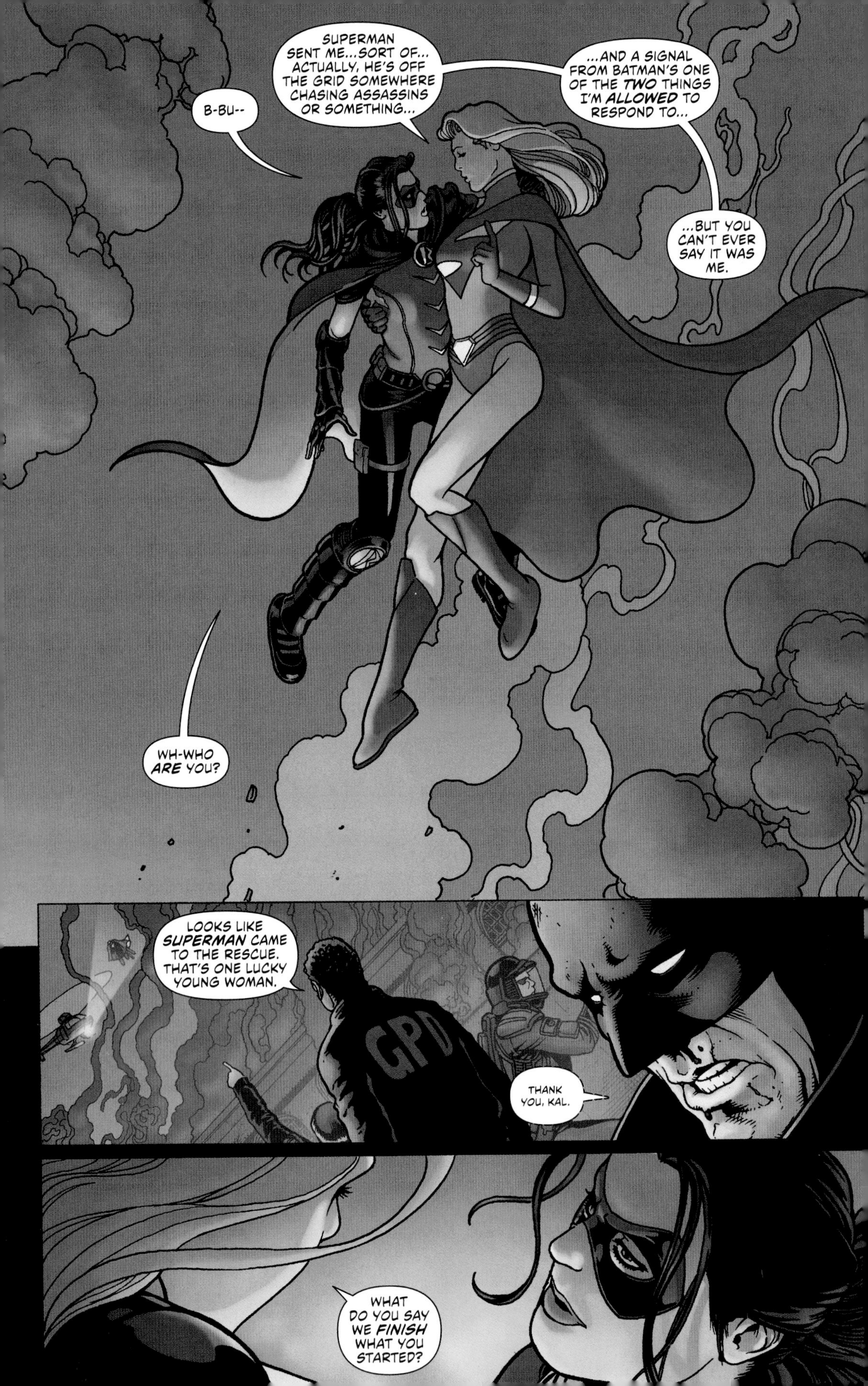
B-BU--
SUPERMAN SENT ME...SORT OF... ACTUALLY, HE'S OFF THE GRID SOMEWHERE CHASING ASSASSINS OR SOMETHING...
...AND A SIGNAL FROM BATMAN'S ONE OF THE TWO THINGS I'M ALLOWED TO RESPOND TO...
...BUT YOU CAN'T EVER SAY IT WAS ME.
WH-WHO ARE YOU?
LOOKS LIKE SUPERMAN CAME TO THE RESCUE. THAT'S ONE LUCKY YOUNG WOMAN.
GPD
THANK YOU, KAL.
WHAT DO YOU SAY WE FINISH WHAT YOU STARTED?

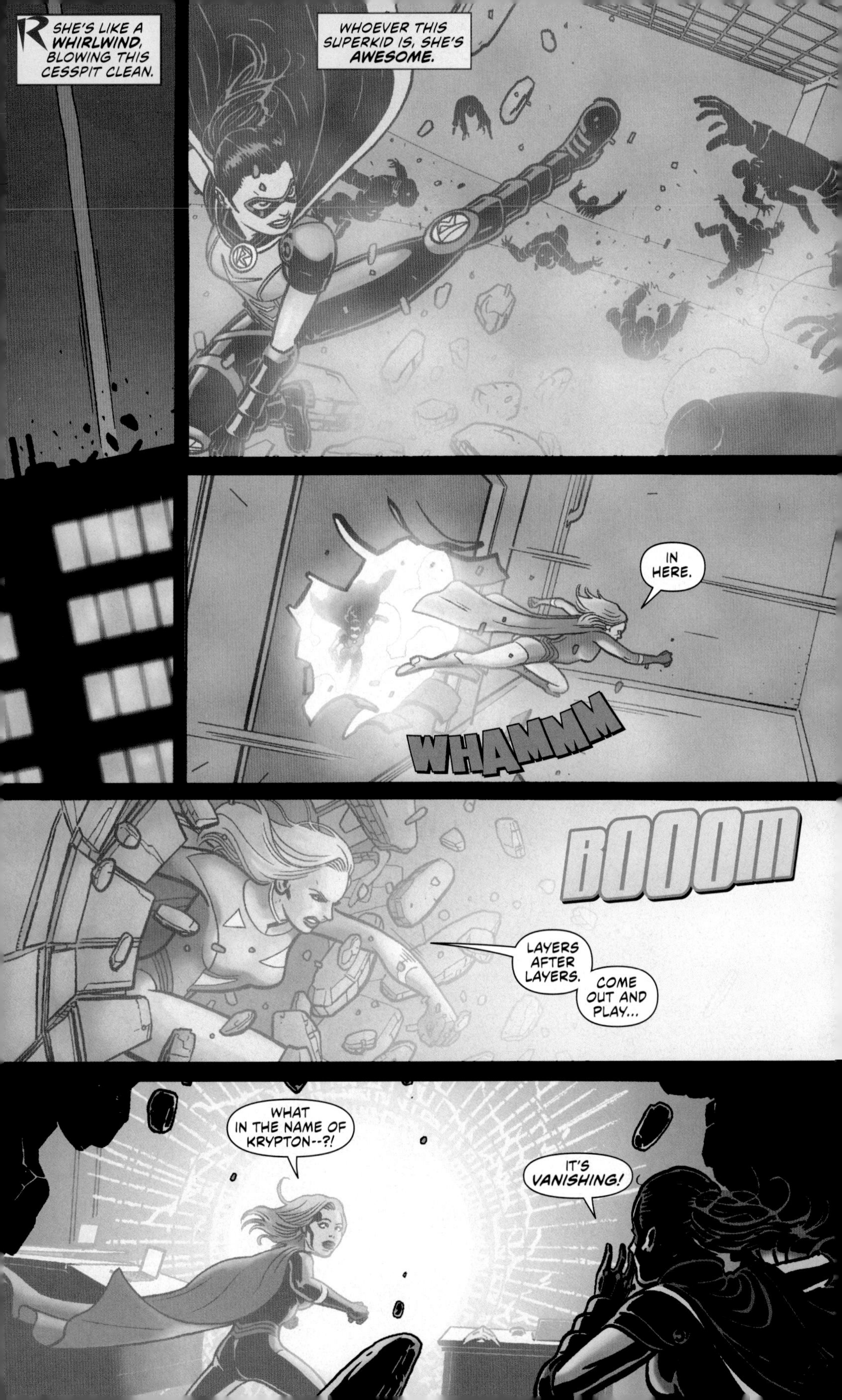
SHE'S LIKE A WHIRLWIND, BLOWING THIS CESSPIT CLEAN.
WHOEVER THIS SUPERKID IS, SHE'S AWESOME.
IN HERE.
WHAMMM
BOOOM
LAYERS AFTER LAYERS.
COME OUT AND PLAY...
WHAT IN THE NAME OF KRYPTON--?!
IT'S VANISHING!

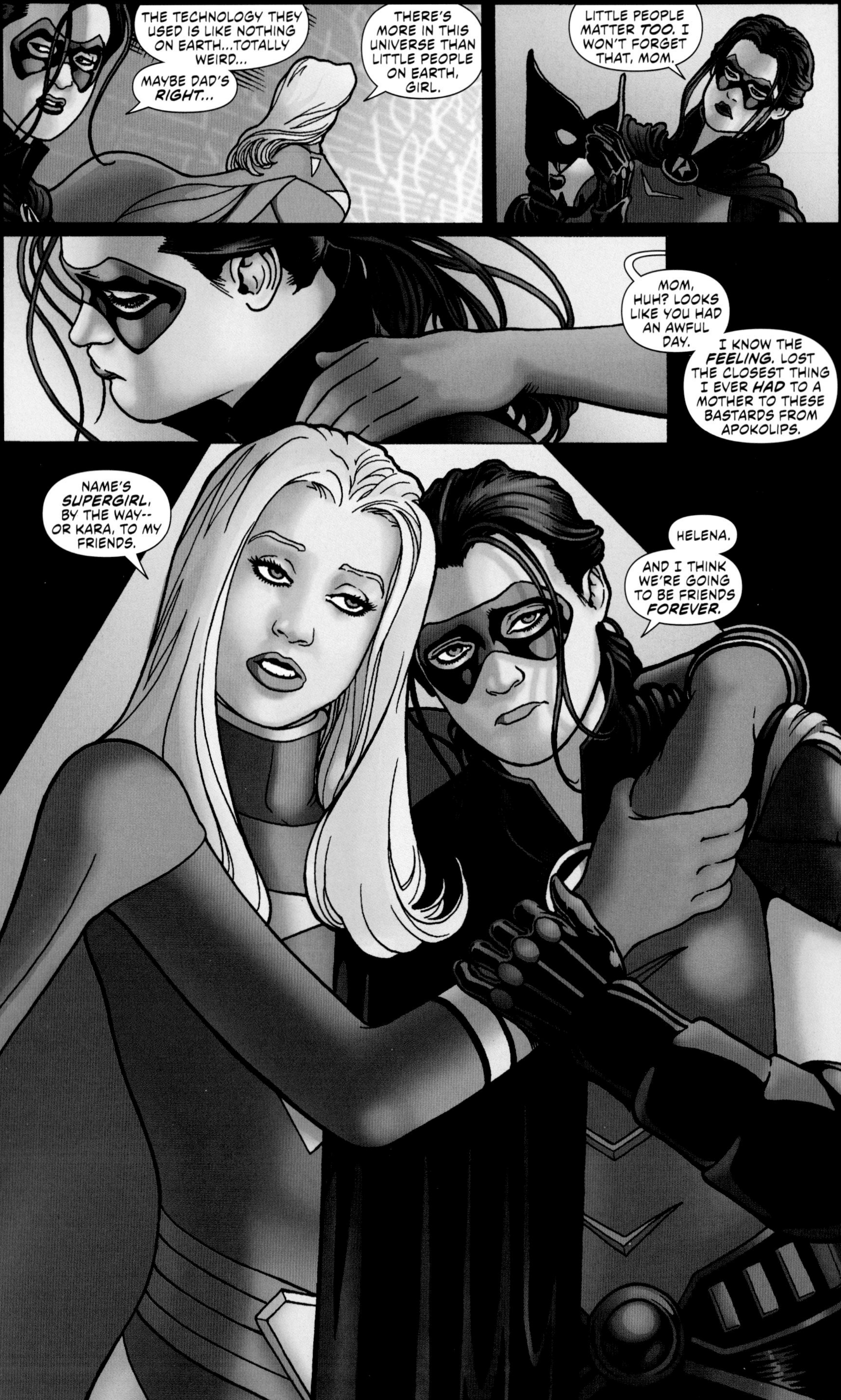
THE TECHNOLOGY THEY USED IS LIKE NOTHING ON EARTH...TOTALLY WEIRD...
MAYBE DAD'S RIGHT...
THERE'S MORE IN THIS UNIVERSE THAN LITTLE PEOPLE ON EARTH, GIRL.
LITTLE PEOPLE MATTER TOO. I WON'T FORGET THAT, MOM.
MOM, HUH? LOOKS LIKE YOU HAD AN AWFUL DAY.
I KNOW THE FEELING. LOST THE CLOSEST THING I EVER HAD TO A MOTHER TO THESE BASTARDS FROM APOKOLIPS.
NAME'S SUPERGIRL, BY THE WAY--OR KARA, TO MY FRIENDS.
HELENA.
AND I THINK WE'RE GOING TO BE FRIENDS FOREVER.

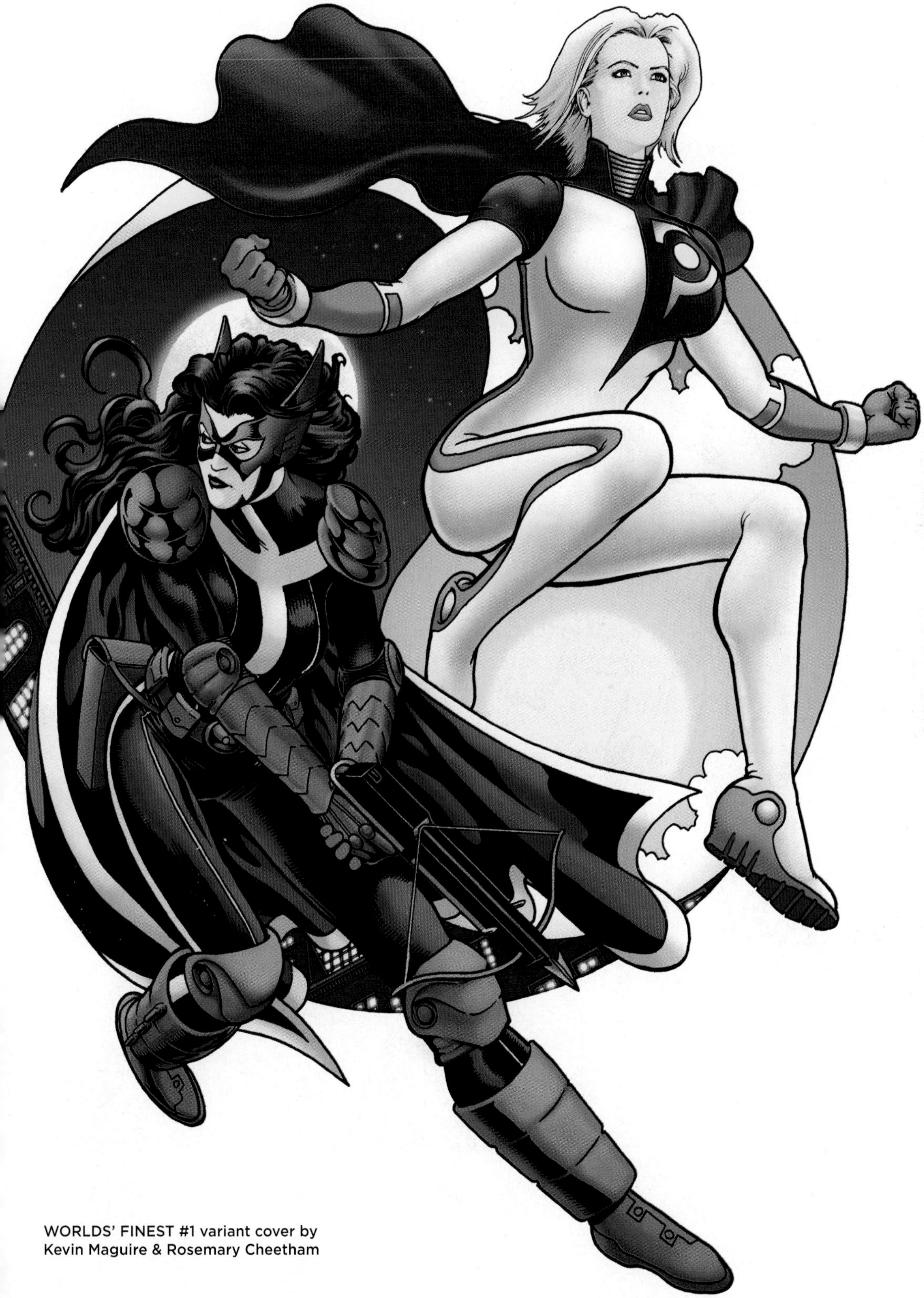

WORLDS' FINEST #1 variant cover by
Kevin Maguire & Rosemary Cheetham

Power Girl costume ideas by Jim Lee (left), Kevin Maguire (top right),
Cully Hamner (bottom right) and Kenneth Rocafort (opposite page)

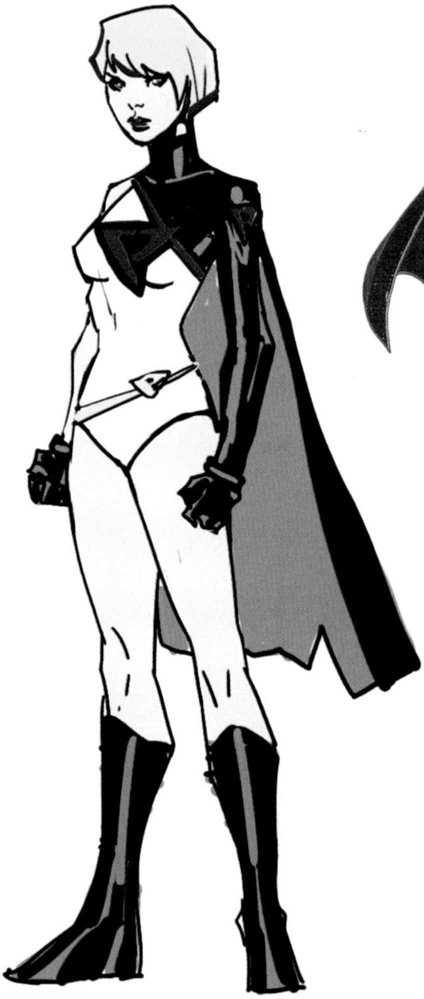

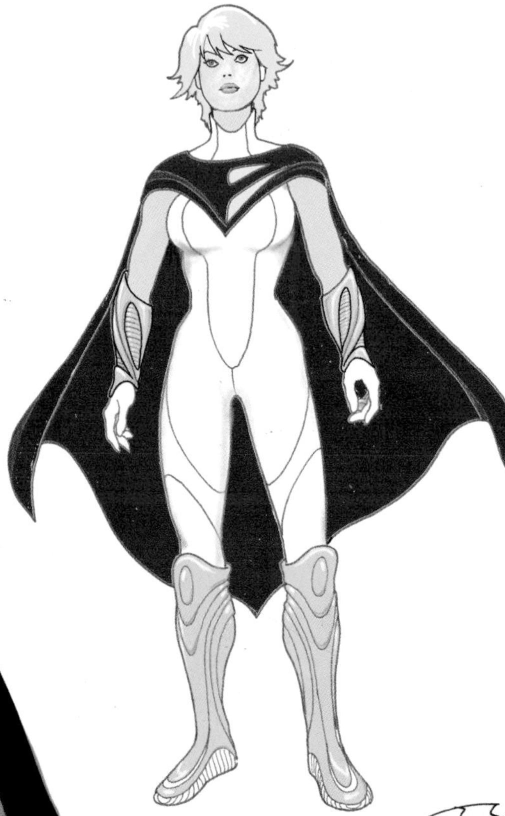

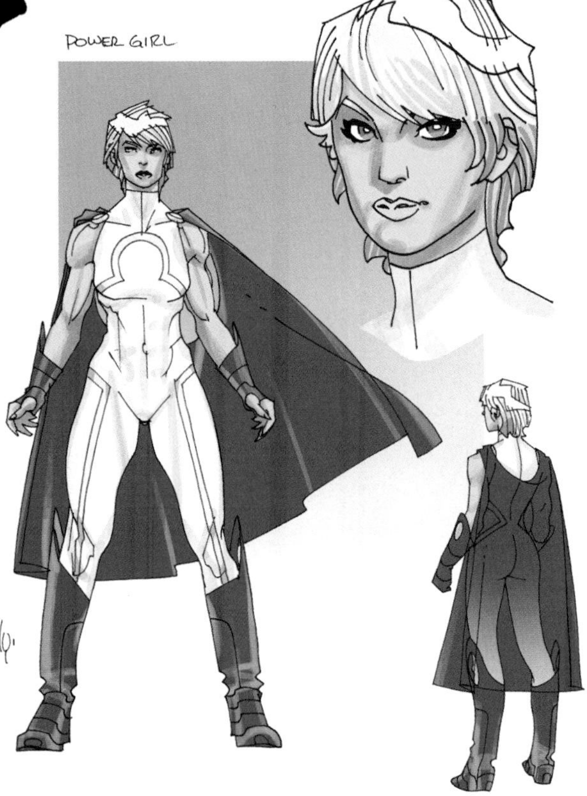
POWER GIRL

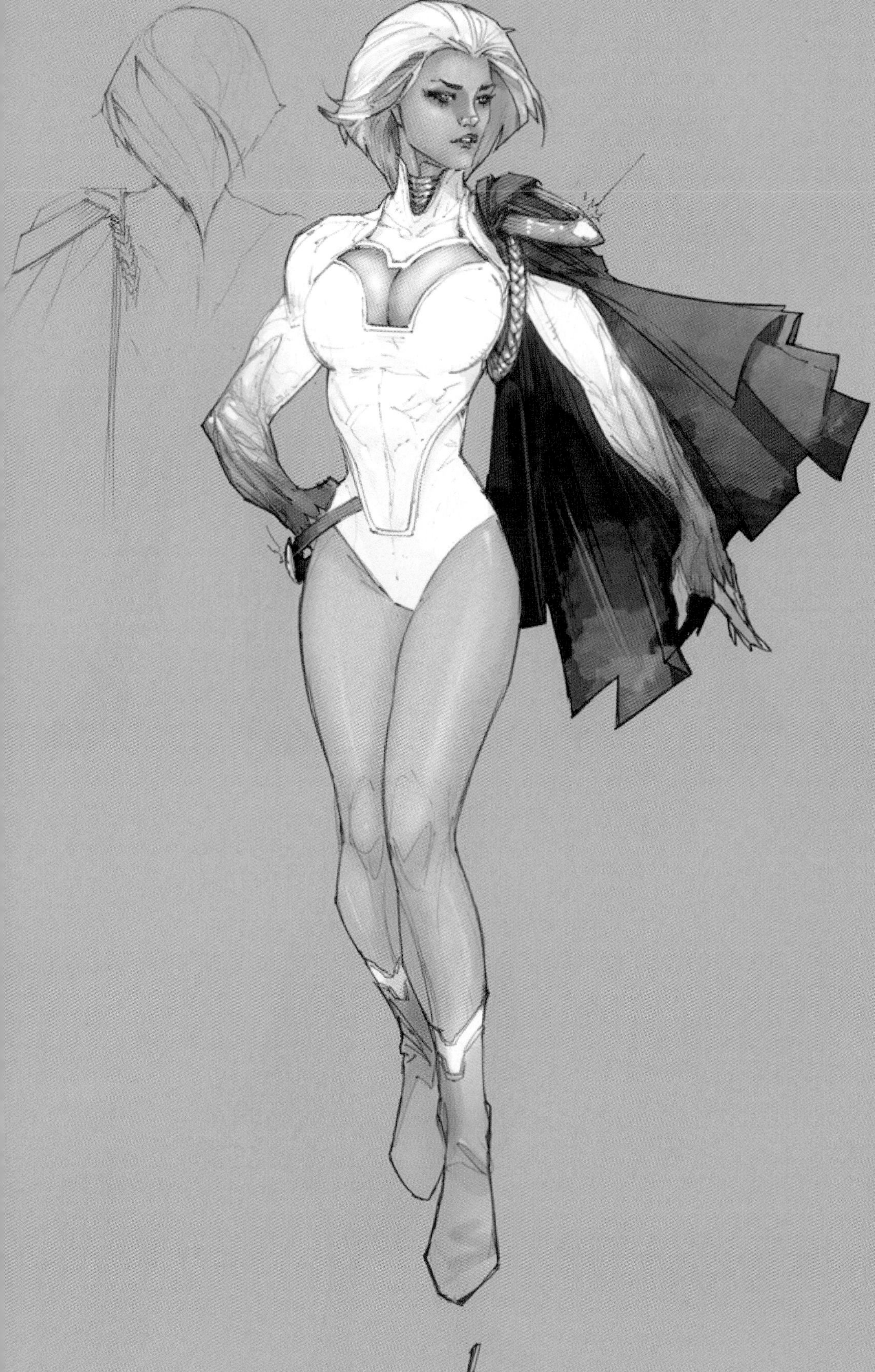

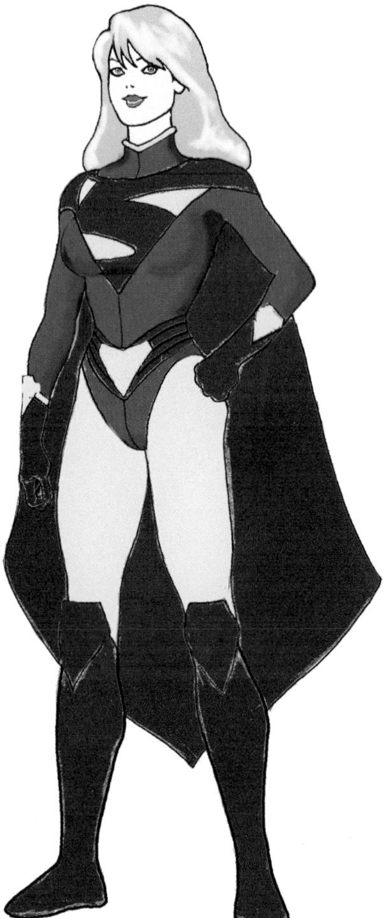

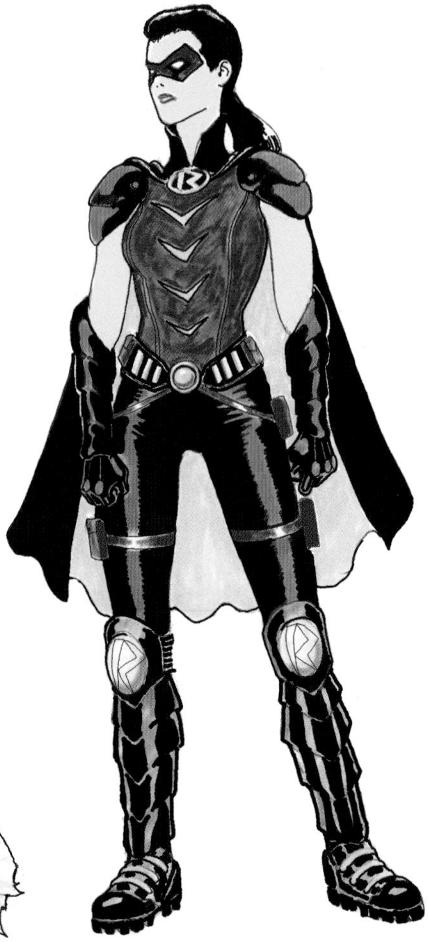

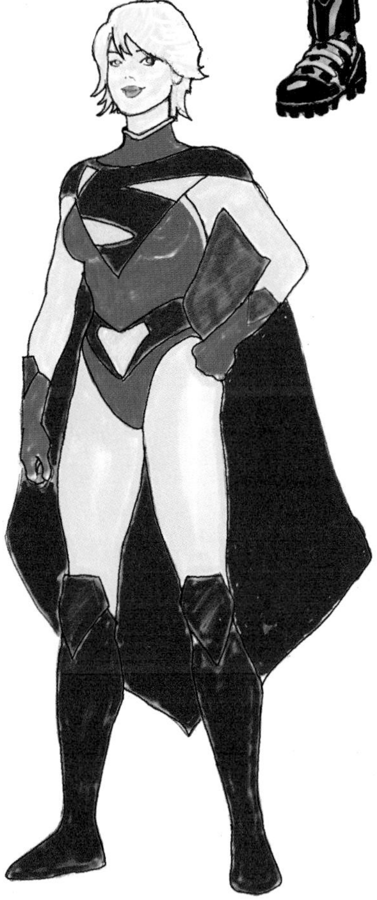

Kevin Maguire's final designs for
Earth 2 Supergirl and Robin (top) and
his initial Supergirl design (bottom)

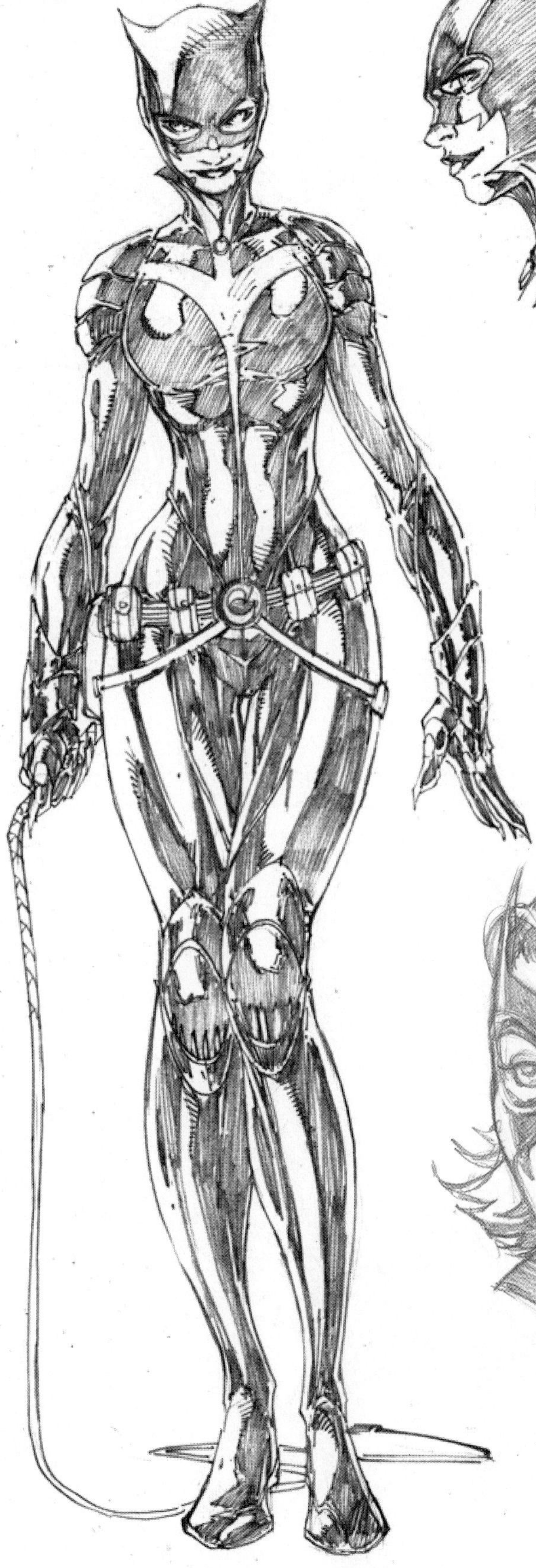

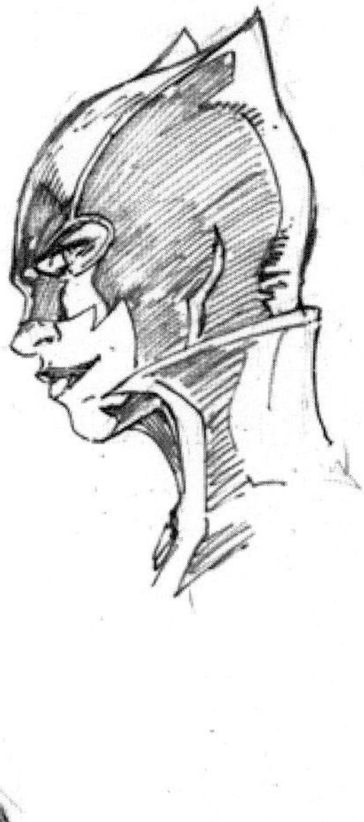

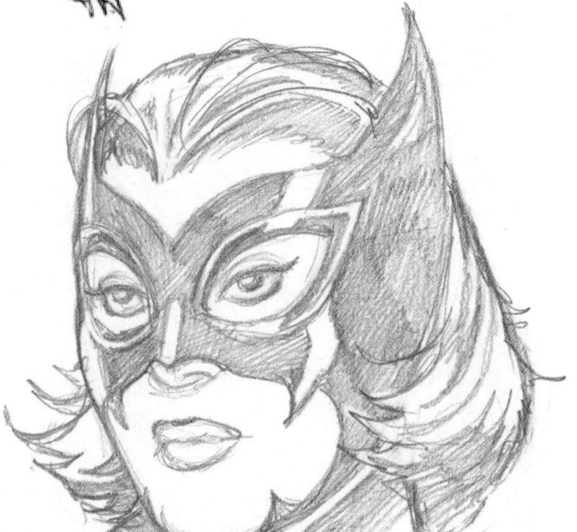

Earth 2 Catwoman sketch by Brett Booth; final
Catwoman mask by Kevin Maguire

Cover sketches for WORLDS' FINEST #1-4 by George Pérez

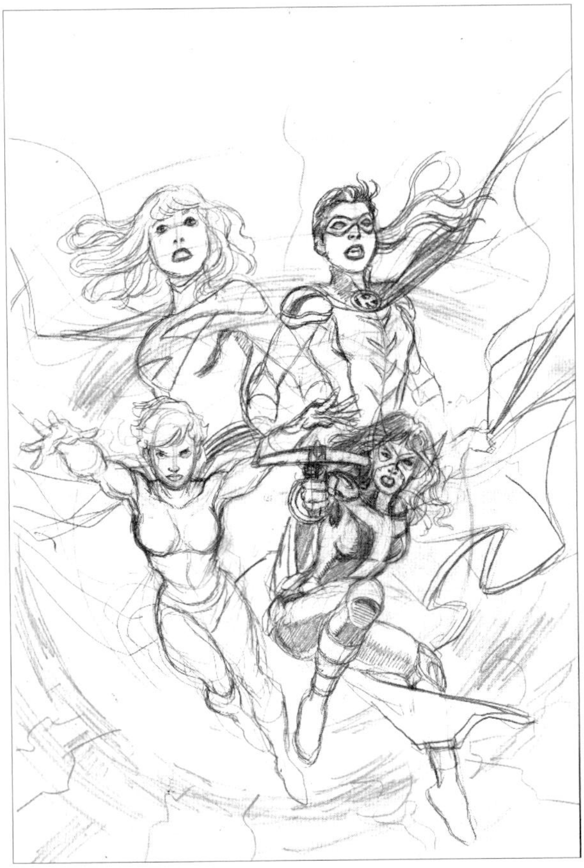

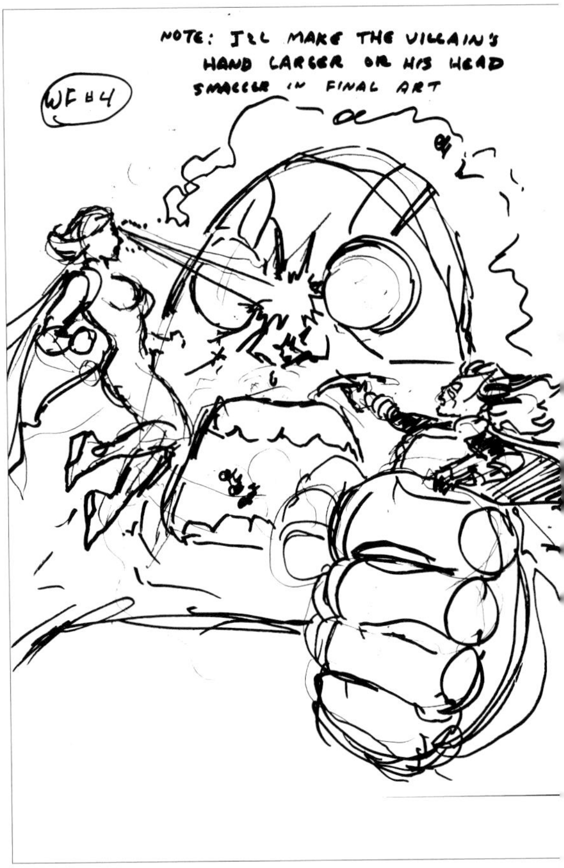
NOTE: I'LL MAKE THE VILLAIN'S HAND LARGER OR HIS HEAD SMALLER IN FINAL ART
WF #4

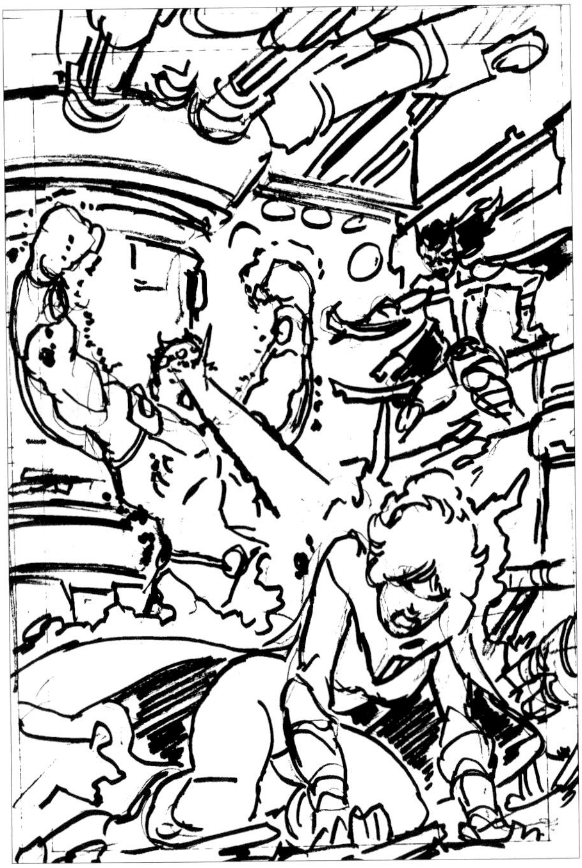

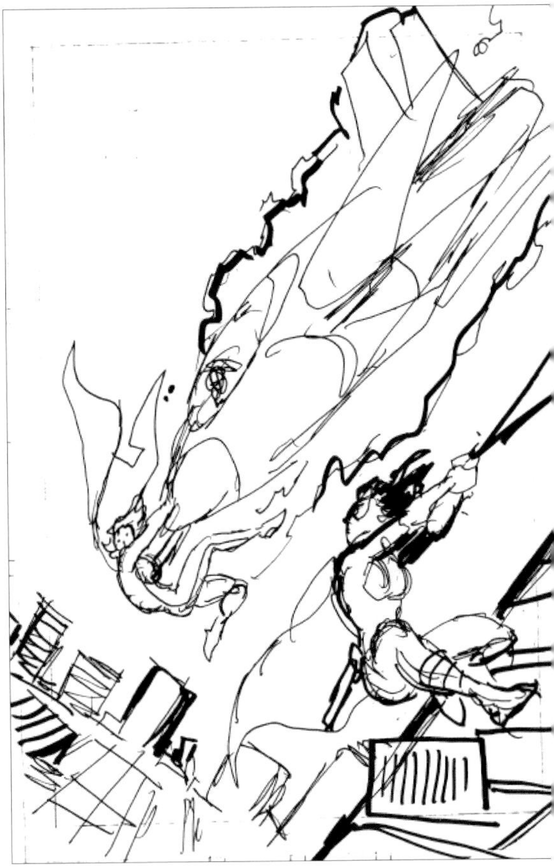

Cover sketches for WORLDS' FINEST #1 variant and WORLDS' FINEST #0 by Kevin Maguire

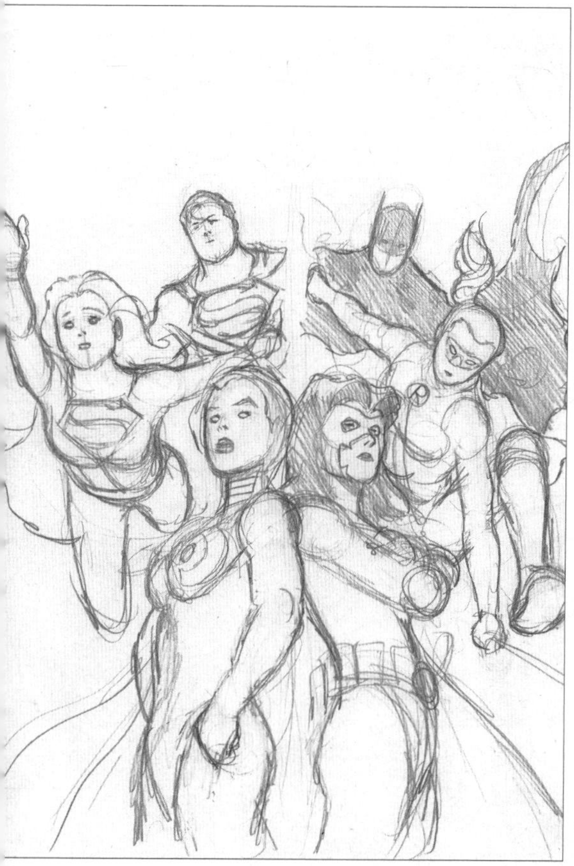

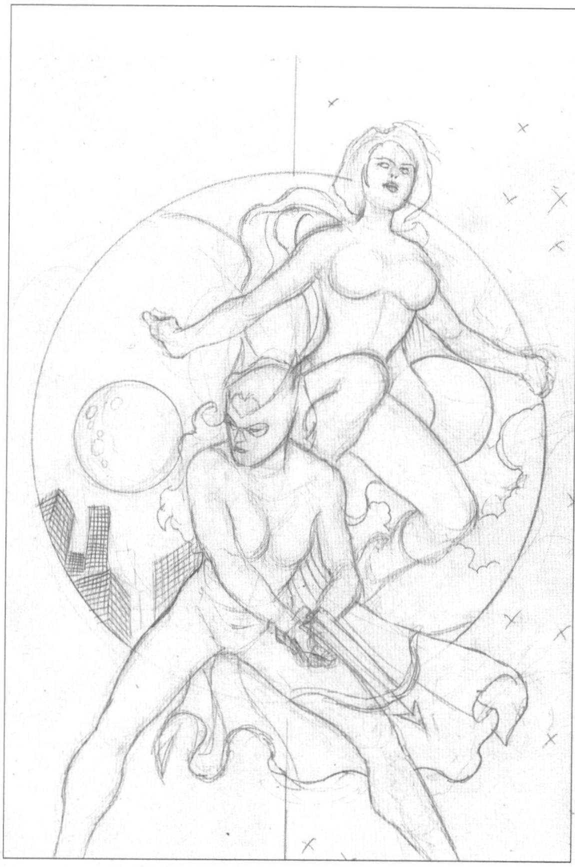

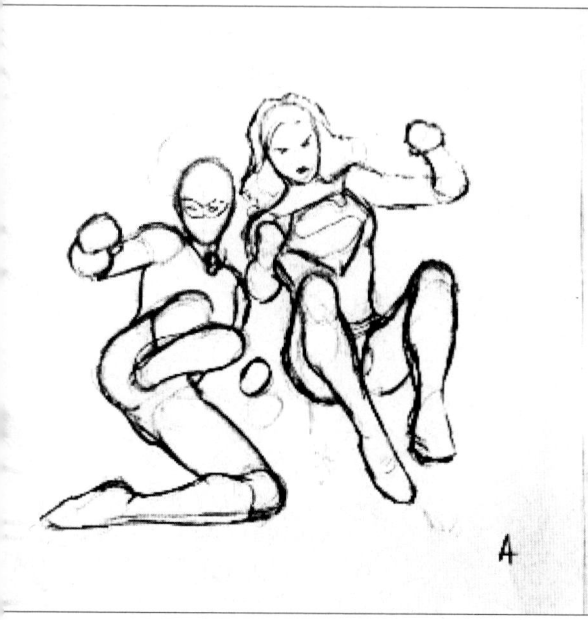
A

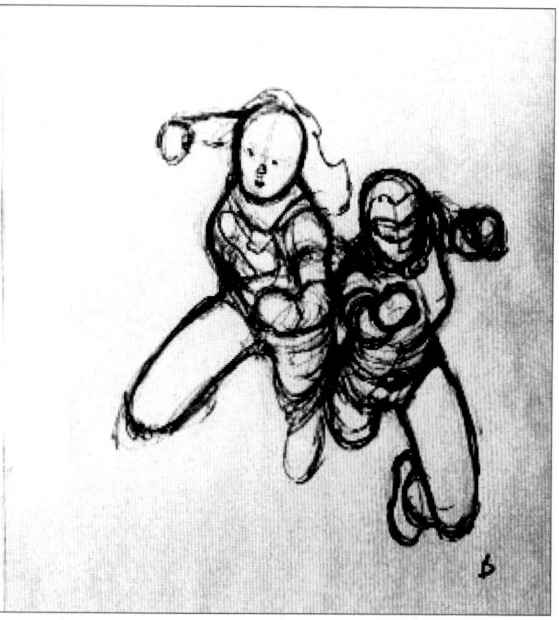
B

Cover sketch for WORLDS' FINEST #5 by Jerry Ordway

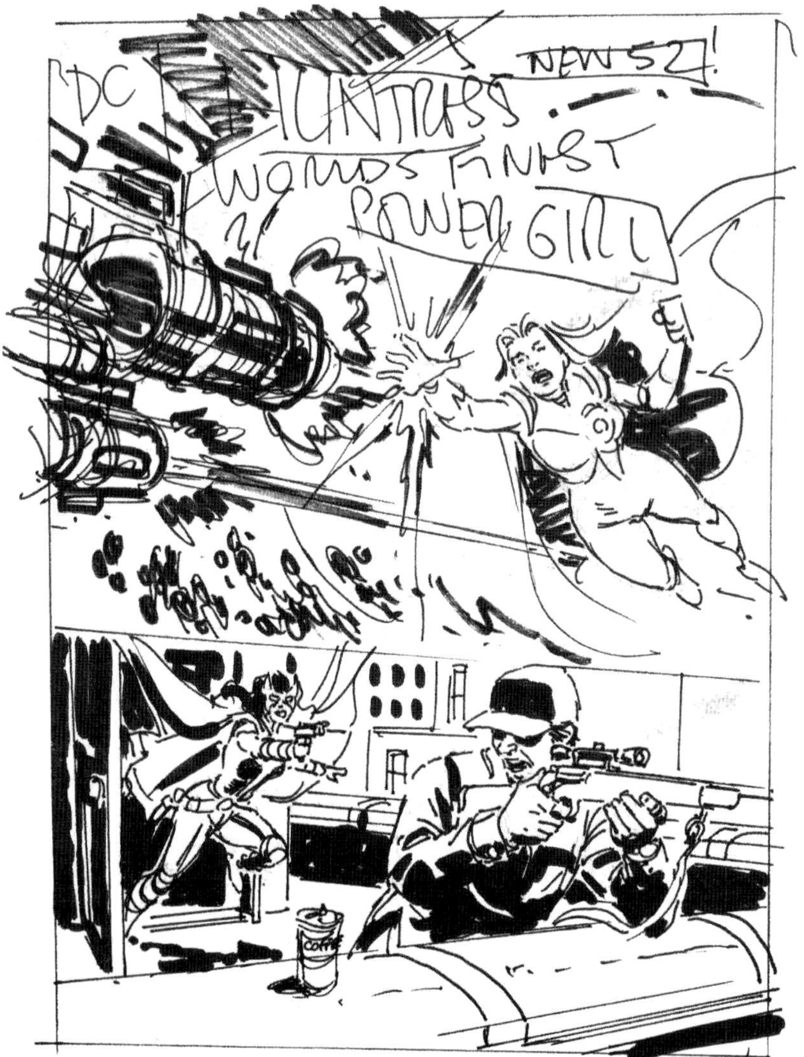
DC
NEW 52!
HUNTRESS
WORLDS FINEST
POWER GIRL

JERRY ORDWAY
6/25/12

POWER GIRL
CHARGES VORTEX
PROBE SHOOTING
AT HER (PAUL DESCRIBES
A FLYING TYPE
WEAPON, SO IM
DRAWING GUN BARRELS
FIRING. IT'S STILL
IN VORTEX
SO CIRCULAR
ENERGY
SURROUNDS
P.G.

---

HUNTRESS CHARGES
SHOOTER ON
ROOFTOP